IMPORTANT:

HERE IS YOUR REGISTRATION CODE TO ACCESS
YOUR PREMIUM McGRAW-HILL ONLINE RESOURCES.

MCGRAW-HILL
ONLINE RESOURCES

For key premium online resources you need THIS CODE to gain access. Once the code is entered, you will be able to use the Web resources for the length of your course.

If your course is using **WebCT** or **Blackboard**, you'll be able to use this code to access the McGraw-Hill content within your instructor's online course.

Access is provided if you have purchased a new book. If the registration code is missing from this book, the registration screen on our Website, and within your WebCT or Blackboard course, will tell you how to obtain your new code.

Registering for McGraw-Hill Online Resources

TO gain access to your McGraw-Hill web resources simply follow the steps below:

1. USE YOUR WEB BROWSER TO GO TO: **register.dushkin.com**

2. CLICK ON **FIRST TIME USER**.

3. ENTER THE REGISTRATION CODE* PRINTED ON THE TEAR-OFF BOOKMARK ON THE RIGHT.

4. AFTER YOU HAVE ENTERED YOUR REGISTRATION CODE, CLICK **REGISTER**.

5. FOLLOW THE INSTRUCTIONS TO SET-UP YOUR PERSONAL UserID AND PASSWORD.

6. WRITE YOUR UserID AND PASSWORD DOWN FOR FUTURE REFERENCE.
KEEP IT IN A SAFE PLACE.

TO GAIN ACCESS to the McGraw-Hill content in your instructor's **WebCT** or **Blackboard** course simply log in to the course with the UserID and Password provided by your instructor. Enter the registration code exactly as it appears in the box to the right when prompted by the system. You will only need to use the code the first time you click on McGraw-Hill content.

Thank you, and welcome to your McGraw-Hill online Resources!

REGISTRATION CODE

housewives-91787719

Mc Graw Hill **Higher Education**

* YOUR REGISTRATION CODE CAN BE USED ONLY ONCE TO ESTABLISH ACCESS. IT IS NOT TRANSFERABLE.

0-07-292171-4 T/A COKER: MOTOR LEARNING AND CONTROL FOR PRACTITIONERS

Motor Learning and Control
for Practitioners

Motor Learning and Control for Practitioners

CHERYL A. COKER, PH.D.

New Mexico State University
Las Cruces, New Mexico

Boston   Burr Ridge, IL   Dubuque, IA   Madison, WI   New York   San Francisco   St. Louis
Bangkok   Bogotá   Caracas   Kuala Lumpur   Lisbon   London   Madrid   Mexico City
Milan   Montreal   New Delhi   Santiago   Seoul   Singapore   Sydney   Taipei   Toronto

MOTOR LEARNING AND CONTROL FOR PRACTITIONERS

Published by McGraw-Hill, a business unit of The McGraw-Hill Companies, Inc.,
1221 Avenue of the Americas, New York, NY 10020. Copyright © 2004 by The McGraw-Hill
Companies, Inc. All rights reserved. No part of this publication may be reproduced or
distributed in any form or by any means, or stored in a database or retrieval system,
without the prior written consent of The McGraw-Hill Companies, Inc., including, but
not limited to, in any network or other electronic storage or transmission, or broadcast
for distance learning.

Some ancillaries, including electronic and print components, may not be available to
customers outside the United States.

This book is printed on acid-free paper.

1 2 3 4 5 6 7 8 9 0 DOC/DOC 0 9 8 7 6 5 4 3

ISBN 0-7674-1645-7

Vice president and editor-in-chief: *Thalia Dorwick*
Publisher: *Jane E. Karpacz*
Executive editor: *Vicki Malinee*
Senior developmental editor: *Michelle Turenne*
Senior marketing manager: *Pamela S. Cooper*
Senior project manager: *Marilyn Rothenberger*
Production supervisor: *Enboge Chong*
Media technology producer: *Lance Gerhart*
Associate designer: *George Kokkonas*
Cover/interior designer: *Mary Spanburg*
Cover image: *Courtesy of the Author*
Art editor: *Jen DeVere*
Senior supplement producer: *David A. Welsh*
Compositor: *GAC–Indianapolis*
Typeface: *9.75/12 Palatino*
Printer: *R. R. Donnelley/Crawfordsville, IN*

Library of Congress Cataloging-in-Publication Data

Coker, Cheryl A.
    Motor learning and control for practitioners / Cheryl A. Coker
      p. cm.
    Includes bibliographical references (p.) and index.
    ISBN 0-7674-1645-7
      1. Motor learning. I. Title.
  BF295.C645 2004
  152.3'34—dc21

                                                2003052745

This text was based on the most up-to-date research and suggestions made by individuals
knowledgeable in the field of motor learning. The author and publisher disclaim any
responsibility for any adverse effects or consequences from the misapplication or
injudicious use of information contained within this text.

www.mhhe.com

BRIEF CONTENTS

CONTENTS

CHAPTER 10

Diagnosing Errors 199

CHAPTER 11

Correcting Errors 215

PREFACE

Human movement is a complex phenomenon. For the practitioner concerned with movement enhancement, that complexity presents a constant challenge. The key to meeting this challenge lies in the understanding of how people learn. *Motor Learning and Control for Practitioners* introduces the practitioner to the processes that underlie human movement learning. Bridging the gap between research and practice, this text provides the practitioner with the necessary tools to build a solid foundation for assessing performance, providing effective instruction, and designing practice, rehabilitation and training experiences that will optimize skill acquisition and performance.

APPROACH

The purpose of this textbook extends beyond simply presenting the concepts and principles of motor learning and control. The intent of *Motor Learning and Control for Practitioners* is to provide the student with the opportunity to become actively engaged with its content through an applications-based approach. Before a student can be challenged to apply theoretical constructs however, they must first understand them. To facilitate this understanding, the material is presented in an easy to read manner that incorporates a wide range of examples from everyday life, teaching, coaching and rehabilitation. It offers abundant opportunities for student interaction with the text's key concepts, principles, and basic terminology. Students are then challenged to apply that information to real-life situations.

AUDIENCE

This text is designed for the practitioner in Physical Education, Kinesiology, Exercise Science, Athletic Training, Physical and Occupational Therapy, Dance and Coaching. Special care was taken to accommodate the diverse needs of this multifaceted audience and is reflected in the examples, scenarios, and activities provided throughout the text. Also interspersed throughout the text are numerous opportunities to apply principles and concepts to each reader's specific content area to assist in the development of a working knowledge of motor learning and control as it applies to his or her chosen profession.

ORGANIZATION

The focus of chapters one through four is on the behavioral and neurological processes that influence performance. The text begins by introducing the reader to the foundational concept that human movement is a complex phenomenon that is a function of the interaction of the learner, the task and the environment in which the task is performed (Chapter 1). The reader's working knowledge of this interaction is further developed in Chapter 2, which begins the dialogue on the underlying processes that govern movement execution and control. While Chapter 2 focuses on the factors that influence movement preparation, Chapter 3 explores the theoretical constructs underlying the coordination and control of human movement. Movement is then examined from a neurological perspective (Chapter 4).

Chapters five through eleven build on this foundational knowledge of how skilled movements are produced and examine the factors involved in their acquisition and refinement. This discussion begins with an introduction to the changing characteristics of learners as they progress from novices to experts and their role in guiding the practitioner's decision making throughout the instructional process (Chapter 5). Starting with Chapter 6, the sequence in which concepts are introduced parallels that which would be used in the instructional process. First, pre-instruction considerations to facilitate learning such as learning styles, transfer, and motivation to learn are discussed (Chapter 6). Methods of presenting skills, specifically instructions, demonstrations, and discovery learning are then examined in Chapter 7. Next, learners must be provided with ample opportunities to practice the skills presented. Chapter 8 examines a number of practice variables, including sequencing and psychological strategies that a practitioner can manipulate to optimize gains in skill proficiency. This focus on practice design continues in Chapter 9 where practice organization and scheduling are highlighted. Once the learner begins to practice a skill, the role of the practitioner becomes one of error detection and correction. Chapter 10, unique to this text, investigates the role of motor learning and control in diagnosing errors while Chapter 11 addresses principles and guidelines regarding the provision of feedback for their correction. Finally, an epilogue is presented that contains two real life scenarios designed to test the readers' abilities to apply what they have learned.

FEATURES

Accessible for all Students The writing style, easy readability and numerous applications and examples throughout the chapters make this text appealing to students who plan on pursuing careers as practitioners.

Broad Range of Examples Integrates examples from sport, physical education, dance, exercise science, athletic training, rehabilitation and "everyday life" to accommodate the variety of students in the course.

Theoretical Coverage Provides equal coverage of Schema Theory and Dynamic System Theory.

Introduction to Learning Styles In Chapter 6, students are introduced to unique coverage of individual learning styles and their influence on the learning process, reinforcing the importance of both recognizing and accommodating individual differences.

Functional Anatomy of the Nervous System Chapter 4 connects basic nervous system anatomy to motor learning and control concepts.

Error Diagnosis and Correction Chapter 10 presents unique coverage by exploring errors based on motor learning and control issues and their diagnosis. The chapter presents critical factors for conducting an observation, a categorical model for the determination of an error and its resolution, and discusses situational factors that should be considered before correcting an error.

Exploration Activities Includes experiential activities that enable students to use typical classroom and household items to translate chapter content into practice. These activities can also serve as a starting point for classroom discussion.

Cerebral Challenges are critical thinking exercises interspersed throughout the text that require the reader to engage in problem-solving activities.

Research Notes These boxes provide examples of key research conducted on the topics discussed in the chapter.

Pedagogical Features Numerous teaching tools appear throughout the text, including case studies/vignettes, Cerebral Challenges, Common Myths and review questions all to help students to understand and apply the material presented.

PEDAGOGICAL FEATURES

Exploration Activities that only require everyday classroom equipment are found in each chapter to further illustrate key concepts. They can serve as an instructor directed starting point for class discussion or can be conducted by the student outside the classroom.

Critical thinking is incorporated throughout the text in boxed elements entitled **Cerebral Challenges.** Cerebral challenges pose higher order questions to the reader and provide the opportunity for them to become actively engaged with the principles and concepts presented. This feature can further serve as an instructor directed starting point for class discussion.

A **Pretest** is presented at the beginning of the text to determine students' current level of knowledge with respect to Motor Learning and Control. The test is composed of **Common Myths** that are later dispersed in boxes throughout the text to introduce students to common misconceptions in the field.

Broad Range of Examples from sport, physical education, dance, exercise science, athletic training, rehabilitation and "everyday life" accommodate the variety of majors and future professionals in the course.

Bolded Key Terms have been included with an accompanying comprehensive Glossary at the end of the text.

Opening Scenarios or Vignettes focusing on the key concepts to be presented begin most chapters.

Research Notes provide an example of research conducted on a topic discussed within the text.

Each chapter concludes with a section entitled **A Look Ahead,** which briefly summarizes the emphasis of the chapter and previews the next chapter. This feature serves to create more comprehensible connections between chapters.

Bulleted Summaries of key concepts are located at the end of each chapter.

Review Questions are found at the end of each chapter for students to test their comprehension of presented material.

The text concludes with an **Epilogue** that presents two real life scenarios and associated questions for students to test their ability to incorporate multiple concepts in an applied setting.

ANCILLARIES

Instructor's Resource
Computerized Test Bank CD-ROM
Brownstone's Computerized Testing is the most flexible, powerful, easy-to-use electronic testing program available in higher education. The Diploma system (for Windows users) allows the test maker to create a print version, an online version (to be delivered to a computer lab), or an Internet version of each test. Diploma includes a built-in instructor gradebook, into which student rosters and files can be imported. The CD-ROM includes a separate testing program, Exam VI, for Macintosh users.

Internet Resources
PowerPoint
www.mhhe.com/coker1e
A complete PowerPoint lecture for the course is included on the accompanying website at *www.mhhe.com/coker1e*. This presentation, ready to use in class, corresponds to the content in each chapter of this text, making it easier for you to teach and ensuring that your students can follow your lectures point by point. You can modify the presentation as much as you like to meet the needs of your course.

PowerWeb
www.dushkin.com/online

The PowerWeb website is a reservoir of course-specific articles and current events. Students can visit PowerWeb to take a self-scoring quiz, complete an interactive exercise, click through an interactive glossary, or check the daily news. An expert in each discipline analyzes the day's news to show students how it relates to their field of study.

PowerWeb is packaged with many McGraw-Hill textbooks. Students are also granted full access to Dushkin/McGraw-Hill's Student Site, where they can read study tips, conduct web research, learn about different career paths, and follow fun links on the web.

Health and Human Performance Website
www.mhhe.com/hhp

McGraw-Hill's Health and Human Performance website provides a wide variety of information for both instructors and students, including monthly articles about current issues, downloadable supplements for instructors, a "how to" technology guide, study tips, and exam-preparation materials. It includes information about professional organizations, conventions and careers.

PageOut: The Course Website Development Center
www.pageout.net

PageOut, free to instructors who use a McGraw-Hill textbook, is an online program you can use to create your own course website. PageOut offers the following features:

- A course home page
- An instructor home page
- A syllabus (interactive and customizable, including quizzing, instructor notes, and links to the text's Online Learning Center)
- Web links
- Discussions (multiple discussion areas per class)
- An online gradebook
- Links to student web pages

Contact your McGraw-Hill sales representative to obtain a password.

ACKNOWLEDGEMENTS

A journey such as this is never traveled alone and there are many people to which I am indebted. I would like to thank my family, friends, teachers, colleagues, and students for their support, encouragement, knowledge, suggestions, ideas, posing for pictures, lending me a digital camera (thanks Jim!), proofreading, listening, providing elusive words, and always challenging me to aspire to greater heights. I would also be remiss if I did not specifically recognize several individuals. Special thanks to Michele Sordi who initiated this project and provided valuable insights into the world of publishing. Appreciation is also extended to the publishing team at McGraw-Hill for their efforts and expertise. To my mentors Linda Bunker and Dan Pfaff, for cultivating my passion for learning and believing in me, I am truly grateful. I would also like to express my gratitude to Gib Darden for his open ear and unique pronunciations. Finally, my deepest appreciation to Kim and Oakley for keeping my soul and my feet warm.

I would also like to thank the following individuals who served as reviewers for their input into the development of this text:

William Berg, Ph.D.
Miami University (OH)

John Billing, Ph.D.
University of North Carolina at Chapel Hill

Gordon Chalmers, Ph.D.
Western Washington University

Geffrey Colon, Ph.D.
Eastern Michigan University

Lanie Dornier, Ph.D.
Texas Tech University

William H. Edwards, Ph.D.
California State University at Sacramento

Shirl Hoffman, Ed.D.
University of North Carolina at Greensboro

Christopher Janell, Ph.D.
University of Florida

Claudia Lange, Ph.D.
University of San Francisco

Chuck Layne, Ph.D.
University of Houston

Yuhua Li, Ph.D.
University of Memphis

Gerard G. Lyons, Ed.D.
Idaho State University

Monica Magner, Ed.D.
Morehead State University

Sue Ellen Miller, P.E.D.
Ohio University

Robert J. Rausch, Jr., Ph.D.
Westfield State College (MA)

Shannon D. Ringenbach, Ph.D.
Arizona State University

Clifford Singh, Ph.D.
California State University at San Bernardino

Thomas Stoffregen, Ph.D.
University of Minnesota at Minneapolis

Phillip D. Tomporowski, Ph.D.
University of Georgia

Cynthia D. Williams, Ph.D.
Winston-Salem State University

Cheryl A. Coker
Las Cruces, New Mexico

As a student of human movement, you bring to this course extensive knowledge from your past experiences. To determine your current level of knowledge with respect to motor learning and control, complete the following pretest.

TRUE OR FALSE?

1. Future success in a specific skill can easily be predicted.   True   False

2. The higher the level of arousal, the better the performance.   True   False

3. All sensory messages must go to the brain for integration.   True   False

4. Unless the learner displays some overt changes in performance, he or she is no longer learning.   True   False

5. All learners are motivated to learn the skills presented to them.   True   False

6. Experts are always the most effective instructors.   True   False

7. For an observer to learn a movement, the demonstration must be performed correctly.   True   False

8. Practice makes perfect.   True   False

9. Long-term retention of a motor skill is best achieved by practicing the skill repeatedly before moving to either a different version of the task or a different task altogether.   True   False

10. When teaching a youngster how to catch, you should toss the ball with a high arch in order to give them enough time to follow it and get underneath it for a successful catch.   True   False

11. The more frequently a practitioner provides feedback to the learner, the greater the gains in learning.   True   False

12. A practitioner should give the learner feedback immediately following a movement/performance attempt.   True   False

ANSWERS:

The answer to all of the above questions is false. These questions represent many myths that exist regarding motor learning and control. Myth boxes have been placed throughout the textbook to discuss each of these concepts in detail. Look for them as you begin your journey through the field of motor learning and control.

CHAPTER ONE

Introduction to Motor Learning and Control

I have come to a frightening conclusion. I am the decisive element in the classroom. It is my personal approach that creates the climate. It is my daily mood that makes the weather. As a teacher, I possess the tremendous power to make a child's life miserable or joyous. I can be the tool of torture or an instrument of inspiration. I can humiliate or humor, hurt or heal. In all situations, it is my response that decides if a crisis will be elevated or de-escalated, and a child humanized or dehumanized.

Haim Ginott,
Educator

The above message is clear: the role of instructor is a very powerful one. The climate you create will determine the level of success that your students, patients, clients or athletes will achieve. Fundamental to creating an effective climate is having an understanding of how people learn. *Motor Learning and Control for Practitioners* focuses on the processes that govern movement acquisition and control and provides a foundation for the development of effective instructional strategies that facilitate learning and performance. By studying this book you

FIGURE 1.1
The interaction of the learner, the task and the environment in which the task performed is fundamental to the understanding and facilitation of motor skill acquisition and performance.

Learner

Do they possess underlying abilities to perform the task?
Is the task developmentally appropriate?
Have they had any past experiences that are relevant to the task?
Are they motivated to learn the task?
What individual differences might influence the acquisition of this task?

Environment

In what context will the task be performed?
Is that context predictable or unpredictable?
Is there a time limitation?

Task

Does the task have a high perceptual component?
Is objective manipulation required?
What body movements are required?
Must the task be performed under a variety of conditions, or must the learner be able to consistently and accurately replicate the movement pattern?

will learn that human movement is a complex phenomenon that is a function of the interaction of three elements: the learner, the task and the environment in which the task is performed.

When assessing performance and making instructional decisions, you must remember that none of these elements exists in isolation. Practitioners are therefore challenged to go beyond simply reading and developing a basic understanding of the theoretical constructs presented in this text. Instead, you are challenged to reinvent yourself as a human movement specialist by developing a working knowledge of motor learning and control so that you can empower your learners and maximize their potential.

Motor Learning, Control and Performance

How, exactly, do people acquire motor skills? What processes allow the musculoskeletal system to produce intended movements? What variables facilitate or hinder skill acquisition? Questions such as these have led to the evolution of a field of study known as motor learning. **Motor learning** is the study of the processes involved in acquiring and refining motor skills and of variables that promote or inhibit that acquisition. A related field of study, **motor control,** focuses on the neural, physical and behavioral aspects of human movement. An understanding of both motor learning and control is necessary to develop a complete understanding of motor skill acquisition. Such an understanding provides the human movement practitioner with foundational knowledge that not only explains why a certain behavior manifests but provides the basis for assessing performance, providing effective instruction and designing optimal practice, rehabilitation and training experiences.

motor learning: The study of the processes involved in acquiring and refining motor skills and of variables that promote or inhibit that acquisition.

motor control: The neural, physical and behavioral aspects that underlie human movement.

WHAT IS LEARNING?

The first question we should ask if we are going to look at how people learn is what is learning? Before continuing, please complete Exploration Activity 1.1 on the following page.

When used in reference to motor learning and control, **learning** is defined as a relatively permanent change in a person's capability to execute a motor skill as a result of practice or experience. To claim that you have learned how to juggle as a result of your participation in Exploration Activity 1.1, then, you must determine whether a persistent change in your juggling behavior has occurred. Part of the problem we face when attempting to resolve whether a motor skill has been learned is that we can't actually *see* learning because the underlying or internal processes that result in a relatively permanent change cannot be directly observed. What we can see, however, is performance. **Performance** is the act of executing a skill. Through repeated observations of an individual's performance, we infer whether an individual has learned a skill. These inferences are based on changes that are observed in an individual's performance over time, such as improvements in movement proficiency and consistency. Caution must be exercised, however, to ensure that the inferences made are indeed accurate. For example, numerous variables, such as fatigue, anxiety and problems with equipment, can impair performance but do not necessarily indicate a loss of capability. Alternatively, a learner may suddenly become consistent in performing a given skill at a higher level of proficiency during one practice, only to return to their original level at the next practice.

learning: A relatively permanent change in a person's capability to execute a motor skill as a result of practice or experience.

performance: The act of executing a skill.

The Nature of Motor Skills

In order to begin our exploration of factors that influence skill acquisition and performance, the term *skill* must first be defined, and that definition

EXPLORATION ACTIVITY 1.1 Learning to Juggle

EQUIPMENT NEEDED:

2 tennis balls
Some space to move!

GOAL:

The goal of this exercise is to successfully juggle two tennis balls using your nondominant hand.

PROCEDURE:

To start, place both tennis balls in your nondominant hand. Toss one ball upward. As that ball reaches its peak height, toss the second ball upward, leaving the hand empty to catch the first ball. Continue this pattern, attempting to achieve as many successive catches as possible. Repeat for 10 minutes, recording the number of successful catches you achieve on each trial (from the starting position to the time you drop or miss a catch).

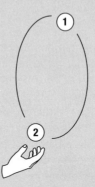

QUESTIONS:

1. Assuming that you were eventually able to make two or more catches, can you conclude that you have learned how to juggle two balls with your nondominant hand? Why or why not?
2. Let's say that in your first nine minutes of juggling, you spent more time chasing balls than catching them. Up until the nine-minute mark, your record number of catches was two. All of a sudden, in that last minute, you catch six! Does this mean you have learned how to juggle?
3. Based on this juggling experience, formulate a definition for learning.
4. What learner, task and environmental factors affected your performance and learning?

depends on the context in which the term is used. First, the term *skill* can be used to depict the quality of a performance. If one is identified as skillful, it is implied that one has achieved a high degree of proficiency. Kristi Yamaguchi, for example, is considered a highly skilled figure skater.

A **motor skill** is an act or task that satisfies four criteria. First, it is goal-oriented, meaning it is performed to achieve some objective. Second, body and/or limb movements are required to accomplish the goal. Third, those movements must be voluntary. Given this stipulation, reflexive actions, such as the stepping reflex in infants, are not considered to be skills, because they occur involuntarily. Finally, motor skills are developed as a result of practice. In other words, a skill must be learned or relearned. Crutch walking would therefore be considered a skill, as it satisfies these four criteria: it requires voluntary body and or limb movement to achieve a goal (e.g., move across a room), and it must be learned.

motor skill: A goal-oriented act or task that requires voluntary body and/or limb movement and must be learned.

CEREBRAL CHALLENGE #1

Determine which of the following can be classified as a motor skill. Explain why you selected or omitted each option.

a. Grasping an object
b. Tapping your pencil
c. Solving a word problem
d. Driving a car
e. Drawing back after touching a hot stove
f. Sewing on a button

g. Walking
h. Playing the trumpet
i. The parachute reflex displayed by an infant
j. Performing proprioceptive neuromuscular facilitation (PNF) exercises

SKILL CLASSIFICATIONS

The nature of a skill imposes specific demands on the learner that must be considered when designing learning experiences. To assist practitioners in understanding the nature of motor skills and the demands they impose, several classification systems or **taxonomies** have been developed that organize motor skills by their common elements. Knowing the relationships among diverse skills can assist the practitioner in planning learning and practice experiences as well as provide a starting point for performance assessment.

taxonomy: A model into which skills are classified.

Fine vs. Gross Motor Skills Frequently used in adapted physical education and motor development is the classification system that distinguishes between fine and gross motor skills. This scheme is based on the precision of movements and the corresponding size of the musculature required for their successful performance. Those skills involving very precise movements, which are accomplished using smaller musculature, are known as **fine motor skills**. These skills tend to be manipulative in nature; examples

fine motor skill: A motor skill involving very precise movements normally accomplished using smaller musculature.

gross motor skill: A motor skill that places less emphasis on precision and is typically the result of multi-limb movements.

include sewing on a button, tying a fly (fishing), controlling dental or surgical instruments and installing additional memory into a desktop computer. Larger muscles are used in the performance of **gross motor skills,** which place less emphasis on precision and are typically the result of multi-limb movements. Examples include running, hopping and skipping, which are generally known in physical education as fundamental motor skills.

While this classification system categorizes skills as either gross or fine, many skills require the combined effort of both large and small muscle groups. In bowling, for instance, the large muscles of the legs propel the body forward in the approach and those of the shoulder create the arm swing necessary to launch the ball. However, a high degree of fine motor control is needed to manipulate the spin of the ball upon release. In fact, fine motor control has a significant impact on the extent to which many skills can be performed proficiently (Payne & Isaacs, 1999), accordingly, the degree of fine motor control displayed during the performance of a skill can be used to assess skill development.

Also of interest to practitioners is the fact that children tend to achieve gross motor skill proficiency before developing control over fine motor skills (Eichstaedt & Kalakian, 1993). Developmental readiness must therefore be a consideration when designing teaching progressions, with the sequence in which skills or skill components are introduced moving from gross to fine.

CEREBRAL CHALLENGE #2

Determine where along the fine-to-gross continuum the following skills would be placed:

a. Signing a check
b. Dribbling a basketball
c. Throwing a discus
d. Walking with crutches

e. Tackling
f. Making a surgical incision
g. Picking up a paper clip
h. Setting a volleyball

discrete skill: A skill whose beginning and end points are clearly defined.

serial skill: A motor skill composed of a number of discrete skills whose integrated performance is crucial for goal achievement.

continuous skill: A skill whose beginning and ending points are either arbitrary or determined by some environmental factor rather than by the task itself.

Nature of Movement Organization A second taxonomy classifies skills into one of three categories based on the nature of their organization. A **discrete skill** is one whose beginning and end points are clearly defined. Examples are a golf swing, moving from sitting to standing and throwing a horseshoe.

Other tasks, such as a melange in classical ballet, roping a calf and performing a figure skating routine, are composed of a number of discrete skills whose integrated performance as **serial skills** is crucial for goal achievement. Finally, **continuous skills** are those whose beginning and ending points are either arbitrary or determined by some environmental factor (such as a finish line) rather than by the task itself. Typically, continuous skills are repetitive in nature and include cycling, speed skating, rowing, locomotion in a wheelchair and tracing a picture.

Sewing on a button is a fine motor skill.

Jumping is a gross motor skill.

Because serial skills are a collective sequence of multiple discrete skills, their complexity is greater than that of a single discrete skill. Due to their nature, however, serial skills can be simplified when necessary by practicing their components separately. The time spent practicing components in isolation, however, should be limited as the successful performance of both serial and continuous skills is dependent on the performers' ability to combine movements (Rink, 1998). In basketball, for example, an outlet pass commonly follows a rebound. How the rebound is performed in a given situation will determine how the learner will have to execute the pass. Consequently, practice should emphasize the entire movement sequence as well as other possible movement combinations (e.g., rebound, dribble and pass). This will enable learners to discover how the skill's components interact, which will better prepare them to adjust their movements in different situations (Rink, 1998).

CEREBRAL CHALLENGE #3

Categorize each of the following skills as either discrete, serial or continuous:

a. Performing the triple jump
b. Executing a crochet shot
c. Punting a football
d. Hurdling
e. Vaulting in gymnastics

f. Transferring from a wheel chair to a bed
g. Walking with an assisted device
h. Cross-country skiing

Predictability of the Environment The predictability of the environment in which the skill is performed is the determinant of the third classification system. This particular classification system is based on a continuum, as the degree of predictability can vary between low and high. On one end of the continuum are skills performed in stable, predictable environments. These are called **closed skills.** In closed skills, the performer controls the performance situation, because the object being acted on or the context in which the skill is being performed does not change. For example, in bowling, the pins are stationary and the performer chooses when to initiate the movement. Other examples of closed skills include chopping wood, picking up a cup of coffee, zipping up a jacket and taping an athlete's ankle.

Open skills are at the other end of the continuum, as they are performed in an unpredictable, ever-changing environment. Mountain biking is a good example of an open skill, because the performer must continually adapt his or her responses to conform to the trail. Other examples of open skills include pursuing an opponent in field hockey and walking through a crowd after a concert, movie or sporting event.

The closed/open distinction is an important one for practitioners, as the instructional goals for each differ significantly. For closed skills, consistency is the objective, and technique refinement should therefore be emphasized. For closed skills performed in a variety of contexts, exposure to those contexts is also important. In bowling, for example, the learner's performance must be adjusted depending on the placement of the pins during any given

closed skill: A skill for which the object or context to be acted on or within is very stable and predictable, allowing the performer to control the performance situation.

open skill: A motor skill that is performed in an unpredictable, ever-changing environment.

trial, so potential pin combinations should be practiced. Open skills, on the other hand, are performed in complex, unpredictable environments. Successful performance of such skills becomes more dependent on the learner's capability to select the appropriate response in a given situation than on mastering technique. Consequently, practice should emphasize development of the capability to respond to the ever-changing demands imposed by the performance environment.

The closed/open distinction can also assist practitioners in the regulation of task complexity. For example, throwing a football can be considered a closed or an open skill, depending on the context. Throwing at a stationary target would be considered a closed skill. As other variables are added, such as a moving receiver and a pursuing defense, throwing a football becomes progressively more open and, in turn, more complex.

CEREBRAL CHALLENGE #4

Determine where along the closed–open continuum the following skills would be placed:

a. Walking with a cane
b. BMX racing
c. Playing a video game
d. Guiding a patient through PNF exercises

e. Kicking a field goal
f. Mowing the lawn
g. Snowboarding
h. Balancing on a wobble board

Can any of the above be placed in more than one location along the continuum? Give an example, and explain your answer.

Multidimensional Classification System A complete understanding of the demands a task places on a performer, according to Gentile (2000), cannot be realized using a single-dimensional system. Instead, Gentile proposed a taxonomy that categorized skills according to two general characteristics. Skills are first analyzed according to the context in which they are performed, and then the action requirements of the skill are assessed. Combined, these two dimensions provide insight into the processes involved in skill acquisition.

Regulatory Conditions Skills are not performed in a vacuum. To successfully perform a jump header in soccer, for example, the performer must conform his or her movement to the height, size, speed and trajectory of the ball, as well as to the location of the intended target. A number of environmental factors therefore exist for any given skill that specifies the movement characteristics necessary for successful performance. These factors are known as **regulatory conditions** (Gentile, 2000), and their determination can be used to differentiate skills.

regulatory conditions:
Environmental factors that specify the movement characteristics necessary to successfully perform a skill.

CEREBRAL CHALLENGE #5

Determine the regulatory conditions for each of the following:

a. Performing a bicep curl
b. Hiking along a forest trail
c. Diving from a springboard
d. Cross-country skiing
e. Stepping onto an escalator

f. Picking up your change from the counter
g. Dusting the furniture in your house
h. Retrieving your suitcase from the baggage carrousel

The first question of interest when examining the environmental context of a task is whether the regulatory conditions are stationary, as in shooting at a stationary target, or in motion, such as in skeet shooting. Notice that this concept parallels that of the open vs. closed skill classification in that the regulatory conditions for closed skills tend to be stationary, while those for open skills tend to be in motion. As indicated earlier, when a learner must conform to constraints imposed by the environment, more complex processes must take place to assess the environment and select an appropriate response.

The second question of interest is whether there is inter-trial response variability, that is, whether the regulatory conditions remain fixed or change with each successive performance attempt. A free throw, for example, has low inter-trial variability because the context in which it is performed does not change from one shot to the next. The basket does not change, the distance from which one must shoot remains constant and defenders do not oppose the performer. A great deal of inter-trial variability would be experienced by a tailback, on the other hand, as his running pattern must change each time he receives the ball to avoid tackles and gain maximum yardage.

Action Requirements The other dimension proposed by Gentile (2000) pertains to the action requirements of a skill, specifically with respect to body movement and object manipulation. Body movement in this context refers to whether the performer must change locations when performing the skill. Cross-country skiing, performing the high jump and using an assisted walking device are examples of skills that require the performer to move from one place to another. On the other end of the spectrum are skills that require body stability. Push-ups, lifting a coffee mug while seated, a golf putt and playing the drums would all fall into this category.

A second determinant of action requirements is object manipulation. A variety of skills require the performer to manipulate objects or opponents. Wrestling, knitting and grasping would fall into this category. Other skills, including step patterns in aerobics and performing pelvic tilt exercises, do not require object manipulation. Notice that object manipulation generally involves the use of the hands.

Practical Application To use this classification system to understand the demands that a task imposes on a learner, one must ask four questions: (1) Are the regulatory conditions stable or in motion? (2) From trial to trial, do the regulatory conditions remain fixed or do they change? (3) Is the performer required to change locations or maintain body position when performing the skill? and (4) Does the task require the performer to manipulate an object or opponent or not? Once the answer for each question is determined, the skill can be classified into one of sixteen resulting categories (see Table 1.1).

Gentile's multidimensional classification system was originally developed for physical therapists and offers the human movement practitioner several uses. First, as you move diagonally from the top left box to the bottom right box, task complexity increases with a subsequent increase in the demands placed on the performer. Accordingly, the simplest skill would be one that is stationary, involves no inter-trial variability or body transport and does not require object manipulation. On the other end of the spectrum, the most complex skill is performed in an environmental context that is in motion, involves high inter-trial variability and requires both body transport and object manipulation. To successfully perform such a skill, learners must be able to scan their environment to identify and process relevant information, decide how to respond and allocate attentional resources to concurrently control body transport and object manipulation. By understanding the level of complexity of a skill, practitioners can better design challenging yet realistic learning experiences. Logical progressions that move from simple to complex can be created, ultimately leading to simulations of the actual context in which the skill will be performed.

TABLE 1.1
Task examples for Gentile's (2000) multidimensional classification system.

Action Requirements				
	Neither body transport nor object manipulation	**Object manipulation only**	**Body transport only**	**Both body transport and object manipulation**
Stationary and fixed	Doing a sit-up	Moving a chess piece	Climbing a ladder	Heaving a shot put
Stationary and variable	Writing ABC's with foot for ankle rehabilitation	Playing "round the clock" in darts	Following a dance pattern that has been placed on the floor	With a partner, following a dance pattern that has been placed on the floor
Moving and fixed	Floating on a river in an innertube	Playing with a yo-yo	Running down a hill	Walking on crutches in a clear hallway
Moving and variable	Riding in a tube pulled by a speedboat	Playing fooze ball	Skating on a crowded ice rink	Skiing a downhill slalom course

Regulatory Conditions

CEREBRAL CHALLENGE #6

Determine a simple to complex progression that might be used to teach dribbling (basketball) using Gentile's taxonomy.

Gentile's model can further be used to systematically evaluate a learner's movement capabilities and limitations. This assessment affords practitioners a better understanding of the degree of complexity that a learner is able to handle and can provide insight into what performance demands (e.g., scanning the environment, processing information, allocating attention) are problematic.

Individual Differences

individual differences: Relatively stable and enduring characteristics that make each of us unique.

One challenge faced by practitioners is the fact that all learners are unique. This uniqueness is a function of relatively stable and enduring characteristics known as **individual differences.** Factors such as height, body type, physiological makeup (e.g., number of white twitch muscle fibers), learning styles, type and amount of previous movement experience, motivation, developmental level, cultural background, psychological makeup, attitude and confidence all affect the rate of and potential for developing skill proficiency. Because of individual differences, not all teaching strategies will be equally effective for all learners.

MOTOR ABILITIES

ability: A genetic trait that is prerequisite to the development of skill proficiency.

Of interest to human movement practitioners are individual differences in motor abilities. **Abilities** are genetic traits that cannot be modified through practice and are prerequisite for skilled performance. Accordingly, the degree to which a learner could potentially develop proficiency at a particular motor skill is dependent on whether he or she possesses the necessary underlying abilities.

Although many different abilities have been identified to date, it was initially hypothesized that there existed a single general motor ability (Brace, 1927; McCloy, 1934). The impetus behind this notion was the observation that accomplished athletes often were able to quickly pick up new skills and excel at numerous other skills without much practice. It therefore seemed reasonable to surmise that there existed a high correlation between one's level of general ability and one's potential for skill proficiency at a variety of tasks. In other words, if you had inherited a high level of general motor ability, you should be able to achieve a high level of proficiency in all motor skills, from golf to bobsledding to kayaking.

Refuting the existence of a general motor ability, the author of the specificity hypothesis proposed that not only do individuals inherit a large number of motor abilities but also that those abilities are independent of one another (Henry, 1968). In addition, each skill requires a set of particular abilities for successful performance. Consequently, an individual who obtains a high degree of proficiency in archery will not necessarily achieve that same degree of proficiency in wrestling, as these two skills have different underlying ability requirements.

Research examining the strength of interrelationships between motor abilities silenced the debate between proponents of the general and specificity hypotheses. In general, researchers found low correlations between an individual's performances of two different tasks (including those that appeared to be closely related), which supported the specificity hypothesis (Drowatzky & Zucatto, 1967; Henry, 1968; Robertson, Zelaznik, Lantero, Bojczyk, Spencer, Doffin & Schneidt, 1999; Zelaznik, Spencer & Doffin, 2000). However, because the correlations were found to be low, instead of there being no correlation at all, it was possible that some of the same underlying abilities were required by different tasks. Recognizing this, Fleishman (1962) set out to not only identify underlying motor abilities that were predictive of high skill proficiency levels, but to create a taxonomy from which skills could then be classified.

CATEGORIZING MOTOR ABILITIES

Fleishman's taxonomy groups motor abilities into two categories: (1) perceptual motor abilities and (2) physical proficiency abilities. The eleven perceptual motor abilities and nine physical abilities are identified in Table 1.2 along with an example of a skill for which the ability is elemental. It should be noted that this list is not all-inclusive, nor is it likely that all abilities have yet been identified.

TABLE 1.2
Fleishman's taxonomy of motor abilities

Abilities	Definition	Illustration
Perceptual Motor Abilities		
Control Precision	Ability to make highly controlled movement adjustments, especially those involving larger muscle groups	Dribbling a soccer ball
Multi-limb Coordination	Ability to coordinate numerous limb movements simultaneously	Spiking a volleyball
Response Orientation	Ability to rapidly select a response from a number of alternatives, as in choice reaction time (RT) situations	Tailback trying to find an opening
Reaction Time	Ability to rapidly initiate a response to a stimulus	The start in a swimming competition
Speed of Limb Movement	Ability to make a gross rapid limb movement without regard for reaction time	Executing a slapshot in hockey

(continued on next page)

TABLE 1.2 Fleishman's taxonomy of motor abilities *(continued)*

Abilities	Definition	Illustration
Perceptual Motor Abilities		
Rate Control	Ability to make continuous speed and direction adjustments with precision when tracking	Mountain biking
Manual Dexterity	Ability to control manipulations of large objects using arms and hands	Playing water polo
Finger Dexterity	Ability to control manipulations of small objects primarily through use of fingers	Dialing a number on a cell phone
Arm-Hand Steadiness	Ability to make precise arm-hand positioning movements where involvement of strength and speed are minimal	Working as a dentist
Wrist-Finger Speed	Ability to move the wrist and fingers rapidly	Dealing a deck of cards
Aiming	Ability to quickly and accurately direct hand movements at a small object	Tapping the keyboard of a pocket PC with a stylus to enter text
Physical Proficiency Abilities		
Static Strength	Ability to generate maximum force against weighty external object	Pushing a car out of snowbank
Dynamic Strength	Muscular endurance or ability to exert force repeatedly	Rock climbing
Explosive Strength	Muscular power or ability to create maximum effort by combining force and velocity	Throwing a javelin
Trunk Strength	Dynamic strength of trunk muscles	Pole vaulting
Extent Flexibility	Ability to move trunk and back muscles through large ROM (Range of Motion)	Performing a circus contortionist act
Dynamic Flexibility	Ability to make repeated, rapid flexing movements	Springboard diving or aerial ski jumping
Gross Body Coordination	Ability to coordinate numerous movements simultaneously while the body is in motion	Slalom skiing or synchronized swimming
Gross Body Equilibrium	Ability to maintain balance without visual cues	Tightrope walking while blindfolded
Stamina	Cardiovascular endurance or ability to sustain effort	Climbing Mt. Everest

CEREBRAL CHALLENGE #7

Determine which abilities would be important to become highly proficient in the following skills:

a. Bobsledding
b. Wiring a house (electrician)
c. Accomplishing a triple axel in figure skating
d. Driving a race car
e. Performing heart surgery
f. Juggling
g. Fire fighting
h. Competing in a triathlon

CEREBRAL CHALLENGE #8

Which of the following statements is/are true? Justify your answer.

1. An individual can have abilities but not be skilled.
2. An individual can be skilled without ability.

PRACTICAL IMPLICATIONS

All of us have different abilities that enhance or limit our capability to become skilled at a particular task, but even if we possess the prerequisite abilities for accomplishing a task, there is no guarantee that we will become skillful. We only have the potential to become skillful. Practice and experience also play a role in realizing that potential. Consequently, children should be provided with as many varied movement experiences as possible. In addition, those experiences should be developmentally appropriate. Learners will modify skills according to their current level of ability. For example, successful performance of a regulation free throw requires a prerequisite strength level. A young learner who has not yet developed to that point will modify his or her performance accordingly in an attempt to achieve the goal of the task, making a basket. Consequently, rather than employing correct technique, the learner may instead execute the free throw using more of a "shot put" type movement in order to generate enough force to project the ball high enough and far enough. Rather than reinforce this type of movement, practitioners should lower the baskets to a more suitable height. As learners continue to develop, their level of abilities will increase, though not all learners will progress at the same rate.

The concept of abilities is also useful for skill classification. Through a method known as a **task analysis,** those underlying abilities important to the successful performance of a specific skill can be determined. Skills can then be grouped accordingly. To perform a task analysis, a skill is first broken down into its key elements or component parts. Once the key components have been identified, the important abilities necessary to meet their requirements can be more readily determined. By conducting a task analysis,

task analysis: The breaking down of a skill into its component parts and corresponding underlying abilities.

Starting Position

Approach

Jump

Arm Swing and Contact

Follow Through

> **UNDERLYING ABILITIES**
>
> Control Precision
> Multi-limb Coordination
> Rate Control
> Aiming
> Explosive strength
> Trunk Strength
> Dynamic Flexibility

FIGURE 1.2
Task analysis of the volleyball spike

practitioners can develop a greater understanding of the requirements of the skill. Figure 1.2 illustrates a task analysis and subsequent examples of ability prerequisites for the volleyball spike.

 CEREBRAL CHALLENGE #9

1. For a skill of your choice, perform a task analysis to determine its component parts and the underlying abilities required to achieve a high degree of proficiency.
2. Think about the activities that you tend to participate in versus those you tend to avoid. Speculate as to why you make these choices by comparing the underlying abilities needed to accomplish the activities.

COMMON MYTH

Future success in a specific skill can easily be predicted.

If we can determine the underlying abilities important to the successful performance of a specific skill, it would stand to reason that an individual who possesses those same abilities would be predisposed to achieving a high level of proficiency. Imagine the impact this would have on sports programs, as we could predict future performance by simply screening individuals for certain abilities. In fact, talent identification programs, which have been around for decades, screen children and adolescents using a battery of tests that have been constructed to determine the extent to which they possess certain abilities. The test results are then used to predict those individuals who have the potential to succeed in a given sport. But how successful have these programs been in predicting a person's potential for success in a specific skill? And what can we learn from them to help identify future stars during T-ball?

RESEARCH NOTE

Hoare and Warr (2000) conducted a study to examine the effectiveness of applying an Australian talent identification model that is traditionally used with individual sports to the team sport of women's soccer. Subjects (ages 15–19) with a background in team sports or track and field were recruited to participate in the program. Following two days of testing, which included the assessment of physiological (vertical jump, acceleration, speed, agility and aerobic power), anthropometric (height, mass) and skill (juggling, dribbling, ball control, passing and receiving) attributes, 17 of the original 71 athletes were chosen, based on their abilities, to take part in a 12-month training program. At the conclusion of the 12-month program, which included 25 competitions, 10 players (59%) were selected for regional teams, with two being selected for the state team within six months. Based on their results, the authors recommended that speed and acceleration should be weighed more heavily in the future and suggested that selection procedures would benefit from the development of an objective test of "game sense" (technical and tactical competence).

Results of talent identification programs have been mixed. To understand why, we must consider three limitations of such programs. First, as was indicated earlier, it is likely that all of the abilities that contribute to skilled performance have yet to be identified. Second, a high level of performance in the early stages of learning does not always correlate to advanced performance, due to changes in the requirements of the skill. For example, a child may be an outstanding hitter in T-ball where the ball remains stationary, but the results may be different when he or she moves to the next level, where the ball is pitched. Third, abilities alone cannot predict performance; other individual differences must be considered. Because of differences in reaching physical maturity, for example, players that possess the underlying abilities to excel in a sport may get cut from a team. A great example is Michael Jordan, who was cut from his high school basketball team when he was a sophomore, yet went on to become one of the greatest basketball players ever to play the game!

While it is apparent that individual differences must be taken into account for the development of a successful talent identification program, these differences' impact on learning should be the practitioner's primary concern. Practitioners must remember that all learners are unique in what they bring to the learning environment. Consequently, one teaching strategy doesn't work for everyone. Practitioners should, therefore, develop a large repertoire of instructional strategies so they can accommodate the needs of all learners. Furthermore, practitioners should take the time to get to know each learner. What types of past experiences have they had? What motivates them? What situations lead to increased anxiety? Because of the influence of individual differences, it will be time well spent.

A Look Ahead

Human movement is a complex phenomenon that is a function of the interaction of three elements: the learner, the task and the environment in which the task is performed. Because this concept is foundational to the development of optimal learning experiences, practitioners must develop a working knowledge of this interaction in order to help learners realize their potential. Further development of this working knowledge requires an understanding of the underlying processes that govern movement execution and control. The following chapter begins this discussion, focusing on the factors that influence movement preparation.

Can future success in a skill be predicted?

Summary

- The interaction of the learner, the task and the environment in which the task is performed is fundamental to the understanding and facilitation of motor skill acquisition and performance.
- The field of motor learning examines the processes and variables that influence the acquisition and refinement of motor skills, while motor

control focuses on the neural, physical and behavioral aspects that underlie movement.

- Learning and performance are not synonymous. Learning is a relatively permanent change in the capability to execute a motor skill as a result of practice or experience, while performance is simply the act of executing a skill.
- Motor skills are categorized using several classification systems:
  - The gross–fine motor skills continuum is based on the precision of execution of a movement.
  - Skills can be classified as discrete, serial or continuous according to the nature of their movement organization.
  - The open–closed motor skills continuum is based on the predictability of the environment.
  - Gentile's multidimensional classification categorizes skills according to both the context in which they are performed and the action requirements of the skill.
- All teaching strategies will not be equally effective for all learners due to individual differences.
- Each of us possesses different abilities, which are genetically determined traits that enhance or limit our capability to become skilled at a particular task.
- By conducting a task analysis, one can identify those underlying abilities important to the successful performance of a specific skill.
- Talent identification programs where athletes are screened using a battery of tests to predict future success based on whether they possess certain abilities have shown mixed results.

Review Questions

1. Compare and contrast motor learning and motor control.
2. Define learning. What is the relationship between learning and performance?
3. What four criteria must a task meet if it is to be classified as a skill?
4. How are skills and abilities different?
5. Explain why most of the classification systems discussed involve a continuum.
6. Briefly summarize each classification system.
7. Explain how Gentile's taxonomy differs from the other classification types. Why is this significant?
8. Explain the controversy over general vs. specific motor abilities.
9. Explain why predicting future performance success is not always accurate.
10. What is the relevance of the interaction of the learner, the task and the environment in human movement?

References

Brace, D.K. (1927). *Measuring motor ability*. New York, NY: A.S. Barnes.

Drowatzky, J.N. & Zucatto, F.C. (1967). Interrelationships between selected measures of static and dynamic balance. *Research Quarterly, 38*, 509–510.

Eichstaedt, C.B. and Kalakian, L.H. (1993). *Developmental/adapted physical education: Making ability count.* (3rd ed.). New York, NY: MacMillan Publishing Co.

Fleishman, E.A. (1962). The description and prediction of perceptual motor skill learning. In R. Glasser (ed.), *Training research and education* (pp. 137–175). Pittsburgh, PA: University of Pittsburgh Press.

Gentile, A.M. (2000). Skill acquisition: Action, movement, and the neuromotor processes. In J.H. Carr & R.B. Shepard (eds.), *Movement science: Foundations for physical therapy in rehabilitation* (pp. 111–180). Rockville, MD: Aspen Publications.

Henry, F.M. (1968). Specificity vs. generality in learning motor skills. In R.C. Brown & G.S. Kenyon (eds.), *Classical studies on physical activity* (pp. 331–340). Englewood Cliffs, NJ: Prentice-Hall.

Hoare, D.G. & Warr, C.R. (2000). Talent identification and women's soccer: An Australian experience. *Journal of Sports Sciences, 18*, 751–758.

McCloy, C.H. (1934). The measurement of general motor capacity and general motor ability. *Research Quarterly, 5* (Suppl. 5), 45–61.

Payne, V.G., & Isaacs, L.D. (1999). *Human motor development: A lifespan approach* (4th ed.). Mountain View, CA: Mayfield Publishing Company.

Rink, J.E. (1998). Motor learning. In B.S. Mohnsen (ed.), *Concepts of physical education: What every student needs to know* (pp. 15–37). Reston, VA: NASPE.

Robertson, S.D., Zelaznik, H.N., Lantero, D.A., Bojczyk, K.G., Spencer, R.M., Doffin, J.G. & Schneidt, T. (1999). Correlations for timing consistency among tapping and drawing tasks: Evidence against a single timing process for motor control. *Journal of Experimental Psychology: Human Perception and Performance, 25*(5), 1316–1330.

Zelaznik, H.N., Spencer, R.M. & Doffin, J.G. (2000). Temporal precision in tapping and circle movements at preferred rates is not correlated: Further evidence against timing as a general-purpose ability. *Journal of Motor Behavior, 32*, 193–199.

CHAPTER TWO

Understanding Movement Preparation

After 90 grueling minutes of regulation and 30 minutes of overtime, the score was tied: USA 0, China 0. The 1999 Womens' Soccer World Cup would be decided by penalty kicks. China shot first, and Xie Huilin found her mark in the top left corner of the goal. U.S. co-captain Carla Overbek answered back. Next, China's Haiyan Qui and the U.S.'s Joy Fawcett were equally successful, tying it up at 2–2. This brought up Liu Ying. As her kick shot towards the left side of the goal, the U.S. goalkeeper, Briana Scurry, dove with outstretched arms, making an amazing save that sent a record crowd of 90,185 fans into a frenzy. The U.S. then went ahead 3–2 after Kristine Lily easily scored. Ouying Zhang beat Scurry with China's 4th penalty shot, while Mia Hamm answered, putting the U.S. ahead once again. The final kicker for China, Sun Wen, the tournament's top scorer, put her shot far left of Scurry, tying the game at 4–4. The hopes of the U.S. team rested on the fifth and final kicker, Brandi Chastain. The packed stadium was silent as they watched her approach the ball. She drilled it off of her left foot. The Chinese goalkeeper, Gao Hong, responded, but she was too late. The ball soared past her, and history was made: USA 5, China 4.

The interaction of the performer, the task and the environment in the generation of a goal-directed action suggests that some form of movement preparation precedes the execution of a motor response. Faced with the task of blocking a penalty kick, for example, the goalkeeper must somehow assess the situation to determine both where the ball will go and what movement will intercept it. Her task is further complicated by a time constraint, as she has a fraction of a second to not only make these decisions but to organize and execute the motor response before the ball reaches the goal line. So why was Scurry able to make a save, while Hong responded too late?

Theoretical Approaches to Movement Preparation

perception: The process by which meaning is attached to information.

Our senses are constantly being bombarded with information from both internal and external sources (input). Before any of that information can potentially be used to assist a learner in selecting an appropriate response for a given situation, however, it must first be interpreted. The process by which meaning is attached to input is known as **perception**. Two prevailing approaches regarding perception exist. The first, a product of cognitive psychology, maintains that perceptual processes lead to the creation of some form of symbolic representation of environmental and task information that traverses a series of mental processes, including a comparison with existing memory stores, resulting in a decision as to which action, if any, is needed in response to the situation. Because there is a "need for sensory input to be processed or elaborated to provide the perceiver a meaningful description of the world," perception in this paradigm is considered to be indirect (Burton, 1987; p. 258).

This view of perception has generally been associated with a model for movement preparation known as information processing (Figure 2.1). In this model, a performer, such as Gao Hong, will receive an abundance of information, including, in this instance, the foot used to kick the ball; characteristics of the ball itself, including velocity, trajectory, spin and direction; the score; the feel of sweat on her skin; the sight and sound of the crowd; the sound of a plane flying overhead; the smell and color of the grass; memories of prior success or failure in similar situations and an assessment of the area of the net to be covered. Some of this information is relevant or useful in assessing the demands of the task, such as the velocity, trajectory and direction

FIGURE 2.1
Information processing model.

of the ball, while other information, such as the plane flying overhead, is not and should be ignored. By focusing on pertinent **stimuli**, the goalkeeper will receive information crucial to the production of a response that will intercept the shot. Once the information has been gathered, it is transformed into afferent or sensory nerve signals and conducted to the brain, where it is integrated or compared with similar past experiences that are stored in long-term memory. Based on this comparison, a response is selected (dive right, catch, jump), organized and, through efferent (motor nerve) commands, executed. This paradigm further suggests that as the movement is initiated, information regarding its progress is fed back to the performer. This information, which is referred to as **intrinsic feedback**, can be used to make adjustments to the movement, if there is a discrepancy in what was intended and what is actually occurring (time permitting), and it enables the performer to evaluate the outcome of the response.

stimuli: A change in the environment that evokes a response.

intrinsic feedback: Response-produced information that is available to learners from their sensory system both during and as a consequence of performance.

CEREBRAL CHALLENGE # 1

1. Generate a list of possible stimuli, both relevant and irrelevant, that may have been available to the Chinese goalkeeper when facing Chastain.
2. In addition to deciding what response to make, details regarding that response, such as when to initiate it, must also be decided. Generate a list of possible responses and response details for the above situation.
3. Using a skill and situation of your choice, repeat #1 and #2.
4. Speculate as to the differences in processing demands for open vs. closed skills. Give examples to support your answer.

The second prevailing approach regarding perception suggests that the environment and task are perceived or interpreted directly in terms of affordances. **Affordances** are the action possibilities of the environment and task in relation to the perceiver's own capabilities (Burton, 1987; Gibson, 1977, 1979). In other words, the environment is perceived in terms of the actions the perceiver can potentially exert on it (Burton, 1987). Because of individual differences, several learners could be faced with the exact same situation and perceive entirely different affordances. For example, while walking through a clothing store, the affordances perceived by an adult will be much different than those of a small child because of differences in height. Similarly, an adult will likely read a sign, whereas a child may see it as an object to swing on. Since affordances are directly perceived, this perspective, known as the ecological approach to perception, argues against the need to refer to stored representations and views the relationship between perception and action as circular (Summers, 1998).

affordances: Action possibilities of the environment and task in relation to the perceiver's own capabilities.

Using this paradigm, the goalkeeper needs to decide if she will catch the ball or dive to block the shot. Rather than making a decision based on an elaboration of the ball's characteristics and memory stores of similar

FIGURE 2.2
The direct approach to perception suggests a circular relationship between perception and action.

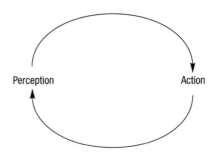

experiences, as suggested by the indirect approach to perception, the goalkeeper directly perceives the ball in terms of its "catchableness" in relation to her own body scaling and capabilities (Burton, 1987). If the goalkeeper perceives herself as being quick enough to position herself in front of the ball to make the catch, this action will be selected. If, however, she doesn't think she can make it, or doubts her catching ability, she may instead choose to block it.

RESEARCH NOTE

Oudejans, Michaels, Bakker and Dolné (1996) examined the relevance of action in perceiving affordances. The purpose of their study was to determine whether perceptual information about the perceiver's own actions has to be available to determine the catchableness of a fly ball. Because catchableness depends on both spatial (distance to be covered) and temporal (time available to cover that distance) aspects, Oudejans et al. speculated that judgments regarding catchableness would be more accurate when information about the catcher's action was available. Six nonexperts and six expert outfielders were tested in two conditions. The first condition, or the perceiving only condition, required subjects, who remained stationary, to determine as quickly as possible whether a ball could be caught if they had been permitted to make an attempt at catching it. The second condition was an actual catching condition. Results revealed that when compared to actual catching, stationary perceivers, regardless of experience, make poor judgments as to the catchableness of a ball. These results suggest that stationary perceivers who were prevented from receiving current information about their running capabilities did not rely on other information, such as what may be stored in memory, to determine the catchableness of a ball.

 ### CEREBRAL CHALLENGE # 2

1. Generate a list of examples of affordances that exist in your everyday environment.
2. Generate a second list of affordances that exist in your chosen professional field.

> **3.** How might the affordance you listed in question 1 be different for a woman who was seven months pregnant?

Preparing a Response

The conceivability of both theoretical approaches to movement preparation, in addition to the possible integration of the two, continues to be debated and explored by scientists. Regardless of the paradigm used to explain the internal processes that occur between input and output, research has clearly shown that a brief time lag occurs between the moment that a stimulus is presented and the initiation of a response. This time interval is known as **reaction time** (RT) and is a measure of the time needed to prepare a response.

Reaction time is not constant; it is dependent on the processing demands imposed by a given situation. As those demands increase, a corresponding increase in reaction time occurs, indicating the need for more time to prepare a response. The result, however, is a delay that can be detrimental to successfully avoiding a collision, catching an item that has fallen from the kitchen counter or stopping a penalty kick in soccer. Understanding the variables that cause such delays is therefore paramount in developing strategies for their reduction and, in some cases, avoidance during the performance of open skills. Of equal interest to coaches and athletes is how to elicit delays in an opponent's responses in order to gain an advantage.

reaction time: The interval of time between the moment that a stimulus is presented to when a response is initiated.

FACTORS INFLUENCING REACTION TIME

As indicated, a number of variables influence the length of time needed for response preparation. The following section introduces those variables and provides practical suggestions for their manipulation.

Number of Response Choices In the sprint start, there is one stimulus, the firing of the gun, and one response choice, exploding out of the blocks. Because there is only one choice in this situation, uncertainty as to how to respond is essentially eliminated. Conversely, in a penalty kick, there are a number of possible shots that can be taken, and a corresponding increase in the number of the response choices available to the goalkeeper. Because of the uncertainty of the impending shot, the goalkeeper must be prepared for anything. The processing demands for the goalkeeper are therefore much higher than for the sprinter. You can see that as the number of movement choices in a given situation increases, the amount of time needed to prepare a response increases. This increase in processing demands is reflected by an increase in RT.

This relationship between the number of choices and time to prepare a response was found to be so stable that it has become known as **Hick's Law** (Hick, 1952), named for its discoverer. Hick's Law states that **choice RT**, the

Hick's Law: Relationship between the number of movement choices and the time needed to prepare a response where the higher the degree of uncertainty in a given situation, the longer the time needed to decide which response to make.

choice RT: The reaction time resulting from a situation involving a choice as to how to respond.

EXPLORATION ACTIVITY 2.1: Choice Reaction Time

EQUIPMENT:

2 12-inch rulers
1 Partner

PROCEDURE

Activity 1: The objective of this task is to see how fast your partner can catch a ruler once you let it go. Hold one ruler vertically in the hand of your choice at its highest point so that the 12-inch line is closer to the holding point (see figure). Have your partner line up his or her thumb and forefinger of one hand on either side of the ruler at its bottom (zero). Once you are both in position, let the ruler go. Be sure not to give any indication to your partner of when you are going to let it go. Note the numerical value of the point of the catch.

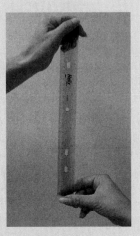

Activity 2: Now, hold a ruler in each of your hands as described above while your partner places both hands in the starting position. This time, explain to your partner that you will drop only one ruler and that the goal is to catch the dropped ruler with the corresponding hand as fast as possible. Again, it is imperative that you do not give your partner any indication of when you are going to let go. Note the results.

QUESTIONS

1. Was there a difference in where the ruler was caught for the two tasks? Explain your results.
2. Why is it important not to let your partner know when you are going to drop the ruler? Explain. What is the relationship of your answer to the concept of number of response choices?

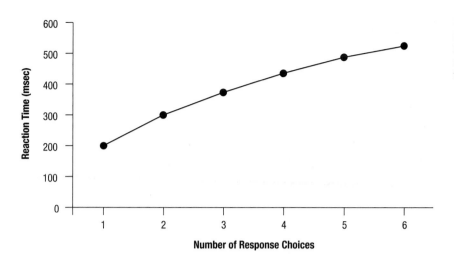

FIGURE 2.3
Predicted relationship between number of stimulus-response choices and reaction time.

reaction time resulting from a situation involving a choice as to how to respond, is logarithmically related to the number of stimulus choice alternatives. This relationship is illustrated in Figure 2.3.

Notice that in a situation requiring one definitive response, such as the sprint start discussed earlier, RT is approximately 190 ms, but in the situation faced by the goalkeeper, RT can be two to three times that amount. This increase in RT has important implications when the movement situation demands a quick and accurate response.

Response time is determined from the moment that a stimulus is presented to when a response is completed and involves not only RT but also **movement time** (MT) (Figure 2.4). Movement time is the interval between the initiation of the movement and its completion. Both of these times must be considered when analyzing the goalkeeper's task of intercepting the ball. Because of ball placement and speed, a goalkeeper has approximately 360 ms from the time the ball leaves the kicker's foot to decide how to respond and execute that movement (RT + MT) before the ball crosses the plane of the goal. Assuming that she has only two response choices, according to Hick's Law, RT will be approximately 300 ms. This leaves only 60 ms to execute the response. When examined from this perspective, it is not surprising that Gao Hong was unable to block Chastain's shot.

response time: The time interval from the moment that a stimulus is presented to when a response is completed; a combination of RT and MT.

movement time: The interval of time between the initiation of a movement and its completion.

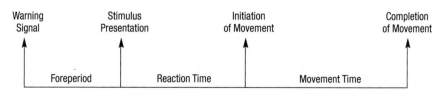

FIGURE 2.4
Components of response time.

CEREBRAL CHALLENGE # 3

1. Explain why a racquetball player who can perform five different serves proficiently has an advantage over an opponent who has only two. Use Hick's Law to justify your answer.
2. Provide other examples of Hick's Law and its influence on skills of your choice.

Since, according to Hick's Law, increased uncertainty leads to delayed or even inaccurate responses, practitioners should be aware of strategies that can both create or reduce this uncertainty, depending on the situation, to facilitate learning and performance. The goal of many competitive situations, for example, is to gain an advantage over an opponent. By having a large repertoire of proficient serves, plays, moves, pitches and the like, the uncertainty of which response will be required increases and the ability of the opponent to respond quickly and accurately will be diminished. On the other hand, the successful performance of other tasks is dependent on quick decision making. When a quarterback is executing an option play, trying to read all of the stimuli in order to choose the best of three options to execute can be overwhelming and, as illustrated by Hick's Law, time-consuming. As a result, coaches teach their quarterbacks to systematically look for key defensive characteristics to reduce the number of choice alternatives. In play, the quarterback assesses the potential success of the first option. If that option looks good, he takes it; if not, he will look for the second option, and so on. Emergency medical personnel use this same strategy when they arrive at the scene of an accident. Using what's known as the ABC's (airway, breathing and circulation) they systematically assess the situation, reducing their response preparation time.

Reducing uncertainty by systematically reducing the number of possible response alternatives is also a technique used to facilitate skill learning. When teaching the forearm pass in volleyball, instructors often organize practice such that learners are working in pairs. Within each pair, one person will toss the ball while the other passes it back. At first, the tosses are thrown directly to the learner. Once the learner has developed some proficiency, the tosses may be directed to the right, left, in front of or behind the learner, forcing him or her to move into the correct position and perform the skill. The first step of a normal progression for this drill is for the tosser to tell the passer which direction the toss will be made. Because the learner knows in advance where the ball will go, the number of response alternatives are reduced, subsequently reducing the processing demands of the task. The next step would be to eliminate the pre-toss information, forcing the passer to be prepared for any of the four possible response alternatives.

(Partially obscured by overlapping ticket)

8:55p CENTURY 16 EASTPORT PLAZA
DISTRICT 9
8/30/2009 9:00 PM
Ticket: 965242
$8.00
CENTURY THEATRES
8/30/09
Sun 08/30/09
STUDENT
St
2
AUDITORIUM
R

CEREBRAL CHALLENGE # 4

...eral video games on the market is to shoot the bad characters but ...good characters. The trick is that the characters literally jump out ...ınd the player must quickly decide whether they are "good" or ...ı were playing this video game, what strategies might you use to ...ıcertainty and response time and accuracy? ...ıt you suggest to police officers who face this same situation? ...kill of your choice, explain how you would increase or decrease ...nty, depending on your objective.

...ı Being given advanced information about not only what event ...r but also when it will occur has a positive impact on optimizing ...nt preparation and reducing response delays. Although situations ...here the performer is directly told in advance what to expect (for ex- ...use of a car's turn signals communicates an intent, and highway ...tell drivers about driving and road conditions), this is obviously not always the case. Consequently, performers must learn how to functionally reduce temporal and/or event uncertainty through anticipation.

Anticipation involves predicting what event will happen (**event anticipation**) and/or when an event will occur (**temporal anticipation**). The more predictable a stimulus, the quicker and more accurately a learner can respond. This concept is closely related to reducing the number of response choices as the learner essentially narrows down the possible options.

event anticipation: Prediction of what event will happen.

temporal anticipation: Prediction of when an event will happen.

CEREBRAL CHALLENGE # 5

Provide a list of examples from a movement situation or sport of your choice for both event and temporal anticipation.

Example:

Goalkeeping in Soccer

Event Anticipation:	What type of kick?
Temporal Anticipation:	When will the ball cross the goal line?
	When should I move in order to intercept the ball?

Prediction is dependent on the performer's ability to detect clues, or **precues**, that are often present in the environment. Therapists, for example, may watch for subtle changes in a patient's posture to anticipate when they should intervene. Similarly, parents use precues to anticipate when to catch a toddler who is learning to walk. In athletic contests, opponents are scrutinized to determine tendencies that can serve as precues. An offense may, for example, use the same play in a given situation, or a batter may expect a

precue: Clues in the environment that if detected can assist a learner in anticipating.

certain pitch depending on the count. Perhaps right before making a pass, a basketball player always looks at the player he or she is going to pass to. A racquetball player may change his or her back swing depending on the serve about to be performed.

CEREBRAL CHALLENGE # 6

"Briana Scurry looked at the Chinese midfielder Liu Ying as she walked to the penalty spot. Liu's head was down and her shoulders drooped, and it seemed to Scurry that she did not want the burden of the kick. 'This is the one,' Scurry said to herself. Liu set the ball down, backed up at a sharp angle, and began her approach with a tentative jog. Her intention became obvious, and her hips rotated in a way that gave the shot away. Scurry lunged with an explosive step, then planted her feet wide and dived to her left. . . ."

Longman, J. (2000). The Girls of Summer.
Women's Sports and Fitness, July/Aug p. 72.

Liu's hips served as a precue for Scurry, allowing her to anticipate what response she would have to make to block the shot. Using a skill of your choice, generate a list of precues that serve to increase the predictability of a certain response.

Regardless of whether a precue is based on an individual performer's idiosyncrasies or tendencies elicited in certain situations, research has shown that as the probability of a particular response increases (at a level of approximately 80 percent), performers will likely bias their response preparation in its direction (Larish & Stelmach, 1982). The result is that the action can be prepared in advance, decreasing RT. However, anticipation is not without risks. If the response required is anything other than that which the performer was preparing, the consequence will be a RT that is even slower than if the response had not been biased at all (Larish & Stelmach, 1982).

Practical Applications Through practice, learners' capability to recognize cues, idiosyncrasies and tendencies of opponents will improve, resulting in better anticipation of predictable events and the capacity to prepare required actions in advance. By identifying potential predictors, focusing learners' attention to where in the environment they might be located and designing drills in which they are incorporated, practitioners can facilitate this development.

The extent to which a learner is prepared to respond in a given situation can also influence anticipation. The provision of a warning signal, for example, leads to significantly faster reaction times, as it alerts the performer to the approach of an impending stimulus (Brebner and Welford, 1980). The "set" command issued prior to the firing of the starting gun, the toss of the ball in the tennis serve and the turn signal on a car all serve as warning signals. But the mere presence of a warning signal is not enough for a performer to achieve and maintain optimal preparedness. Ideally, the interval of time that transpires between the presentation of the warning signal and the stimulus, called the **foreperiod**, should range from one to four seconds. Foreperiod durations that fall short of this range do not permit adequate time to prepare, while expectancy levels fall when durations are too long.

Foreperiod consistency also influences one's ability to capitalize on anticipation. When foreperiod lengths are constant or predictable, temporal anticipation becomes possible (Queseda & Schmidt, 1970). Provided that the response to the signal is predetermined, such as in a sprint or swimming start, reaction time will be significantly reduced. Good starters prevent this by continually varying the foreperiod length prior to firing the starting gun. Yet foreperiod consistency considerations are not solely restricted to racing events. To avoid anticipation and quick responses from the defense for example, a quarterback varies the snap count. Randomizing foreperiod length is therefore essential in preventing an opponent from gaining an advantage. Situations do exist, however, where a constant foreperiod is desirable. Successful performance in music and the performing arts for example is highly dependent on temporal anticipation as the performers must be able to initiate their movements at a precise moment.

foreperiod: The time interval between the presentation of a warning signal and a stimulus.

Psychological Refractory Period If you have ever been faked out, you have experienced what happens when two stimuli, each of which requires a different response, are presented in succession within a short period of time. Those who haven't directly experienced this phenomenon have probably seen it occur: when a performer buys into a head fake to the right, for example, he or she will prepare and initiate the corresponding response, but if the opponent then quickly moves in the other direction, there is a momentary delay in response to this second stimulus. This delay, known as the **psychological refractory period (PRP)**, is reflected in a RT that is slower than the RT for the first stimulus, the fake.

psychological refractory period (PRP): Delay in responding to a second stimulus in a situation where two stimuli, each of which requires a different response, are presented in succession within a short period of time.

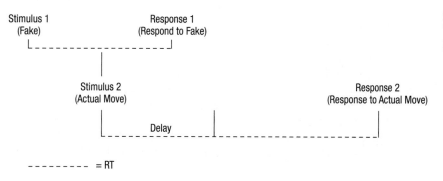

FIGURE 2.5
The psychological refractory period (PRP).

To execute a successful fake, several performance factors are fundamental. First, the fake must be realistic. When volleyball players want to draw a block in order to tip the ball around it, for example, they have to execute a convincing spike approach or the defense will read their actual intentions. Second, timing is critical. If the fake and the actual move are executed too closely in time, the opponent will not have enough time to buy into the fake and will ignore it. On the other hand, if the faker allows too much time to elapse between the fake and the actual move, the opponent has enough time to effectively respond to both. This timing comes with practice. Through practice, performers can also learn how to read a fake, and the occurrences of being fooled will decrease. Teaching learners to focus on an opponent's center of gravity, for example, provides clues as to the impending motion, because an opponent's center of gravity must first be shifted towards the desired direction of movement before a change in course can be made.

While fakes clearly illustrate the psychological refractory period, a performer who anticipates incorrectly experiences the same phenomenon. An excellent example is the batter who, having anticipated a fastball because the pitcher was behind in the count, suddenly realizes that the pitch is a change up (Shea, Shebilske & Worchel, 1993). Similarly, goalies often fall victim to PRP delays when the puck or ball is deflected in front of the net.

Stimulus-Response Compatibility Another factor found to affect movement preparation time when a number of stimulus-response (S-R) choices are available, is **stimulus-response compatibility**, which refers to the extent to which a stimulus and its required response are naturally related. When stimulus-response compatibility is low, additional time is needed to prepare

stimulus-response compatibility: The extent to which a stimulus and its required response are naturally related.

Goalies experience delays due to the psychological refractory period when the puck is deflected in front of the net.

a response, as reflected in increased reaction times. A classic example involves the arrangement of stovetop burners and their corresponding controls. Traditionally the burners are arranged in a rectangular pattern, while the controls are positioned horizontally. The spatial discrepancy in arrangement creates confusion and results in response delays. A more compatible organization would be to arrange the knobs in the same pattern as their corresponding burners.

You may have experienced this concept if you have gone into a skid with your car. The natural response when faced with this situation is to turn the wheel in the opposite direction of the skid, but the correct response is to turn into the skid. Fortunately, with practice the disadvantages of stimulus-response incompatibility can be overcome.

Aerobics instructors also pay attention to the S-R compatibility issue when conducting classes. Because of the imitative nature of an aerobics class, instructors must remember to mirror each move. This means that when facing the group, if the instructor wants the participants to raise their right hands, the instructor must raise his or her left hand. Mirroring increases the compatibility of the stimulus-response choice and reduces response delays or incorrect movements, facilitating participants' ability to successfully replicate the routine.

Finally, equipment manufacturers in the therapeutic modality and fitness industries have not ignored the issue of compatibility. Start and stop buttons on ultrasound machines or treadmills are colored in the corresponding green and red that we are accustomed to. In addition, the buttons/switches used to manipulate intensity level are often depicted by + and – signs, which indicate increasing and decreasing, respectively.

REDUCING RESPONSE TIME: BEYOND MOVEMENT PREPARATION

While strategies targeted at reducing movement preparation delays can be effective at decreasing response time, they are not always sufficient to lead to successful performance. Recall that response time is the combination of both reaction time and movement time. Consequently, slow responses can also be due to prolonged movement time (Figure 2.4). One strategy for decreasing response time would therefore be to increase the speed at which the movement is executed. Another strategy would be to reduce the length of the movement. This technique is used frequently in self-defense classes, where learners are taught not to cock back their arm prior to striking. Likewise, in hockey, shots in front of the net have little or no backswing in order to get the shot off as quickly as possible.

Rather than changing the speed or distance of the movement, an alternative approach is to increase the distance between the performer and the opponent. Tennis provides an excellent example of this strategy, where players will stand behind the baseline to receive the serve, which gives the receiver more time for decision making and/or movement execution.

Attention

Before a number of the strategies suggested earlier for the reduction of response delays can be successfully implemented, another factor must be considered. There is a limit to how many things an individual can pay attention to or process at any given time. When this limit is exceeded, a competition for attentional resources occurs, the consequences of which can be a reduction in the speed or quality of the performance of one or both activities or even a complete disregard for one of the activities.

EXPLORATION ACTIVITY 2.2 Limited Attentional Capacity

EQUIPMENT NEEDED:

Flat surface of approximately waist height

PROCEDURE

Stand perpendicular to the flat surface so that your dominant side is closer to it (see illustration below).

Now, lift your non-dominant foot slightly off of the ground and make a figure eight. Repeat this movement continuously. Now, while continuing to make figure eights with your nondominant foot, trace the numeral '6' on the flat surface with the index finger of your dominant hand.

QUESTION

What happened when you attempted to perform the two tasks simultaneously? Discuss this task with respect to attention.

Sensory
Input

Information
Attended To

FIGURE 2.6
Bottleneck theory of attention,
where information flow is
impeded by an attentional
filter that separates what will
be processed further.

THEORETICAL MODELS OF ATTENTION

Early theories of attention speculated that while we are subjected to a continuous flow of information, that flow is impeded at some point by an attentional filter that separates that which will be processed further and that
which will not (Broadbent, 1958; Deutsch & Deutsch, 1963; Norman, 1968;
Welford, 1952). Stimuli selected for further processing then pass (via processing) through the filter in a serial fashion. Because the filter essentially
creates a bottleneck in the flow of information traffic, this theory is often referred to as the bottleneck theory (Figure 2.6).

While the bottleneck theory accounts for phenomenon such as the psychological refractory period, it lacks flexibility and cannot explain situations
such as walking on a treadmill and reading a magazine, where an individual
can successfully attend to more than one stimulus at a time. Alternatively,
more contemporary theories suggest the existence of limited attentional resources or space (Kahneman, 1973; Wickens, 1984). According to this view,
two tasks can be successfully performed simultaneously provided that combined they do not exceed the attentional resources available. In other words,
if walking on a treadmill requires 25 percent of the total available attentional
space and reading a magazine requires 50 percent, the combined total of
75 percent falls within the amount available (Figure 2.7a). However, if another task was introduced, such as watching a news report on the TV across
from the treadmill, that combined with walking on the treadmill and reading a magazine required more attentional space than is available, interference occurs, and either the level of performance on one or more tasks
declines or a task may be ignored (Figure 2.7b).

FIGURE 2.7
Representation of attentional
demands on available
attentional resources.
In (a) the two tasks can be
performed simultaneously,
as they do not exceed the
attentional capacity. In (b) the
combination of these tasks
requires more attentional
space than is available, and
the level of performance on
one or more tasks will decline
or a task may be ignored.

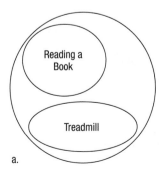

Reading a
Book

Treadmill

a.

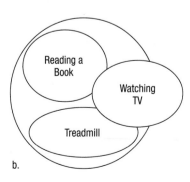

Reading a
Book

Watching
TV

Treadmill

b.

TIPS FOR PRACTITIONERS

Complicating the issue of limited attentional capacity is the fact that the attentional demands for a given task are not constant. Practitioners should be aware that environmental, task and learner characteristics all influence the attentional demands placed on the performer. These characteristics therefore have important implications with regard to designing instructional experiences.

Environmental and Task Complexity As the environment or task increases in complexity, the attentional demands required will undergo a corresponding increase, reducing the amount of attentional space available for additional tasks. For instance, sufficient processing space appeared to be available in the example of reading a magazine while walking on a treadmill. However, these same two tasks would likely interfere with one another if, rather than a treadmill, the performer was walking down a crowded sidewalk. By decreasing the complexity of the environment or task, attentional limits will not be exceeded, enabling learners to allocate the necessary attentional resources to the task being learned. For example, an optimal environment for a first-time driver might be a large empty parking lot instead of a city street in the middle of rush hour. Similarly, by removing defenders while individuals are learning skills such as lay-ups, dribbling and offensive plays, a coach can ensure that attentional capacity is less likely to be exceeded.

Attentional consideration should also be given to gait training. Research has shown that the attentional demands of an individual can vary according to the type of assistive device used and the patient's familiarity with that device (O'Sullivan, 1988). It appears that while both a standard pick-up walker and a rolling walker were attention demanding, the rolling walker required less attention to use.

CEREBRAL CHALLENGE # 7

1. Observe an individual performing a closed skill and another individual performing an open skill. How do the attentional demands differ for the two performers?
2. For a skill of your choice, explain how you might design the instructional environment to reduce the attentional demands imposed on the learner.

Skill Level of Performer Beginners, characteristically, have difficulty attending to more than one thing at a time when learning a new skill. Remember your juggling experience from Chapter 1? Imagine having to carry on a conversation while attempting to juggle. You probably needed every ounce of your attentional resources to focus on the task at hand. The addition of a conversation would have overloaded your attentional space, and the two tasks would have interfered with one another. A skilled circus performer, on the other hand, can not only juggle and carry on a conversation but do so while riding a unicycle. Consequently, when teaching beginners new skills, be sure that they have been given sufficient practice on the first task before teaching them additional tasks.

Numbers of Cues Attentional limitations are also exceeded when a performer tries to think about too many things at one time. This can be remedied with a few simple teaching strategies. First, when teaching a new skill, focus on only a small number of meaningful cues. Second, when correcting performance, avoid overloading the learner with information. Again, provide only one or two cues for the learner to think about. Finally, most performance situations present an abundance of information. Some of this information is relevant to the skill (relevant cues) while some is not (irrelevant cues). Teaching learners to selectively attend to relevant cues and ignore irrelevant ones will also reduce the competition for attentional space.

SELECTIVE ATTENTION

As you just read, the performance environment is teeming with information, some of it relevant and some of it irrelevant to the impending response. Because there appears to exist a limited attentional capacity, successful performance is dependent on the performer's ability to attend to meaningful information. Fortunately, we have the capacity to do this through **selective attention**.

selective attention: The ability to attend to or focus on one specific item in the midst of countless stimuli.

The classic example demonstrating our ability to selectively attend to or focus on one specific item in the midst of countless stimuli comes in the form of what is known as the cocktail party phenomenon (Cherry, 1953). Let's say that you are at a large tailgate party in the midst of many other tailgate parties. Although there are countless conversations taking place around you, you are still able to selectively attend to the conversation in which you are engaged. Of further interest is the fact that the mention of your name in another conversation will divert your attention to the individual from which it came. For another example of selective attention, try Exploration Activity 2.3.

EXPLORATION ACTIVITY 2.3: Selective Attention

Read the bold print in the following paragraph:

Somewhere **Among** hidden **the** in **most** the **spectacular** Rocky Mountains **cognitive** near **abilities** Central City **is** Colorado **the** an **ability** old **to** miner **select** hid **one** a **message** box **from** of **another.** gold. **We** Although **do** several **this** hundred **by** people **focusing** have **our** looked **attention** for **on** it, **certain** they **cues** have **such** not **as** found **type** it **style.**

What conclusions can you draw regarding selective attention based on this example? Include what you remembered about the regularly printed text in your response.

ATTENTIONAL FOCUS

The process used to selectively attend to specific environmental information is known as **attentional focus**. Attentional focus can be subdivided along two intersecting dimensions: direction and width (Nideffer, 1993). The width dimension ranges from a broad to narrow attentional focus, while the direction dimension ranges between internal and external. These two dimensions interact to create four types or styles of attentional focus: broad-external, broad-internal, narrow-external and narrow-internal (Figure 2.8).

Different performance situations place different attentional demands on the performer. Consequently, success is often contingent on the performer's ability to employ the appropriate attentional focus for a given situation. For instance, situations requiring proficient environmental awareness and assessment, such as a bicycle courier maneuvering through New York City traffic, necessitate the use of a broad-external attentional focus. On the other hand, the employment of a broad-internal focus would be necessary in situations where strategic analysis is required, such as when a billiard player plans the next shot. Mentally rehearsing the impending action requires a narrow-internal focus, while a volleyball player executing a set is an example of the use of a narrow-external focus.

It is important to understand that many situations require performers to continually shift their attentional focus throughout the performance. For example, Brandi Chastain likely used all four attentional focus types during

FIGURE 2.8
Four attentional styles based on the interaction of two intersecting dimensions: direction and width.

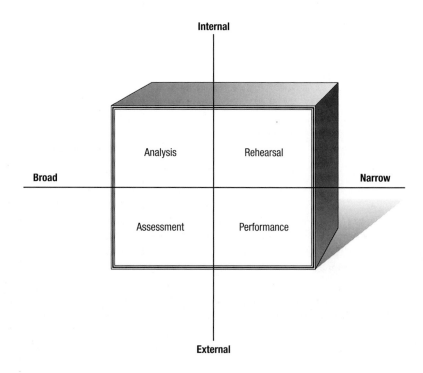

her penalty kick. First, she assessed the environment (goalie position, wind, etc.) through a broad-external focus. Once this information was gathered, her focus became broad-internal so she could decide what shot to take. Next, she switched to a narrow-internal focus, as she mentally rehearsed the shot and finally, her attentional focus became narrow-external as she initiated and executed the penalty kick (Nideffer & Sagal, 2001).

Other situations, such as those presented in the performance of open skills, demand that performers not only be able to shift their attentional focus but do it quickly and at the appropriate times. Performers who know where and when to focus their attention are able to disregard irrelevant information that will cause response delays. By teaching learners to recognize the attentional demands of their sport or movement as well as providing ample practice opportunities, practitioners can help learners sharpen their attentional switching skills.

CEREBRAL CHALLENGE # 8

1. Explain the possible attentional shifts that would be required to successfully perform the following:
   a. Manuevering through a restaurant with a wheelchair
   b. Cooking using a new recipe
2. On your next trip to the grocery store, record the attentional shifts that occurred from the time you entered the store to the time you got into your car to leave.
3. Explain, in detail, the attentional shifts required to execute a skill/situation of your choice.

Arousal

COMMON MYTH 2.1

The higher the level of arousal, the better the performance.

Arousal is "a general physiological and psychological activation of the organism that varies on a continuum from deep sleep to intense excitement" (Gould & Krane, 1992, pp. 120-121). It should not be confused with **anxiety**, which is an emotion resulting from an individual's perception of a situation as threatening, although changes in anxiety levels do lead to changes in arousal levels. While a performer's level of arousal does influence his or her performance, the manner in which it affects performance is not as simple as the myth states.

The actual relationship between arousal and performance has been captured by the **inverted-U principle**, also known as the Yerkes-Dodson Law (1908). According to the inverted-U principle, there exists an optimal level of arousal for peak performance (Figure 2.9).

arousal: A general physiological and psychological activation of the organism that varies on a continuum from deep sleep to intense excitement.

anxiety: An emotion resulting from an individual's perception of a situation as threatening.

inverted-U principle: The relationship between arousal and performance where there exists an optimal level of arousal for peak performance.

FIGURE 2.9
Inverted-U principle.

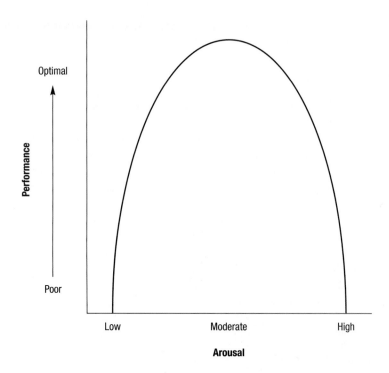

That optimal level is not a constant, however, and is dependent on both task and performer characteristics. As a task increases in complexity due to increased fine motor control, decision-making and attentional requirements, lower levels of arousal will be optimal. On the other hand, higher arousal levels are desired for tasks involving gross movements, minimal decision making and low attentional demands. Performing a delicate surgical procedure versus executing a power clean is therefore quite different with respect to optimal level of arousal for maximum performance.

A second consideration is the performer. Individual differences exist with respect to arousal and anxiety. As a result, the natural arousal level for one individual may be significantly higher than that of another individual. In addition, if an individual perceives a situation as threatening, given the relationship between arousal and anxiety mentioned earlier, arousal levels will rise. These factors, a naturally high level of arousal and perception of the situation as threatening (e.g., possible performance failure), both make an individual more susceptible to exceeding his or her optimal level of arousal.

AROUSAL AND MOVEMENT PREPARATION

cue utilization hypothesis:
A paradigm where changes in attentional focus occur according to arousal levels.

Explanations for the relationship between arousal and performance come in the form of the **cue utilization hypothesis** (Easterbrook, 1959). According to the hypothesis, changes in attentional focus occur according to arousal levels (Figure 2.10). Under low arousal conditions, a performer's attentional focus

A higher arousal level would be optimal for peak performance of a power clean.

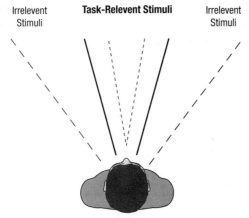

Irrelevent Stimuli   **Task-Relevent Stimuli**   Irrelevent Stimuli

FIGURE 2.10
Relationship between level of arousal and attentional focus. The area between matching line types indicates the stimuli to which one would attend according to level of arousal. (– – – – too broad; ········· too narrow; ——— optimal focus).

Sources: Weinberg & Gould (1995) and Martens (1987).

is relatively broad. If attentional focus becomes too broad, both task relevant and irrelevant cues become available to the performer. Because of our limited attentional capacity, as we saw earlier, a competition for attentional resources will occur, resulting in response delays and a corresponding decrement in performance. As arousal approaches optimal levels, however, attentional focus narrows, enabling the performer to concentrate on task relevant cues while ignoring irrelevant ones. This narrowing of attentional focus is termed **perceptual narrowing**. But, if arousal continues to increase beyond optimal levels and the performer becomes over-aroused, perceptual narrowing can become problematic. At some point, transitions (switching) between different attentional styles will be impaired and attentional focus will be so narrow that the performer may no longer be capable of effectively scanning the environment, leaving potentially significant stimuli undetected. This, in turn, may lead to inaccurate responses, as the performer lacks the necessary information for appropriate decision making.

perceptual narrowing: The narrowing of attentional focus with increasing levels of arousal.

CEREBRAL CHALLENGE # 9

1. The focus of a performer whose arousal levels are too low may become too broad and as a result, he or she may direct some attention to irrelevant stimuli. One example of such irrelevant stimuli is a heckler in the crowd. From your own experience, generate a list of other examples of irrelevant stimuli that might draw the attention of an individual with low arousal and affect overall performance.
2. On the other hand, an emergency room physician who is overly excited may experience perceptual narrowing to the degree that he or she becomes susceptible to making poor decisions. Generate a list of other professions and/or situations that may lend themselves to this situation. Fully explain your answer, using specific examples.

CEREBRAL CHALLENGE # 10

Are team pep talks before the game beneficial for performance? Fully explain your answer.

A Look Ahead

In this chapter we have examined many variables that influence the time it takes to gather information and make a decision before a movement can be organized and an overt response can be made. The following chapter will add to our knowledge of movement production as it discusses theoretical information regarding how responses are organized, executed and controlled once the decision has been made as to how to respond.

Summary

• The process by which meaning is attached to input is known as perception.

- Two prevailing theoretical approaches to perception exist: the direct approach, where the environment and task are perceived in terms of affordances, and the indirect approach, which is generally associated with information processing.
- A time lag occurs between the moment when a stimulus has been presented to the moment when a response is initiated. This interval of time is known as reaction time and is indicative of the time needed to prepare a response before it can be executed.
- Reaction time is not constant and depends on the processing demands imposed by a given situation.
- Numerous variables influence the time needed to prepare a response, including the number of response choices available, temporal and/or event anticipation, the psychological refractory period, stimulus-response compatibility and amount of practice.
- There exists a limit to how many things an individual can pay attention to or process at any given time. When that limit is exceeded, interference between those items competing for attentional resources occurs and performance declines.
- Selective attention is the ability to attend to or focus on specific aspects of the environment while ignoring others.
- Successful performance is often contingent on whether the learner can employ the appropriate attentional focus (attend to relevant while ignoring irrelevant information) for a given situation. Performers must also be able to shift that focus according to the changing demands of the task to avoid response delays.
- An optimal level of arousal exists for each performer. When that level is too low, attentional focus is too broad and the learner attends to both relevant and irrelevant cues. When arousal is too high, perceptual narrowing occurs and learners may no longer be capable of effectively scanning the environment, which may cause them to miss potentially significant cues.

Review Questions

1. Compare and contrast direct and indirect perception.
2. What are "affordances"?
3. What is the relationship between reaction time and movement preparation?
4. Give an example of a situation where your goal would be to reduce response delays.
5. In World War II, pilots were given a deck of cards, and each card had a different picture of an enemy aircraft. What might have been the purpose of these cards? Support your answer.
6. According to an ABC News report (June 18, 2000), there is a 400% greater chance of getting in an accident when talking on a cell phone.

In addition, the report stated that 87% of the drivers who use computer maps (global positioning maps) while driving veer out of their lane when watching the map. Discuss these data with respect to attention. Provide suggestions that may reduce these statistics.

7. Explain the cost-benefit trade-off associated with anticipation.
8. You are driving along a divided highway when a deer crossing sign on the side of the road catches your eye. When you look back to the road, you suddenly notice the illuminated brake lights of the vehicle in front of you. There is a car approaching in the opposite lane and a ditch on your right.
   a. What objects in this scenario served as warning signals?
   b. List the possible relevant and irrelevant stimuli that might be available in this situation.
   c. How is Hick's Law a factor in this situation?
   d. Identify an example of stimulus-response compatibility in this situation.
   e. The car in front of you swerves to the right. As you begin your response, it suddenly changes direction back to the left. What impact will this sudden change in direction have on your performance? Fully explain your answer.
   f. What attentional style(s) are necessary to successfully avoid a collision?
   g. Discuss how arousal may be a factor in this situation.
   h. Explain the two-second safe following distance driving rule based on the information you have learned in this chapter.

References

Brebner, J.T. & Welford, A.T. (1980). Introduction: An historical background sketch. In A.T. Welford (ed.), *Reaction Times*. New York: Academic Press, pp. 1–23.

Broadbent, D.E. (1958). *Perception and communication*. London: Pergamon Press.

Burton, A.W. (1987). Confronting the interaction between perception and movement in adapted physical education. *Adapted Physical Education Quarterly, 4*, 257–267.

Cherry, E.C. (1953). Some experiments on the recognition of speech, with one and two ears. *Journal of the Acoustical Society of America*, 25, 975–979.

Deutsch, J.A. & Deutsch, D. (1963). Attention: Some theoretical considerations. *Psychological Review, 70*; 80–90.

Easterbrook, J.A. (1959). The effect of emotion on cue utilization and the organization of behavior. *Psychological Review, 66*, 183–201.

Gibson, J.J. (1977). The theory of affordances. In R. Shaw & J. Bransford (eds.), *Perceiving, Acting and Knowing: Toward an Ecological Psychology*. Hillsdale, NJ: Erlbaum.

Gibson, J.J. (1979). *The Ecological Approach to Visual Perception*. Boston, MA: Houghton Mifflin.

Gould, D., & Krane, V. (1992). The arousal-performance relationship: Current status and future directions. In T.S. Horn (ed.), *Advances in Sport Psychology* (pp. 119–142). Champaign, IL: Human Kinetics.

Hick, W.E. (1952). On the rate of gain of information. *Quarterly Journal of Experimental Psychology, 4*, 11–26.

Kahneman, D. (1973). *Attention and effort*. Englewood Cliffs, NJ: Prentice-Hall.

Larish, D.D. & Stelmach, G.E. (1982). Preprogramming, programming and reprogramming of aimed hand movements as a function of age. *Journal of Motor Behavior, 14*, 322–340.

Martens, R. (1987). *Coaches Guide to Sport Psychology*. Champaign, IL: Human Kinetics Publishers.

Nideffer, R.M. (1993). Attention control training. In R.N. Singer, M. Murphy, and L.K. Tennant (eds.), *Handbook of research on sport psychology*. New York: MacMillan, pp. 542–556.

Nideffer, R.M. & Sagal, M.S. (2001). Concentration and attention control training. In J.M. Williams (ed.), *Applied sport psychology; Personal growth to peak performance*. Mountain View, CA: Mayfield Publishing Company, pp. 312–332.

Norman, D.A. (1968). Toward a theory of memory and attention. *Psychological Review, 75*; 522–536.

O'Sullivan, S. (1988). Clinical decision making: Planning effective treatments. In S. O'Sullivan, & T. Schmitz (eds.), *Physical rehabilitation: Assessment and treatment*. Philadelphia, PA: FA Davis.

Oudejans, R.D., Michaels, C.F., Bakker, F.C., & Dolné, M.A. (1996). The relevance of action in perceiving affordances: Perception of catchableness of fly balls. *Journal of Experimental Psychology: Human Perception and Performance. 22*(4), 879–891.

Queseda, D.C. & Schmidt, R. A. (1970). A test of Adam-Creamer decay hypothesis for the timing of motor responses. *Journal of Motor Behavior, 2*, 273–283.

Shea, C.H., Shebilske, W.L. & Worchel, S. (1993). *Motor learning and control*. Englewood Cliffs, NJ: Prentice Hall.

Summers, J.J. (1988). Has ecological psychology delivered what it promised? In J.P. Piek (ed.), *Motor behavior and human skill: A multidisciplinary approach*. Champaign, IL: Human Kinetics, pp. 385–402.

Weinberg, R. S. & Gould, D. (1995). *Foundations of sport and exercise psychology*. Champaign, IL : Human Kinetics Publishers.

Welford, A.T. (1952). The psychological refractory period and the timing of high-speed performance—A review and a theory. *British Journal of Psychology, 43;* 2–19.

Wickens, C.D. (1984). Processing resources in attention. In R. Parasuraman & D.R. Davies (eds.), *Varieties of attention.* New York: Academic Press, pp. 63–102.

Yerkes, R.M. & Dodson, J.D. (1908). The relation of strength of stimulus to rapidity of habit-formation. *Journal of Comparative Neurology and Psychology, 18,* 459–482.

CHAPTER THREE

Behavioral Theories of Motor Control

We have all watched in awe as elite athletes perform incredible feats: the pole-vaulter who becomes one with the pole while being projected into the sky, the trapeze artist who completes a flip and is caught at just the right moment and the skier with a disability, completing the downhill slalom course in record time. We look with equal wonder at the Parkinson's patient who has difficulty raising a glass to take a drink, or the crash victim who must relearn how to walk. Indeed, the human body and its ability to perform both simple and complex movements is truly fascinating. How the nervous system organizes the muscles to perform skilled movements is a complex puzzle that continues to challenge movement scientists.

In this chapter, we will examine the theories behind the organization and execution of skilled movements. Understanding theory is important for practitioners, as it is the foundation on which all instructional decisions should be made. After all, how can effective instruction be designed and implemented if we don't understand how people learn?

Coordination and Control

The complexity of determining how skilled movements are acquired and performed is known as the **degrees of freedom problem** (Bernstein, 1967). In the body, most joints are capable of moving independently in one or more planes. As a result, each joint has at least one degree of freedom, which must be controlled in order to carry out a desired movement. However, each joint also has a number of muscles surrounding it, and each of these muscles contains hundreds of individual motor units [a motor unit contains a motor neuron and all the muscle cells that it stimulates (an average of 150); Marieb & Mallatt, 2002]. All of these independent elements (nerves, muscles and joint movement possibilities) must be constrained into an organized movement pattern that must be controlled to meet the goal of the task. When considered from this perspective, even seemingly simple tasks become somewhat daunting.

To illustrate this concept, highlight the word "coordination" in the above subtitle. To accomplish this task, you must somehow manipulate your highlighter and produce a limb pattern that corresponds with the dimensions and location of the word on the page. The process of constraining the system's (in this case the body and highlighter) available degrees of freedom to organize an efficient movement pattern that will effectively achieve the goal of the task is defined as **coordination** (Sparrow, 1992; Turvey, 1990). But this alone does not solve the movement problem. What if you were asked instead to highlight the word "is" in the text, or your highlighter was running low on ink? Variables within the movement pattern such as how hard to push, where to start and finish, and how fast to complete the movement must also be resolved to achieve the goal of the task. The manipulation of those variables within the movement to meet the demands of a given situation is known as **control.** The performance of skilled movement therefore requires the learner to not only condense the available degrees of freedom but also to control the resulting movement. Consequently, both the development of a new coordination pattern and its control must be taken into consideration if we are to understand the acquisition and performance of motor skills (Vereijken, Whiting & Beek, 1992).

Skilled Movement: Command Center or Dynamic Interaction?

Currently, two predominant theories offer explanations of how skilled movement is coordinated and controlled. The first suggests the existence of a command center in the brain that is thought to make all decisions regarding the movement. When a decision to act is made, an appropriate movement plan is retrieved from memory and instructions are sent to the rest of the body to carry out the action. The second theory contends that a plan created by a command center couldn't possibly account for all variations and adjustments in skilled movement, and that the load on memory would be too great. Instead, skilled movement results or "emerges" from a dynamic interaction of numerous variables in the body, the environment and the skill.

MOTOR PROGRAMS

The mechanism at the core of the central command-based construct is the **motor program.** A motor program is an abstract representation of a movement plan, stored in memory, that contains all of the motor commands required to carry out the intended action. Early motor program theories proposed that for each movement to be made, a separate motor program existed and was stored in memory. When a specific action was required, the appropriate program was simply retrieved from memory and executed.

Two inherent problems were detected as the idea of motor programs was examined more closely, however. The first involved storage. If a motor program existed for each and every possible movement and movement variation, there would have to be limitless storage space in memory. The second problem lies in the production of novel responses. If a movement or variation of a movement has never been performed before, where does the program for that specific action come from?

THE GENERALIZED MOTOR PROGRAM

Unlike the authors of earlier motor program theories, Schmidt (1975) proposed that every movement does not require a separate motor program for its execution and that the motor program is more general in nature. This **generalized motor program** represents a class of actions or pattern of movement that can be modified to yield various response outcomes. Consequently, some elements of the generalized motor program (called invariant features) are thought to be relatively fixed from trial to trial, defining the motor program itself, while others (called parameters) are more flexible and define the program's execution (Schmidt, 1985). Before continuing, please complete the Exploration Activity 3.1 on the following page.

Invariant Features Regardless of how you were instructed to write your name in Exploration Activity 3.1, several underlying features of your signature remained constant. These underlying features, or **invariant features,** are similar to fingerprints. Just as our fingerprints can identify each of us, each motor program can be identified by its invariant features. To date, researchers have identified three possible invariant features: the sequence of actions or components, relative timing and relative force.

In Exploration Activity 3.1, regardless of the constraints imposed by the instructions, you spelled your name the same way each time. For example, if

motor program: An abstract representation of a movement plan, stored in memory, that contains all of the motor commands required for carrying out the intended action.

generalized motor program: Abstract representation of a class of actions or pattern of movement that can be modified to yield various response outcomes.

invariant features: Relatively fixed underlying features that define a motor program.

your name is Kim, the "i" always follows the "K" and precedes the "m." Any disruption of that specific order would result in an error in your signature. Similarly, regardless of where the ball has been set, the approach, the jump, the arm swing and ball contact in a volleyball spike must be sequentially executed. The sequence of actions, or the order of components, is therefore an invariant characteristic.

Not only do the components of a skill occur in a specific order, but they are also related to one another in certain invariant ways. One such relationship, relative timing, has been suggested with supporting evidence offered from a variety of activities, including walking (Shapiro, Zernicke, Gregor & Diestal, 1981), throwing (Roth, 1988), hurdling (Hay & Schoebel, 1990) and gait initiation (Brunt, Lafferty, Mckeon, Goode, Mulhausen & Polk, 1991). In essence, relative timing refers to the internal rhythm of the skill. The arm movement in the freestyle stroke, for example, can be broken down into 5 components. Of the total time needed to complete one cycle, let's say that 35% is accounted for by the entry, 13% by the catch, 8% by the mid-pull, 12% by the finish and finally 32% by the recovery. Because relative timing is considered invariant, these percentages should remain the same regardless of whether the athlete is swimming fast or slow.

EXPLORATION ACTIVITY 3.1
Signature Analysis: Fixed vs. Flexible Features

On a blank sheet of lined paper write your name (signature) according to the following instructions:

1. with your dominant hand
2. with your nondominant hand
3. holding the pen/pencil in your mouth
4. holding the pen/pencil between your toes
5. pressing down very hard
6. pressing very softly
7. slowly, while maintaining legibility
8. quickly, while maintaining legibility

According to early motor program theories, each of the above variations of your signature would have its own separate motor program stored in memory. Those theories were modified to suggest that the motor program is a more general representation of a class of actions and consists of elements that are relatively fixed and elements that can be modified.

Which aspects of the above instructions and of your corresponding responses were flexible and defined how to execute the motor program? Which aspects were relatively fixed from trial to trial?

RESEARCH NOTE

Shapiro, Zernicke, Gregor and Diestal (1981) tested the notion of relative timing by having subjects walk on a treadmill at different speeds. Hypothetically, the relative timing of the components of the walking cycle should not change as the overall speed of the treadmill increased. The results showed that for speeds up to 6 km/hr, the relative timing of the step cycle components did indeed remain intact. However, as the speed increased to 8 km/hr and beyond, the relative timing changed. Since members of a class of actions share similar characteristics in relative timing, we can infer that at speeds above 8 km/hr, a different motor program is controlling the action. Interestingly, the shift in relative timing characteristics corresponded to the participants' shift from walking to running.

A similar internal relationship has also been proposed with respect to ratios of force. When the overall force used to execute a skill is changed, the actual force characteristic of each component should change proportionately. Thus, the third invariant characteristic that has received some attention is relative force.

Parameters The features of the motor program that are flexible and define how to execute the program are termed **parameters.** Parameters are easily modified from one performance to another to produce variations of a motor response. This "adaptability" of parameters enables a center fielder to throw to third base from different areas of the field and allows an individual to walk up and down steps of varying heights. Three parameters have been proposed: overall duration, overall force and muscle selection.

parameters: Flexible features that define how to execute a generalized motor program.

The time taken to perform a well-learned motor skill can be increased or decreased as a unit according to changes in the overall duration parameter. Similarly, the overall force and amplitude (size of the movement) can be modified. Consequently, patients can learn to lift off plastic container lids of various sizes (e.g., the lid on a margarine container and the lid on a yogurt container), swimmers can increase the overall speed of their stroke as they approach the finish line and soccer players can make both long and short passes depending on the situation. Finally, as was demonstrated in Exploration Activity 3.1, the hand, foot or even mouth can be used to write one's name; in other words, the specification of muscles and/or limbs to perform the movement is considered a parameter.

 CEREBRAL CHALLENGE #1

1. The use of overweight implements is a common training method for conditioning in many sports. Throwers use heavier shots, discuses and javelins than normally used in competition; pitchers will throw heavier baseballs; hitters swing heavier than normal bats. Does this technique involve a manipulation of invariant features or parameters? Can you think of a situation/condition when the use

A swimmer can increase overall stroke speed without changing the underlying or invariant features of the motor program.

of overweight implements could hinder the development of correct technique? What signs might a practitioner look for to avoid this problem?

2. Another training technique used to prepare athletes for competition is to practice under fatigued conditions. Based on your understanding of invariant features and parameters, is this a good idea? Why or why not?

Specifying Parameter Values—The Schema

According to the generalized motor program concept, a shortstop is able to throw to different bases from various positions on the field by assigning appropriate parameter values to the program. But how does the performer know exactly how much force to create or how fast the ball should be thrown in each situation? The answer lies in the second aspect of Schmidt's theory (1975, 1985), the development of a **schema.**

schema: A rule or relationship that directs decision making when a learner is faced with a movement problem.

A schema is a rule or relationship that directs decision making when a learner is faced with a movement problem. The schema's development is the result of accumulated experiences within a class of actions. Each movement attempt provides the learner with information about the movement that is translated into a relationship that will then be used to guide future attempts. The more movements executed, the more developed the rule.

Let's say you go to the fair and come across a ball toss game whose prize is a huge stuffed animal. The objective of the game is to toss a softball into a peach basket in such a way that it does not bounce out. Feeling confident that you can accomplish this goal, you purchase three chances. Having assessed the attempts of some of the previous players, you decide that the best approach will be an underhand toss. On your first toss, the ball ricochets off of the bottom of the basket. On your second attempt, you decide to lean over the barrier and adjust the toss, decreasing the height of the arch and aiming more towards the front of the basket. Again, the ball bounces out of the basket, but this time with less force. On your final attempt, you again lean over the barrier as far as possible and throw the same low-arched toss, but with a little less force. Unfortunately, the ball barely bounces out of the basket again.

According to the schema concept, on each attempt you subconsciously abstract four pieces of information. The first piece of information involves the initial conditions that were present at the start of the movement. This information includes limb and body position as well as the environmental conditions when the movement was performed. Leaning over the barrier as far as possible is an example of initial position information. The second piece of information involves the response specifications or the parameters used in the execution of the movement, such as the speed and force of your throw. Next, the sensory consequences of the movement are abstracted and consist of the response-produced sensory information or sensory feedback. Information regarding what the throw felt like, for example, would be assessed. Finally, the success of the response in relation to the originally intended goal or outcome is obtained. This is known as the response outcome. Although none of the three attempts actually stayed in the basket, the response outcome for each of the three tosses was different. In the first attempt, the ball ricocheted out of the basket, implying that it had a great deal of force. In subsequent attempts, the magnitude of that force was reduced, indicating that the movement produced was approaching the movement needed to achieve the goal.

These four sources of information are briefly stored in memory following a movement attempt, to allow the performer to abstract some relationship among them. For example, in the first toss of our example, the initial conditions (e.g., the starting position), the response specifications (whatever parameter values were assigned to the program), the sensory consequences (what the performer's sensory system perceived) and the response outcome (the ball ricocheting out of the basket) and their relationship with one another

With practice, a schema for a skill is developed.

are all assessed, leading to an inference about how to successfully perform the task. The schema has begun to develop. Not only does this process occur for each additional attempt, but the resulting relationship becomes incorporated with the former relationship already developed in the existing schema. Consequently, the strength of the overall relationship increases with each successive attempt. The result is the development of the motor response schema, which is thought to be composed of two such relationships, the recall schema and the recognition schema.

The recall schema is responsible for organizing the motor program capable of initiating and controlling the desired movement. When an individual attempts to perform a movement, the desired outcome for that movement and the initial conditions are considered. A recall schema is then selected based on the relationship between actual outcomes and response specifications that have been developed through past experiences with similar movements. From this relationship, the performer determines what specifications will be required to achieve the intended outcome. The individual then executes the motor program according to the movement parameter values determined, and the movement is performed.

The recognition schema is formulated based on the relationship between the initial conditions, past actual outcomes and past sensory consequences and is responsible for the evaluation of a movement attempt. A set of expected sensory consequences that represent the best estimate of the sensory consequences of the correct movement are generated in response to the relationship between actual outcomes and sensory consequences. By comparing the actual sensory feedback from the initiated movement against the expected sensory feedback, the performer can assess the correctness of the movement. An error signal is generated when a mismatch occurs between feedback and the reference of correctness. This error signal provides the performer with information that is used to update the recall schema. Additional information provided by the teacher or coach also serves to update the recall schema.

By continually revising the estimates of the expected sensory consequences and response specifications, the recall schema updates the instructions to the muscles, which leads to more accurate responses on subsequent attempts. Through this process, the schema becomes more established and the performer can more accurately select the appropriate response specifications or parameter values to accomplish a movement goal.

CEREBRAL CHALLENGE #2

Consider the following teaching strategy used by a hockey coach. Having taught the slapshot and given the athletes an opportunity to develop a basic understanding of the movement, Coach X gives the players the following instructions:

Using the slapshot technique that we have been learning, perform the actions listed from each of the following locations:

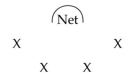

X   X

X   X

1. Shoot the puck so that it misses the net to the right.
2. Shoot the puck so that it misses the net to the left.
3. Shoot the puck so that it goes in the net.

Will this experience help or hinder the athletes' technique development for the slapshot? Why or why not? Use the schema theory to support your answers.

EXECUTING THE PROGRAM

Once a learner decides what movement to execute in a given situation, the performer subconsciously retrieves the appropriate generalized motor program from memory and, based on the existing schema, adds to it the estimated parameter values that will achieve the desired outcome. The details of the desired movement are therefore organized in advance by the motor program and sent to the rest of the body to be carried out. But how is the movement controlled once the motor program initiates it? The answer lies in the detail of the initial movement commands. In other words, does the motor program contain all of the information needed to carry out the action from start to finish, or are continuous adjustments made to the movement based on response-produced feedback?

Open- vs. Closed-Loop Systems Before you can start your workout on a stair-climbing fitness machine, you must select from a number of program options such as the hill profile or interval training. Once you hit the button indicating the desired program, that program will be executed for the specified amount of time. It cannot sense it if you don't like the program you have selected or if the program is too easy or too difficult for you. It simply runs its course. E-mail operates in a similar fashion. If you type a message and hit the send button, the message is automatically sent. Even if you wanted to change the way it was written, you cannot stop the message from being sent once you have hit the button. These two examples illustrate the notion of **open-loop control.**

Open-loop control mechanisms function by way of a two-level hierarchy (see Figure 3.1). An executive level or command center generates action plans that contain all of the information necessary to complete a response. These action plans are then carried out by the limbs and muscles (the effectors)

open-loop control: A mode of control whereby action plans are generated that contain all of the information necessary to complete a response.

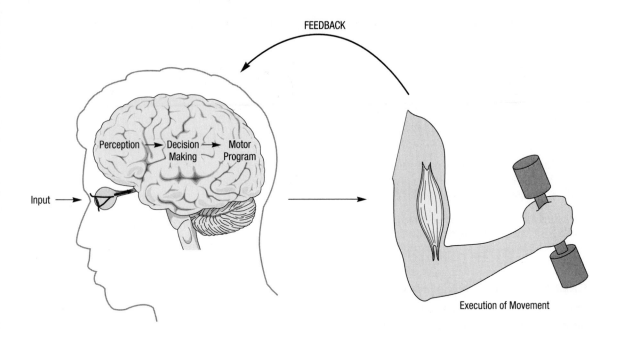

FIGURE 3.1
Representation of open- and closed-loop control systems. Open-loop components are labeled in lowercase letters.

closed-loop control: A mode of control whereby feedback is used in error detection and correction.

without modification. Applying this to human movement, input is perceived via processes in the brain. A decision as to how to respond is made, instructions to execute that response are sent to the muscles via the nervous system, and the response is performed. While feedback is constantly present during movement, it comes too late to adjust the ongoing movement. Consequently, once the prestructured commands are initiated (sent to the nervous system), the action has to run as planned. The feedback received regarding this trial can, however, be used to modify the next trial.

A second kind of control mechanism allows adjustments to be made once a program has been initiated. This is known as **closed-loop control.** A thermostat is a good example of a closed-loop system. Your heating system, once set, continuously monitors the actual room temperature and compares it to the desired room temperature. If a discrepancy is detected, that is, the room becomes too hot or too cold, the corresponding adjustments are made automatically by turning the heater on or off.

Closed-loop systems also function in a hierarchical fashion with one important distinction, the involvement of feedback. Instead of having to generate all of the information needed to complete the response, the command center needs only to generate an action plan that initiates the movement. Sensory information resulting from the movement's progress (response-produced feedback) is then continually compared to the desired movement, and any discrepancies detected are sent to the command center for correction. This cycle continues until the completion of the response. The distinction between open- and closed-loop systems, then, is that the feedback that accompanies a movement can be used to modify an ongoing action in a closed-loop system but cannot be used until the next response in an open-loop system.

CEREBRAL CHALLENGE #3

Compare and contrast open and closed skills with open- and closed-loop control systems.

While open- and closed-loop systems served as precursors to current motor program-based theory, motor control is now seen as a function of both open- and closed-loop mechanisms with motor programs operating in an open-loop fashion. Movements are believed to be planned in advanced, initiated, and carried out with limited modification unless time permits the incorporation of response-produced feedback. Consequently, in rapid movements, the prestructured motor program will control the movement from start to finish, as there is insufficient time to process response-produced feedback and then make the corresponding adjustments. For movements where there is sufficient time to process feedback, the initiation of the skill is controlled by open-loop mechanisms, but closed-loop control is used to continue the movement to its completion.

EVIDENCE SUPPORTING MOTOR PROGRAM CONTROL

Three lines of evidence support the notion of motor program control. First, if the motor program organizes the details of the desired movement in advance, it seems logical that as a task increases in complexity, the amount of time needed to organize the motor program would also increase. Henry and Rogers (1960) tested this notion by measuring the reaction time of subjects performing three tasks that varied in complexity. The tasks, moving from the lowest level of complexity to the highest, were a) lifting the finger from a switch being pressed down, b) lifting the finger from the switch and then reaching and grasping a tennis ball that hung 30 cm away and c) lifting the finger from the key, striking the tennis ball, reversing direction to push a button and finishing by reversing direction again to grasp another tennis ball. Results showed that as the complexity of the movement increased, reaction time increased (165 msec, 199 msec and 212 msec, respectively). Since reaction time measures the time from the onset of a stimulus to the initiation of a response (Chapter 2), their findings supported the idea that movements are planned in advance.

A second experimental approach used to test the notion of motor programs involved deafferentation, a technique where, for example, the sensory nerves of a limb are surgically severed so that the response-produced feedback can no longer reach the central nervous system. Early examples of such studies examined the motor behaviors of monkeys before and after deafferentation (Polit & Bizzi, 1978; Taub & Berman, 1968). In the Polit and Bizzi study, three monkeys were trained in a pointing task prior to undergoing deafferentation of their arm. They were then retested on the same pointing task they had learned earlier, and results revealed that following deafferentation and the subsequent loss of sensory feedback from the limb, the monkeys were still able to accurately move their arm and point to the target, further supporting the notion of motor program control.

Experiments exploring the effects of unexpectedly blocking a limb during movement are the basis of the third line of research supporting motor program control. Using electromyography (EMG), researchers compared the electrical activity in the muscles during limb movements and when those same limb movements were suddenly and unexpectedly blocked (Wadman, Dernier van der Gon, Geuze & Mol, 1979). Researchers inferred that if a motor program does indeed organize all of the instructions needed to carry out the movement prior to the movement's initiation, without regard to feedback, then the EMG of the blocked muscle should display a similar pattern to that of an unblocked muscle. Comparisons of the two limb movement conditions (unblocked and blocked) revealed that this was in fact the case.

Many baseball and softball players, much to their dismay, have probably experienced a real-world example of this concept. The changeup has left many accomplished hitters looking like fools at the plate. An effective changeup is designed to look like a regular speed pitch, but the ball is manipulated just prior to release so it leaves the pitcher's hand much more slowly than the hitter is anticipating from the windup. In this situation, a hitter selects the motor program for the swing, assigning to it the parameter values that will successfully contact a regular-speed pitch, as was indicated by the windup. Once that program is organized and initiated, it will run its course even if the hitter recognizes that the pitcher has thrown a changeup. According to motor program-based theory, to change the tempo of the swing, the hitter must not only recognize that an error has been made in parameter selection, but he or she also has to reorganize and initiate the corrected program in order to meet the demands of the task. Because hitting is a rapid movement, there is often not enough time to do this and the hitter swings prematurely.

CEREBRAL CHALLENGE # 4

A good illustration of the difficulty we have in stopping a planned movement was provided by Slater-Hammel (1960). Subjects were asked to lift their finger from a response key at the same instant that the sweep hand of a clock they were watching passed over the number "8". However, if the sweep hand stopped prior to reaching the target (the number 8 on the clock face), subjects were instructed to continue to press down on the response key. Results showed that when the sweep hand was stopped with less than 140 msec remaining before reaching the target, subjects had a difficult time not lifting their finger. Furthermore, in most cases, subjects were not able to stop the action of lifting their finger on those trials where the sweep hand stopped 50–100 msec before the target.

Can you think of real-life examples where you start a movement, recognize that you shouldn't do the movement you started but have difficulty stopping anyway?

GENERALIZED MOTOR PROGRAM SYNOPSIS

Schmidt's theory (1975, 1985) is an open-loop theory of motor control that combines the basic idea of a schema, or an abstract representation of rules governing movement, and the generalized motor program. The theory proposes that for a given class of actions, such as the overhand throw, we abstract different pieces of information from every throwing experience we've had that involved an overhand pattern (Magill, 1993). We then construct schemas that will enable us to use the overhand thrown in a number of situations and circumstances.

The schema theory proposes that movements are generalized and are run by complex rules that are revised with each movement experience. The stronger the rule (schema), the more skilled the performance. According to the schema theory, the task of the instructor, once the fundamental movement pattern has been achieved, is to provide the learner with appropriate activities designed to strengthen the schema.

CEREBRAL CHALLENGE # 5

Answer the following questions using Schmidt's schema theory:
1. You are coaching an athlete who has a major competition in three weeks. You have noticed a flaw in his/her performance. Should you correct the flaw? Why or why not? What questions must you ask to help you make your decision?
2. You are coaching an 8th grade volleyball team and are getting complaints from team members about the soreness in their forearms from bumping the ball. To help the athletes you decide to let them wear wristbands on their forearms in practice. Is this a good idea? Why or why not?
3. You are teaching a unit on basketball at middle school, specifically the free throw. Unfortunately, there are only four baskets in your gymnasium and there are 28 students in your class. In addition to a low number of baskets, there are only 10 functional basketballs. You remember reading an article in college that encouraged you to be creative and use substitute equipment to increase time on task. As a result, you come up with the idea to use playground balls in addition to the basketballs and to tape targets on the wall at the same height as the normal basket. Are these good ideas? Why or why not?

Dynamic System Theory

Proponents of the Dynamic System Theory (also termed the Dynamic Pattern Theory) argue that motor program-based theories fall short in their account for the control of complex movements and ignore the fact that movements occur in response to a dynamic interaction of the mover and his or her environment. Rather than functioning in a hierarchical manner, with a command center issuing instructions that are carried out by the limbs and muscles, a movement pattern is thought to emerge or self-organize as a function of the ever-changing constraints placed upon it.

CONSTRAINTS

The optimal pattern of any movement is specified by the interaction of internal constraints placed on the performer by the state of the body's subsystem and external constraints induced by the movement that is to be executed and by the environment within which that movement takes place (Caldwell & Clark, 1990). **Constraints** are defined as the boundaries that limit the movement capabilities of an individual (Clark, 1995; Newell, 1986). When an individual is faced with the task of learning a novel motor skill, changes are imposed by either the organism, the environment, the task or a combination of any of these constraints.

constraints: The boundaries that limit the movement capabilities of an individual.

Organismic Constraints Organismic constraints can be either structural or functional. Examples of structural constraints include body shape, weight, and height, while psychological, cognitive and emotional characteristics of an individual are functional constraints (Newell, 1986). A stroke patient's partial loss of arm function, for example, would be considered a constraint that would reduce the ability to perform daily activities such as combing his or her hair. Try Exploration Activity 3.2a to further explore organismic constraints.

Environmental Constraints Gravity, temperature, and natural light are examples of environmental constraints. When throwing the javelin, for example, the wind is an important factor due to the aerodynamics of the implement. The force and direction of the wind place an environmental constraint on the performer, and failure to take them into account will negatively influence the throw. Exploration Activity 3.2b explores this concept further.

Task Constraints The task itself also imposes a number of constraints on motor skill acquisition and performance. Three categories of task constraints have been proposed: (1) the goal of the task, (2) the rules specifying or constraining the movement and (3) the implements or machines specifying or constraining the movement (Newell, 1986). All tasks are governed by goals that relate to the product or outcome of the action. However, a number of sports do have rules that dictate the specific coordination pattern that must be produced. For example, in collegiate fast-pitch softball, a pitcher's feet must remain in contact with the pitching rubber throughout the initiation of the pitch (until the pitcher's weight is transferred forward). This rule prevents the possibility of an unfair advantage gained by taking a step backwards prior to the pitch, which would allow the pitcher to generate added momentum. If the pitcher breaks contact with the rubber during the initiation of the pitch, the base umpire will charge him or her with an illegal pitch. The performer must carry out the specific pattern of coordination, or the movement cannot be called a legal pitch.

In some cases, the set of coordination options that can be performed to achieve the desired outcome are constrained by the rules of the sporting event. For example, boundaries are provided that limit the movement patterns that can be generated by the performer. Sporting examples include tennis strokes, golf swings, the high jump and the basketball free throw. There are a variety of "legal movements" for performance enhancement in these types of motor skills. For example, in a volleyball serve, the performer's feet must be behind the line when the ball is contacted, the ball must pass over the net without touching it and the ball must land within the boundaries of the court. However, the performer can choose to serve underhand or overhand or use a jump serve.

In other cases, the optimal pattern of coordination for a given individual becomes the prominent issue (Newell, 1986). Since the interactions of internal and external constraints determine the optimal movement coordination and control, individual differences must be considered. Because individuals often interpret the imposed constraints differently, one individual may generate one type of response while another will produce a different movement for the same set of task constraints. For example, two figure skaters might execute a triple loop differently based on their interpretation of the ice surface, their approach speed, fatigue level, etc.

The third category of task constraints is the result of the interaction of the individual with an implement or a machine. Examples include stepping on a Stairmaster, walking on a treadmill, using crutches, skiing, kayaking, opening a can with a can opener and performing core stability exercises on a therapeutic ball. The size, dynamics and weight of sporting equipment relative to the body size of the individual are ex-

Equipment can serve as a constraint.

amples of the physical constraints that can be placed on the optimal coordinated movement in regards to the goal of the action. For example, if a client sets the seat for a stationary bike too high, not only will it reduce the efficiency of the exercise but also, over time, it could lead to an injury. Try Exploration Activity 3.2c to gain a better understanding of how an implement can affect the resulting movement pattern.

CEREBRAL CHALLENGE #6

Categorize each of the following as an organismic, environmental or task constraint:

a. Poor flexibility
b. Lack of motivation
c. Height of the curb for an individual in a wheel chair
d. Parkinson's disease
e. Using a regulation-size football with 10-year-olds
f. Catching a pop fly while looking into the sun
g. Using a prosthetic limb

SELF-ORGANIZATION

Self-organization: The spontaneous emergence of a movement pattern as a result of the ever-changing constraints placed on the learner.

As indicated earlier, movement patterns are thought to emerge or spontaneously conform as a function of the ever-changing constraints placed on the learner. Movement, then, is a function of the system **self-organizing** and compressing the available degrees of freedom into a single functional unit that is designed to carry out a specific task. In other words, the arrangement of a movement pattern will be the result of responding to the constraints im-

EXPLORATION ACTIVITY 3.2
Organismic, Environmental and Task Constraints

Perform the following to develop a greater understanding of the role of constraints:

A. ORGANISMIC CONSTRAINTS

Try to touch your elbows together behind your back. What prevents you from being able to do this? Is this a structural or a functional constraint?

Now try to roll your tongue. Are you able to do it? Not everyone can. The ability to roll your tongue is genetically determined. Is this a structural or a functional constraint?

Try to do the splits. Can you do it? What might be some organismic constraints that would prevent you from performing the splits?

B. ENVIRONMENTAL CONSTRAINTS

Equipment needed
  2 pieces of paper
  A small fan

Using two pieces of paper, make two identical paper airplanes. Make a starting point on the ground to ensure the same starting position for each trial. Place the fan approximately three meters to the side, perpendicular to the direction of throw on your throwing side, and approximately three meters in front of the starting line, as depicted below:

Starting
Line   _____

posed by a given situation rather than being generated by a motor program. This concept was demonstrated in Exploration Activity 3.2c, where the movement pattern used to perform the overhand throwing motion changed as a function of the type of ball being used. Because constraints affect the way the system self-organizes, understanding the constraints from which movement patterns/motor skills emerge is necessary in order to comprehend the acquisition of skill.

Turn on the fan, and throw your first plane straight ahead so that it must pass through the stream of air created by the fan. Note the resulting flight path. Now, turn off the fan and throw your second plane using the same throwing motion you used to throw the first plane. Again, note the resulting flight path.

What influence did the airstream produced by the fan have on the flight path of the first aiplane? The second? What adjustments would have to be made to get the plane to land directly in front of you if the fan is turned on?

C. TASK CONSTRAINTS

Equipment needed
1 tennis ball or baseball
1 partially deflated volleyball
1 basketball
1 large playground ball
large open field or play area

Using a mature overhand throwing pattern, throw each ball as far as possible into the open area. If possible, have a friend videotape each attempt.

Compare and contrast each attempt. How did the size of the ball influence the distance of the throw? Were the techniques used to throw the balls the same? What compensations were made, and why? Did any organismic constraints influence the task?

CEREBRAL CHALLENGE #7

Speculate as to how the following would influence the self-organization of an individual's gait pattern:

a. Wearing shoes that were too small
b. Wearing shoes that were too big
c. Wearing high heels
d. Wearing sneakers on the wrong feet
e. Walking on ice
f. Walking on the beach
g. Walking across a log

ATTRACTOR STATES

attractor states: Preferred states of stability or patterns towards which a system spontaneously shifts.

As can be seen, the individual, the task and the environment all have a profound effect on the system and how it self-organizes. The fact that systems prefer states of stability also plays a role in the self-organizing process. These preferred states of stability or patterns are known as **attractor states.** When a change in constraints is imposed on a system, the stability of that system is endangered. If the magnitude of the change is great enough, the system's stability will change and the system will reorganize into a new form within the boundaries established by the constraints (Thelen & Ulrich, 1991). Changes in behavior are therefore the result of a series of shifts, called **phase shifts,** in the state of stability of the system. An example of a phase shift can be seen when a swimmer nears the finish of a close race. In an attempt to generate speed, swimmers may overextend themselves, and the result may be a breakdown in form and a phase shift.

phase shift: Change in the state of stability of a system causing a spontaneous reorganization into a new form.

CEREBRAL CHALLENGE #8

In Cerebral Challenge 7 you were asked to speculate as to how the following would influence the self-organization of an individual's gait pattern:

a. Wearing shoes that were too small
b. Wearing shoes that were too big
c. Wearing high heels
d. Wearing sneakers on the wrong feet
e. Walking on ice
f. Walking on the beach
g. Walking across a log

Expand on your answers to include the concept of phase shifts.

Ennis (1992) suggests that attractors function much like basins or wells in which observable behaviors pool and that their depth is an indication of the stability of the system (see Figure 3.2). Deep attractor basins are characteristic

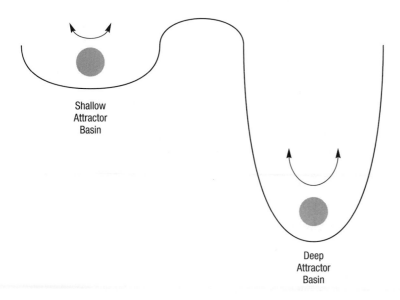

FIGURE 3.2
Shallow vs. deep attractor
basins. Shallow attractor
states are more susceptible
to change than are deep
attractors.

Shallow
Attractor
Basin

Deep
Attractor
Basin

of stable systems, and stable patterns are difficult to change. Conversely, shallow basins are less stable and are more susceptible to change. When a movement is well learned, the pattern is stable and considered a deep attractor. If a major change is now introduced to the original movement, the stability of the system is challenged as a result of the new constraints being imposed. For example, when an athlete moves from high school to college, the new coach will often attempt to change a well-learned technique in order to improve future performance. To make this change, or to cause a phase shift, the practice strategies used must cause instability in an already deep attractor (the current technique). As instability is created, the movement pattern first becomes a combination of the old and new techniques. In addition, there is a temporary period during which the player produces neither the old nor the new pattern, but rather some erratic dysfunctional pattern that varies greatly from trial to trial and reduces performance effectiveness. In time, the pattern will reorganize and the new technique will begin to take over, forming a new attractor. Initially, this new attractor will be somewhat shallow, but with continued practice, it will gain stability.

Constraints, when scaled in magnitude, act as **control parameters** when they lead to changes in the behavior of the system (Clark, 1994; Wallace, 1996). Manipulating control parameters can push an unstable system to a new, more stable state or vice versa. Direction, force, speed and perceptual information are some examples of control parameters. Constraints can also hinder or hold back the ability of the system to change. When constraints function in this capacity, such as a bat that is too heavy for a child, they are known as **rate limiters.** The acquisition of motor skills can, then, be seen as the process of finding the optimum value of control variables (constraints) that will meet the demands of the task for each individual.

control parameters: Variables that move the system into new attractor states.

rate limiters: Constraints that function to hinder the ability of a system to change.

The Dynamic System perspective can be further demonstrated using grasping as an example. Many daily activities involve the grasping of objects of various weights and sizes. An internal constraint on grasping is strength, and a strength deficiency due to an injury would place a constraint on the performer's ability to effectively grasp objects. Through an appropriate strength-building program, grip strength levels can be increased, but with these increased strength levels, the stability of the current attractor state declines. As a result, the system will self-organize, a phase shift will occur and a new form of behavior and attractor state will emerge to establish stability. In the case of grasping, the individual's ability improves to another level that falls within the boundaries established by the newly formed internal constraints.

EVIDENCE SUPPORTING DYNAMIC SYSTEM CONTROL

Supporting the notion of dynamic systems is the fact that spontaneous phase shifts have been demonstrated by manipulating control parameters (Kelso & Schöner, 1988). Participants were asked to place their hands on a table as illustrated in Figure 3.3 a. They were then asked to move their index fingers, keeping in beat with a metronome, such that both fingers pointed to the left or right at the same time. This movement pattern was labeled as an anti-phase pattern because the two fingers were actually performing opposite movements with one in adduction and the other in abduction (Figure 3.3 b). As the speed of the metronome was gradually increased, a sudden phase shift occurred whereby the fingers spontaneously began to perform the same movement pattern (the in-phase pattern; see Figure 3.3 c). Because a motor

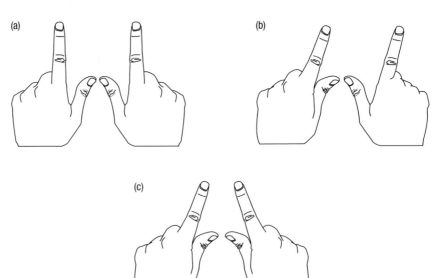

FIGURE 3.3
Finger movement in Kelso and Schöner's (1988) experiment demonstrating spontaneous phase shifts: (a) shows the starting position, (b) shows anti-phase finger movement, and (c) shows in-phase finger movement.

program should have been trying to keep the fingers moving out of phase, this theory falls short in explaining the spontaneous shift to in-phase behavior that occurred. From a dynamic system perspective, speed served as a control parameter that caused the system to self-organize and a phase shift to the new behavior to occur.

DYNAMIC SYSTEM THEORY SYNOPSIS

The complexity of human behavior has led to the development of the dynamic systems approach to understanding motor control. The emphasis of the dynamics of the body and environmental information provide the foundation for the theory wherein human behavior is seen as complex and represents a compression of degrees of freedom. This compression of degrees of freedom allows behavior to emerge in a self-organizing fashion that accounts for the cooperation of the many subsystems in a task context. Movement patterns prefer states of stability or attractor states. New movements self-organize and emerge as a series of phase shifts where attractors stabilize and destabilize as a function of the control parameters of the system, which change over time. For example, a patient relearning to walk after sustaining an injury will display a given gait pattern as a result of the constraints imposed upon the system. If that patient's leg strength reaches a critical level, leg strength could serve as a control parameter, leading to changes in the behavior of the system. In other words, an increase in leg strength could cause a phase shift, and a new gait pattern (attractor state) could self-organize. The task of the instructor, according to the Dynamic Systems Theory, is to identify which constraints act as control parameters that lead to positive changes in the behavior of the system, and which serve as rate limiters.

CEREBRAL CHALLENGE #9

1. Fear often serves as a rate limiter. In hurdling, for example, beginning learners are often afraid that they will not clear the hurdle and will get injured. If you were teaching hurdles, what strategies would you use to overcome this rate limiter? What other rate limiters might be involved? Discuss your answer in terms of the Dynamic System Theory.
2. Explain how orthotics function from a dynamic system perspective.
3. Given what you have learned about dynamic system, can the speed at which a sit-to-stand transfer is executed influence performance? Fully explain your answer.

A Look Ahead

At this point we have explored theoretical constructs underlying the coordination and control of human movement from a behavioral perspective. As you will see in the remaining chapters, these theories will be revisited, as their consideration is imperative for making effective instructional decisions. In the next chapter, movement will be examined from a neurological perspective. What role does the nervous system play in movement, and what clues does it offer movement scientists about the human movement puzzle?

Summary

- Skilled movement requires the learner to not only condense the available degrees of freedom (coordination) but also to control the resulting movement.
- Two prominent theories, motor program-based and dynamic system, offer explanations of how movement is coordinated and controlled.
- Generalized motor programs are an abstract representation of a class of actions that can be modified to yield various response outcomes.
- Some elements of the generalized motor program (invariant features) are thought to be relatively fixed from trial to trial, defining the motor program itself, while others (parameters) are more flexible and define the program's execution.
- Parameters for a given situation are specified according to one's schema, which is a rule or relationship developed through practice that directs decision making.
- Motor control is thought to be a function of both open- and closed-loop mechanisms where movements are planned in advance, initiated and carried out with limited modification unless time permits the incorporation of response-produced feedback.
- Dynamic System Theory argues against the notion of a central command center and suggests instead that movement emerges or self-organizes as a function of the constraints imposed on it at any given time.
- Three categories of constraints have been identified: a) organismic, b) task and c) environmental.
- Systems prefer states of stability known as attractor states, and changes in behavior are the result of phase shifts in states of stability. The ease of creating such shifts is dependent on the depth of the attractor basin.

Review Questions

1. Define the terms coordination and control. Explain their relationship.
2. Explain the degrees of freedom problem.
3. What two major flaws were found in early motor programs? How does Schmidt's Schema Theory solve these two problems? How does the Dynamic System Theory solve these two problems?
4. What is a schema? How do the recall and recognition schema work together?

5. What is the relationship between parameters and schema?
6. How could you determine if snow skiing and water skiing shared the same motor program? Explain your answer using both motor learning terminology and providing specific examples.
7. What three lines of evidence suggest the existence of motor programs?
8. Compare and contrast open- and closed-loop systems.
9. Define self-organization. How is it different from hierarchical control?
10. What is the difference between a control parameter, a constraint and a rate limiter? Provide an example of each using a skill of your choosing.
11. What is a phase shift? Explain how phase shifts are indicative of behavioral changes.
12. Compare and contrast Schmidt's Schema Theory and Dynamic Systems Theory.

References

Bernstein, N. (1967). *The Coordination and Regulation of Movements*. Oxford, England: Pergamon Press.

Brunt, D., Lafferty, M.J., Mckeon, A., Goode, B., Mulhausen, C. & Polk, P. (1991). Invariant characteristics of gait initiation. *American Journal of Physical and Medical Rehabilitation, 70*(4), 206–212.

Caldwell, G. & Clark, J.E. (1990). The measurement and evaluation of skill within the dynamical systems perspective. In J.E. Clark and J.H. Humphrey (Eds.) *Advances in motor development research*. New York, NY: Ams Press, 165–199.

Clark, J.E. (1994). Dynamical Systems perspective on gait. In Craik (Ed). *Analysis: Theory and Application*. St. Louis, MO: Mosby.

Clark, J.E. (1995). On becoming skillful: Patterns and constraints. *Research Quarterly for Exercise and Sport, 66*(3), 173–183.

Ennis, C. (1992). Reconceptualizing learning as a dynamical system. *Journal of Curriculum and Supervision, 7*(2), 115–130.

Hay, L. & Schoebel, P. (1990). Spatio-temporal invariants in hurdle racing patterns. *Human Movement Science, 9*, 37–54.

Henry, F.M. & Rogers, D.E. (1960). Increased response latency for complicated movements and a "memory drum" theory of neuromotor reaction. *Research Quarterly, 31*, 113–121.

Kelso, J.A.S. & Schöner, G. (1988). Self-organization of coordinative movement patterns. *Human Movement Science, 7*, 27–46.

Magill, R. (1993). *Motor Learning: Concepts and Applications*. Dubuque, IA: Wm C Brown Publishers.

Marieb, E.N. & Mallatt, J. (2002). *Human Anatomy*. Menlo Park, CA: Benjamin Cummings.

Newell, K.M. (1986). Constraints on the development of coordination. In M.G. Wade & H.T.A. Whiting (Eds.), *Motor Development in Children*.

Aspects of Coordination and Control. Dordrecht, Germany: Martinus Nighoff, 341–360.

Pollit, A. & Bizzi, E. (1978). Processes controlling arm movements in monkeys. *Science, 201*, 1235–1237.

Roth, K. (1988). Investigations on the basis of the generalized motor programme hypothesis. In O.G. Meijer & K. Roth (Eds.), *Complex movement behavior: The motor action controversy* (pp. 261–288). Amsterdam: North-Holland.

Schmidt, R. A. (1975). A schema theory of discrete motor skill learning. *Psychological Review, 82*(4) 225–260.

Schmidt, R. A. (1985). The search for invariance in skilled movement behavior. *Research Quarterly for Exercise and Sport, 56*(2), 188–200.

Shapiro, D.C., Zernicke, R.F., Gregor, R.J. and Diestal, J.D. (1981). Evidence for generalized motor programs using gait pattern analysis. *Journal of Motor Behavior, 13*, 33–47.

Slater-Hammel, A.T. (1960). Reliability, accuracy, and refractoriness of a transit reaction. *Research Quarterly, 31*, 217–228.

Sparrow, W.A. (1992). Measuring changes in coordination and control. In J.J. Summers (Ed.), *Approaches to the study of motor control and learning*, pp. 147–162. North Holland: Elsevier Science Publishers.

Taub, E. & Berman, A.J. (1968). Movement and Learning in the absence of sensory feedback. In S.J. Freedman (Ed.), *The Neuropsychology of Spatially Oriented Behavior* (pp. 173–192). Homewood, IL: Dorsey Press.

Thelen and Ulrich, (1991). Hidden skills - A dynamical systems analysis of treadmill walking in infants. *Monographs of the Society for Research in Child Development, 56*, serial #223.

Turvey, M.T. (1990). Coordination. *American Psychologist, 45*, 938–953.

Vereijken, B.; Whiting, H.T.A. & Beek, W.J. (1992). A dynamical systems approach to skill acquisition. *The Quarterly Journal of Experimental Psychology, 45A*(2), 323–344.

Wadman, W.J., Dernier van der Gon, J.J., Geuze, R.H. & Mol, C.R. (1979). Control of fast goal-directed arm movements. *Journal of Human Movement Studies, 5*, 3–17.

Wallace, S.A. (1996). Dynamic pattern perspective of rhythmic movement: An introduction. In H.N. Zelaznik (Ed.), *Advances in Motor Learning and Control* (pp. 155–194). Homewood, IL: Dorsey Press.

CHAPTER FOUR

Neural Mechanisms: Contributions and Control

Best known for his role as Superman, Christopher Reeve was a talented actor whose athleticism was evident not only through his stunt work but also in his pursuits away from the big screen. He was an accomplished pianist, an avid outdoorsman, a pilot and a sailor. He also enjoyed scuba diving and skiing.

In the 1990s his passion turned to horses, a passion that would change his life forever. In May 1995, during a competition in Virginia, Reeve's horse, Eastern Express, balked at a rail jump, pitching his rider. Sadly, Reeve's hands got tangled in the horse's bridle, causing him to land headfirst. The impact fractured his uppermost cervical vertebrae.

Tragically, Reeve's spinal cord was severely damaged. The world, as he knew it, would never be the same. The damage to the spinal cord impaired the neurological processes fundamental to movement production. Messages from the receptors could no longer travel to the central nervous system for integration, nor could messages travel from the central nervous system to the muscles to create movement. In a split second, Reeve became a quadriplegic.

Nervous System

The nervous system is responsible for the processes that underlie movement preparation, execution and control. It can be subdivided into two primary components, the central nervous system (CNS) and the peripheral nervous system (PNS). The CNS consists of the brain and the spinal cord. It is within the CNS that sensory information is integrated, decisions are made and signals are generated and sent to the effectors (muscles and glands) to carry out responses. The PNS consists primarily of nerves that extend from the brain and spinal cord, thereby providing a link between the body and the CNS. The PNS can be further subdivided into a sensory or **afferent** division, which detects changes in the environment and conducts nerve impulses from the various sensory receptors towards the CNS, and a motor or **efferent** division, which transmits impulses away from the CNS to the effectors.

afferent: Carrying to; meaning sensory input in the nervous system.

efferent: Carrying away from; meaning motor output in the nervous system.

Sensory Receptors

We are constantly being bombarded with stimuli detected through the component of the nervous system known as the sensory receptors. There are numerous forms of stimuli and a variety of sensory receptors, each of which is sensitive to a particular stimulus. A useful method for classifying these receptors is by location or, more specifically, by the location of the stimuli to which they respond. **Exteroceptors** detect stimuli outside the body and provide information about the environment. They are located at or near the body's surface and include receptors for pressure, pain, touch, temperature, vibrations, hearing, vision, smell and taste. **Interoceptors** detect stimuli from the internal viscera and provide information about the internal environment leading to feelings such as hunger and nausea. Finally, **proprioceptors**, which are located in the muscles, tendons, joints and internal ear, provide information regarding body position and movement by detecting changes in muscle tension, joint position and equilibrium. While each form of receptor is important to overall functioning, this discussion will focus on those receptors particularly important to the performance of skilled movement, namely vision and proprioception.

exteroceptors: Receptors located at or near the body's surface that detect stimuli outside the body and provide information about the environment.

interoceptors: Receptors that detect stimuli from the internal viscera and provide information about the internal environment.

proprioceptors: Receptors that provide information regarding body position and movement by detecting changes in muscle tension, joint position and equilibrium.

VISION

Although numerous sensory receptors exist, our visual system predominates. In fact, our dependence on vision has been shown to be so strong that information from other sensory receptors may even be ignored in its favor (Lee & Aronson, 1974). This dominance of the visual system is also reflected by estimates that 70 percent of all the body's sensory receptors are located in the eyes. Furthermore, 40 percent of the cerebral cortex is thought to be involved in some aspect of processing visual information (Marieb & Mallatt, 2002). It is not surprising then that interest in the role of vision in the production of skilled movement has not only increased but has led to the recent

EXPLORATION ACTIVITY 4.1 Visual Dominance

ACTIVITY #1

Equipment needed
Pencil
Mirror
1 piece of cardboard (20 cm x 20 cm or 8" x 8")

Procedure Sit in front of a mirror with your textbook in front of you on a flat surface such that the diagram below is visible. Now, place the tip of your pencil in between the two lines. You may start anywhere. Using the cardboard, cover up the hand using the pencil so that you can only see your hand and its movements through the mirror in front of you. Using only the image in the mirror, trace the diagram below by moving the pencil around the shape while staying between the lines. You may move in either direction.

How did you do? Were you able to stay in the lines and move around the shape efficiently?

ACTIVITY #2

You will need a partner for this activity. Hold your arms straight out in front of you so that they are parallel with the floor. Now, cross your arms over one another. From this position, turn your palms so that they are facing one another, and then interlock your fingers. Pull your hands down and towards your chest, continuing the rotation until your knuckles are facing the sky. Once you are in position, ask your partner to point to one of your fingers. It is important that they only point to it and that they do not touch it. Your task is to simply move the finger that your partner pointed to.

Do you think the result would have been different if your partner touched the finger to be moved while your eyes were closed? Try it.

In both of these activities, a sensory conflict between vision and proprioception is created. Our vision is so dominant, however, that even when we know that the visual information we are receiving is not accurate, such as when the image is reversed in the first experience, we will often rely on it anyway. The consequence is poorer performance. Lee and Aronson (1974) demonstrated visual dominance in their moving wall study. Subjects stood in a special room where the walls could be moved but the floor remained stationary. The study found that subjects adjusted their posture to compensate for changes in visual information, even though proprioceptive information did not change. Results of this study not only support the notion of visual dominance but also provide insight regarding the role vision plays in the maintenance of posture.

FIGURE 4.1:
Basic structures of the eye.

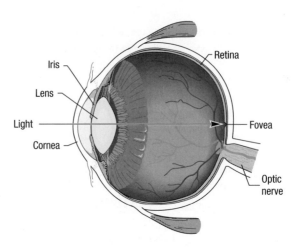

development of a subdiscipline known as sport vision, which focuses on investigating visual contributions to performance with an emphasis on visual correction, enhancement and injury (Kluka, 1999).

Our capacity to see objects clearly at variable distances and under various conditions of light is dependent on the actions of a complex arrangement of structures in and around our eyes (Figure 4.1). Light rays enter the eye, where they are manipulated and focused onto the retina, forming an image that is converted into nerve impulses by light-sensitive cells called **photoreceptors**.

photoreceptors: Light-sensitive cells located in the eyes.

There are two types of photoreceptors, rods and cones. Rods are more numerous and are specialized for vision in dim light. They also enable us to see shapes and movements and discriminate between different shades of light and dark, making them the primary receptor used in night vision. Cones, on the other hand, operate best in bright light and are specialized for color vision and visual acuity (sharpness of vision). Cones are most densely concentrated in the fovea, the area of maximal visual acuity. Given the location of the fovea, our vision is most clear or sharp when we look directly at objects.

The electrical signals generated by the photoreceptors are sent to the brain via the optic nerve. At one point, known as the optic chiasm, some fibers from each of the optic nerves cross (Figure 4.2). Because of this crossing, the visual sensations from the left side of the visual field are sent to the right side of the brain for processing, while those from the right are sent to the left side.

focal system: Visual system that functions to identify objects primarily located in the central region of the visual field.

ambient system: Visual system that functions at a subconscious level and is thought to be responsible for spatial localization and orientation.

Focal vs. Ambient Vision The existence of two separate visual pathways to the brain has led to the belief that two separate but parallel functioning visual systems exist. The **focal system**, which involves the fovea, functions to identify objects primarily located in the central region of the visual field. In addition, focal vision is strongly linked to consciousness and therefore operates under voluntary control. Finally, its function is hampered in low light conditions. In contrast, the **ambient system**, which functions at a subconscious

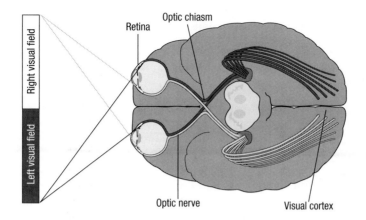

FIGURE 4.2

Visual fields of the eyes and associated neural pathways.

Source: Shea, C.H., Shebilske, W.L. and Worchel, S. (1993)

level, is thought to be responsible for spatial localization and orientation. Unlike focal vision, it involves the entire retina, serves both the central and peripheral visual fields and is not affected by changes in light strength.

During movement, parallel processing of information obtained through each system likely occurs. In mountain biking through a forest, for example, riders rarely identify the trees that are on the side of the trail, but they do need to be aware of where those trees are so they can avoid collisions and successfully follow the trail. Ambient vision serves the rider in this endeavor. At the same time, the rider is using focal vision to identify changes in the trail, such as a fallen tree across it or a rider in front of them. The

EXPLORATION ACTIVITY 4.2 Ambient vs. Focal Vision

ACTIVITY 1

Try walking around your apartment while reading a couple of paragraphs in this book. You should be able to accomplish this without running into your furniture because of the combined efforts of focal and ambient vision. Focal vision was used to read, while ambient vision allowed you to locate obstacles and successfully move about the room.

ACTIVITY 2

Now perform the task again with your sunglasses on. What influence did your sunglasses have on your performance? How can these results be explained?

ACTIVITY 3

For the final activity, you will need a piece of three-hole punched paper. Hold the paper about one inch from your face so that you can see through the middle hole. Wrap the rest of the paper around to touch the sides of your head. Now walk around your apartment again. Explain the results.

A mountain biker uses focal vision to identify changes in the trail.

rider's ability to identify such objects will be hampered when the forest is very dense, or if the tint of their sunglasses is too dark, because of a decrease in focal sensitivity.

Vision and Performance Vision is used throughout all aspects of performance. Not only do we use it to detect environmental stimuli, which are subsequently used to make movement decisions, but it also provides important feedback used to guide the resulting action. The role of various visual abilities on performance therefore warrants exploration.

Eye Dominance Interestingly, information is not processed and transmitted to the brain by both eyes equally. One of your eyes, the dominant eye, carries out these actions a few milliseconds faster. Those individuals whose dominant eye is on the same side of the body as their dominant hand are considered same-side dominant, while those whose dominant eye is opposite that of their dominant hand are considered cross-dominant.

Eye dominance has received attention with respect to hitting performance in baseball and softball. It has been suggested that cross-dominant hitters have an advantage because their dominant eye is closer to and more in line with the pitcher. Although research has not substantiated this claim (Milne, Buckolz & Cardenas, 1995), turning the head to

EXPLORATION ACTIVITY 4.3 Eye Dominance

Find a small object, such as a clock, on a wall. Stand directly in front of it, approximately 10 feet away. Once you are in this position, create a small triangular window with your hands by overlapping your thumbs. Stretch your arms in the direction of the wall so that you can see the object through your triangular window as in the illustration. Close one eye, then open it; repeat with the other eye. Your dominant eye is the one for which the object remained in the triangular window.

give both eyes a clear view of the pitch has been advocated (Kluka & Knudson, 1997).

Time to Contact Many movement situations arise where performers must predict time to contact with an object that they are moving towards or that is moving towards them. Situations involving striking, catching, creating or avoiding a collision, and landing are some examples. As an object approaches, its retinal image enlarges. The rate at which this enlargement occurs is directly related to the speed of the object's approach and is therefore indicative of time to contact. In other words, the faster the enlargement occurs, the faster the object is approaching.

Time of contact information is determined via a single optic variable, *tau*, which is determined by taking the size of the retina image at any position of an object's approach and dividing it by the rate of change of the image (Lee, 1976, 1980). Performers use *tau* to determine when an action should be initiated. When to initiate the interceptive movement required for catching a Frisbee or avoiding a collision while walking down a crowded hallway will be determined by how quickly the size of the approaching object enlarges.

Visual Search The ability to make quick and accurate decisions and to effectively anticipate are dependent on the **visual search** strategies employed by the performer. Visual search is the manner in which the performer directs his or her visual attention while trying to locate critical regulatory cues. **Fixation** is the focusing of one's visual attention on a specific object. During a visual search, numerous fixations may occur. The characteristics of those fixations, such as order, location and duration, are used to infer how and what information performers attend to (Kluka, 1999). For example, Shank and Haywood (1987) found differences in fixations for college and novice baseball players in pitch identification. Interestingly, neither group began to fixate on and track the ball until approximately 150 msec after its release. During the pitcher's windup, however, experts were found to fixate on the release point, while there was a tendency for novices to move their eyes before the release of the ball, alternating their fixations between the release point and the pitcher's head. Given that the expert hitters correctly identified almost all of the pitches, while the novices were accurate only about 60 percent of the time, it appears that experts not only know where to fixate their gaze but can also ignore irrelevant cues. Similar results have been found in tennis (Goulet, Bard & Fleury, 1989) and in soccer (Williams, Davids, Burwitz & Williams, 1994; Williams and Davids, 1998).

Effective visual search strategies that enable a performer to detect task-relevant information can be acquired. For example, according to Abernethy & Wollstein (1989), practitioners can improve learners' anticipation in racket sports by providing visual training videos, identifying opponent tendencies and pointing out relevant cues. However, it may not be necessary to instruct the learner to look for specific cues, such as how the ball leaves the pitcher's hand (Magill, 1998). Instead, it may be equally effective to direct their visual

tau: Optic variable that provides time of contact information by taking the size of the retina image at any position of an object's approach and dividing it by the rate of change of the image.

visual search: The manner by which the performer directs his or her visual attention while trying to locate critical regulatory cues.

fixation: The focusing of one's visual attention on a specific object.

attention to the area at which the ball is released. This suggestion is based on research that has demonstrated that learners whose visual focus is directed at "information-rich" areas can attend to task-relevant cues even if they are not consciously aware of what those cues are (Magill, 1998; Pew, 1974).

While researchers continue to explore the visual search process, Magill (1998) offers several practical tips to help learners develop effective visual search strategies. First, as stated previously, instruction and verbal feedback should direct learners to information-rich areas where the critical cues occur. Second, practitioners must design appropriate learning experiences where extensive practice opportunities in situations that contain common task-relevant cues are provided. Providing opportunities to make connections between cues and ultimate event outcome can facilitate the development of anticipatory skills. Abernethy (1996) further suggests including video training where paused sequences are presented and learners are challenged to anticipate an opponent's action. Finally, the context of those situations developed should include a great deal of variability while still requiring the learner to search for the same cues on each attempt. This variability will prepare the learner to generalize their visual search strategies for performance or game situations.

CEREBRAL CHALLENGE # 1

1. What information-rich area(s) would you point out to beginning drivers to direct their visual attention?
2. Using a skill of your choice, list information-rich areas to which visual attention should be directed.

PROPRIOCEPTION

The continuous flow of sensory information received from receptors located in the muscles, tendons, joints and inner ear regarding movement and body position is called proprioception. Multiple receptors are involved in proprioception. Golgi tendon organs are proprioceptors located at the junction of a tendon with a muscle. When tension is applied to a tendon, golgi tendon organs relay the corresponding sensory information (intensity of the contraction) to the CNS. One of their functions is to protect tendons and their associated muscles from damage due to excessive tension.

Muscle spindles, another type of proprioceptor, are found between the skeletal muscle fibers in the muscle belly. When a muscle is stretched, the spindle sends a signal to the CNS indicating how much and how fast the muscle's length is changing. Muscle spindles can also cause a reflexive contraction known as a stretch reflex, which contributes to the contractile force that can be generated during a skill and is created when a muscle is stretched just prior to contracting. For example, as in many striking skills, the tennis forehand is preceded by a backswing that stretches the involved muscles and sets up a stretch reflex. Elimination of this stretch reflex would change the dynamics of the skill, and practitioners should keep this in mind when designing learning experiences.

Joint kinesthetic receptors are located in and around synovial joints and respond to pressure, acceleration and deceleration and excessive strain on a joint. Joint receptors provide feedback about whether movements are too slow, too fast or in the wrong direction (Kreighbaum & Barthels, 1996).

Finally, the vestibular apparatus is a collective group of receptor organs in the inner ear that respond to changes in posture and balance. The otolithic organs monitor the position of the head, providing sensory information regarding static equilibrium or the maintenance of body position when motionless. They also contribute to dynamic equilibrium, which is the maintenance of body position in response to movement, by monitoring changes in linear acceleration. You have experienced this while moving in an elevator. A second aspect of dynamic equilibrium involves angular acceleration of the head such as when a figure skater does a spin. The cristae in the semicircular ducts of the inner ear are responsible for monitoring changes in the angular acceleration of the head.

What would happen if we did not have proprioception? Ian Waterman knows firsthand. When he was 19, a rare virus attacked his nervous system, rendering his proprioception useless. While his muscles still worked, he could no longer sense body position or movement without looking directly at his joints and limbs (Azar, 1998; Cole, 1995). He has had to learn to rely on vision to control his movements, as it has become his only source of feedback. In order to judge the weight of an object he is picking up, for example, Ian has to watch how his hand reacts instead of receiving feedback from his proprioceptors about the amount of stretch caused in the tendons and muscles as a result of the added weight. The faster and higher the hand moves, the lighter the object. This adaptation was demonstrated in a study that required a deafferented individual to judge different weights in the absence of proprioceptive information (Fleury, Bard, Teasdale, Paillard,

EXPLORATION ACTIVITY 4.4   Proprioception

1. To demonstrate the use of proprioception, close your eyes and hold your arms out to the side, forming a "T." Now touch your nose with the index finger of your dominant hand. Repeat with your nondominant hand. Speculate as to why this exercise is sometimes used to test drivers suspected of drinking.

2. Again, close your eyes. Raise your leg so that your thigh is parallel to the floor. Open your eyes and check your leg's position. Repeat the exercise, bringing your arm in a position parallel to the floor. How accurate was your positioning? How did you accomplish this activity in the absence of vision?

Proprioception helps a backpacker make adjustments while walking across a log.

Cole, Lajoie & Lamarre, 1995). When vision was available the individual could discriminate between weights within 10 g. However, with the eyes closed, the ability to correctly judge the weights was significantly impaired.

Proprioception and Performance Combined, proprioceptors function to "make the motor control system more efficient and flexible for the regulation of goal-directed movements" (Park & Toole, 1999; p. 645). Before a movement is initiated, proprioception provides the information about initial body and limb position that serves as the basis for the programming of motor commands. Once initiated, the movement is continuously evaluated for correctness by comparing proprioceptive feedback to the intended goal. If the two do not correspond, an error is detected. At that point, the adjustments needed to correct the movement must be determined, initiated and accomplished prior to the completion of the response. This, as we saw with open- and closed-loop systems, is dependent on time. If a movement is too rapid, response-produced feedback will be used to make adjustments on the next trial.

As indicated earlier, the intended goal of the movement serves as a frame of reference for error detection, but a learner's level of understanding of that goal is dependent on skill level. Because a beginner is still trying to develop an idea of how a movement should be executed, their frame of reference for movement correctness has yet to be developed. Meanwhile, the instant the ball leaves the hand of a skilled free-throw shooter, he or she can tell whether the shot was a good one by the way it felt at release. To assist beginning learners in developing their frame of reference, practitioners should provide the opportunity for learners to experience a variety of positions and movements across a broad assortment of environments (Kreighbaum & Barthels, 1996). In addition, practitioners should focus learners' attention on the feelings associated with a movement. Because we can often see our limbs relative to the environment, information regarding movement and body position is made available not only through proprioception but also through visual feedback. Often learners rely too heavily on visual feedback when judging a movement's correctness, when kinesthetic feedback should be stressed for optimal learning.

RESEARCH NOTE

To evaluate how visual and proprioceptive information is integrated and modified throughout the learning process, five neurologically normal and one deafferented subject performed a mirror-tracing task (Lajoie, Paillard, Teasdale, Bard, Fleury, Forget & Lamarre, 1992). Subjects were instructed to trace a six-pointed star pattern as fast and accurately as possible while viewing it through a mirror. Normal subjects demonstrated difficulties when drawing oblique lines and changing direction while attempting to trace the star pattern. These difficulties were, however, overcome with practice. Conversely, these same difficulties were not evident in the tracing performance of the deafferented subject, as all trials were consistent in their execution. Because the star was viewed through a mirror, a conflict between visual and proprioceptive information was created for the normal subjects. This same conflict does not exist with the deafferented subject. The results of this study demonstrate that there exists a tight coupling between visual and proprioceptive feedback in the execution of visuomotor tasks.

CEREBRAL CHALLENGE # 2

1. Speculate as to why many practitioners incorporate strategies that focus a learner's attention on the physical feelings associated with a movement.
2. One such strategy is the use of weighted implements (bats, shots, baseballs). Generate a list of other devices designed to enhance the physical feelings associated with a movement.

CEREBRAL CHALLENGE #3

A popular method for teaching a youngster how to swing a bat is to reach around and manually guide them through it. This technique, appropriately termed manual guidance, is also frequently used in a therapeutic setting. The idea of manual guidance is to move the learner through the desired pattern or range of motion so that they can experience the feeling associated with it.

> This technique presents an inherent problem, however. Speculate as to what that problem might be. You might consider trying the strategy prior to formulating your response. Based on your response, what conditions might you adhere to if employing this strategy?

Rehabilitation and Proprioception Training The reestablishment of proprioception, according to Lephart and Swanik (1999) and Prentice (2003), should be a primary concern for athletic trainers when designing rehabilitation programs. Consequently, the inclusion of proprioception training in rehabilitation programs is common practice following a lower limb musculoskeletal injury. The intent is to regain movement and balance sense that has been shown to be lost as a result of inactivity and/or immobilization following an injury or surgery (Leach, 1982; Prentice 1999). Failure to do so can result in functional instability that can impair performance and predispose an athlete or patient to recurrent injury (Laskowski, Newcomer-Aney, & Smith, 1997). The inclusion of functional progressions that incorporate balance and proprioception training, such as one-legged standing, double arm balancing, wobble board exercises and sport-specific exercises such as cutting and defensive slide drills, is therefore an important component of any rehabilitation program designed to return athletes and/or patients to pre-injury performance levels.

Transmission of Information

The continuous flow of information from the receptors to various levels of the CNS is achieved via the conduction of afferent or sensory nerve impulses. Once the information has been perceived and a decision as to how to respond is made, signals are sent by efferent or motor neurons to the corresponding muscles to carry out the desired action. An integral component in this process is the spinal cord.

THE SPINAL CORD

The spinal cord performs two major functions. First, it serves as a route for impulse conduction. Sensory impulses travel up the spinal cord to the brain via ascending pathways, while motor impulses travel in the opposite direction along descending pathways. Second, not all signals travel to the brain for interpretation. Some impulses are integrated at various levels of the spinal cord, which serves as an integrating center for spinal reflexes.

Pathways Sensory information travels up the spinal cord to the brain via two major routes (ascending pathways) on either side of the cord: the spinothalamic pathway and the posterior

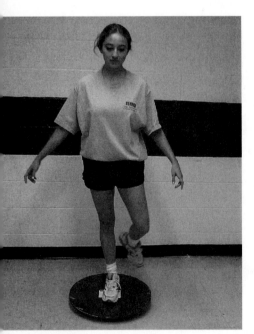

BAPS board exercises help reestablish proprioception.

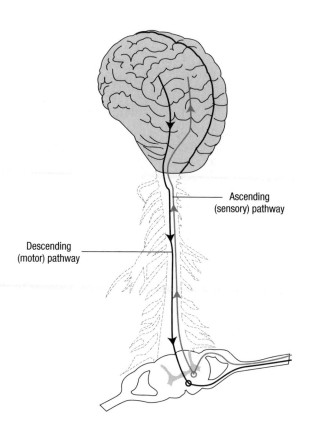

FIGURE 4.3
Transmission of afferent and efferent information between the body and the brain via the spinal cord.

Ascending (sensory) pathway

Descending (motor) pathway

or dorsal column pathway. The spinothalamic pathway conducts impulses associated with pain, temperature, crude touch and deep pressure. Proprioception, discriminative touch, pressure and vibrations travel to the brain via the dorsal column pathway.

The pyramidal and extrapyramidal pathways are descending pathways that transmit motor impulses to the skeletal muscles that will execute movement. Nerve impulses leading to the control of skilled voluntary movements travel down the pyramidal pathway. The extrapyramidal pathway conducts nerve impulses that result in more unconscious control of body movements, such as the control of motor activities associated with posture and balance.

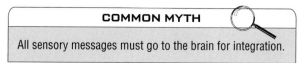

COMMON MYTH

All sensory messages must go to the brain for integration.

Spinal Reflexes As noted above, not all impulses travel to the brain for integration. In some cases, the integration of the sensory information occurs at the level of the spinal cord. The result is an automatic, involuntary response to stimuli called a **reflex.** Because information is integrated at the spinal

reflex: An automatic, involuntary response to stimuli.

cord level, reflexes allow an individual to react to a stimulus faster than if conscious thought was involved in order to make adjustments.

The simplest pathway by which a reflex occurs is known as the **reflex arc**, and its basic components include the 1) receptor, 2) sensory neuron, 3) integrating center, 4) motor neuron and 5) effector. When a sensory receptor detects a change in the internal or external environment, a sensory neuron is stimulated, and it carries an impulse to the integrating center in the spinal cord (or brain stem). The integrating center then triggers an impulse in a motor neuron, which subsequently stimulates a response in a muscle or gland.

Several types of reflex exist, each of which is distinguished by the characteristics of the integrating center. The simplest reflex involves a single synapse. In other words, a sensory neuron communicates directly with a motor neuron. Because it involves only one synapse, this type of reflex is called a monosynaptic or stretch reflex. The knee-jerk reflex is one example of a monosynaptic reflex. When an unexpected stretch of the quadriceps occurs, there is a corresponding stretch of the muscle spindles. As we learned earlier, when a muscle spindle is stretched, it sends a signal to the CNS, more specifically the spinal cord, indicating how much and how fast the muscle's length is changing. A single synapse is then made, prompting an adjustment by increasing the contraction of the quadriceps and resulting in an extension of the leg at the knee. Because only one synapse is involved, the monosynaptic reflex is very fast. Its function in counteracting changes in

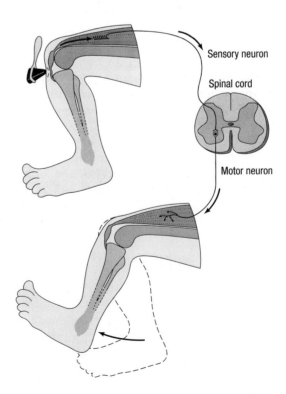

Sensory neuron

Spinal cord

Motor neuron

FIGURE 4.4
Monosynaptic reflex loop.

muscle length, especially those that occur unexpectedly, contributes to our ability to maintain posture and position our limbs.

Other, more common reflex pathways known as polysynaptic reflex arcs consist of one or more **interneurons** that lie between a sensory and motor neuron in a reflex arc (Marieb & Mallett, 2002). Because polysynaptic reflexes involve more than one synapse, they are not as fast as monosynaptic reflexes but still function more quickly than if they had required conscious control. The withdrawal reflex, where we pull back from danger, is a polysynaptic reflex. The classic example of the withdrawal reflex in action is when an individual touches a hot stove. Impulses are generated by heat and pain receptors and sent via sensory neurons to the spinal cord. A synapse occurs there with an interneuron neuron, which then synapses with a motor neuron that signals the muscles to withdraw your hand from the hot stove.

Another reflex often associated with the withdrawal reflex is the crossed-extensor reflex. In addition to an interneuron neuron stimulating the motor neuron responsible for the withdrawal signal, a collateral axon conducts an impulse to the opposite side of the spinal cord to a motor neuron that innervates the muscles on that side of the body, causing them to extend. In other words, when the withdrawal reflex occurs in one limb, the crossed-extensor reflex can be initiated to cause the opposite limb to extend. The crossed extensor reflex can be illustrated in the response of shifting one's body weight to prevent a fall. For example, if you were walking along the beach and accidentally stepped on a sharp shell, the withdrawal reflex would occur in response to the painful stimuli, while the crossed-extensor reflex would cause the opposite leg to extend, thereby creating a weight shift and preventing a fall.

Damage to the Spinal Cord If the nerve fibers of the spinal cord are crushed, torn or severed, as was the case in Christopher Reeve's accident, some of the cord's functions are likely to be permanently lost. If damage occurs to the ascending pathways, sensations arising from receptors below the level of the injury will be lost. If nerve fibers in the descending tracts are cut, the

> **interneuron:** Nerve cell that lies between a sensory and a motor neuron in a reflex arc.

EXPLORATION ACTIVITY 4.5 Knee Jerk Reflex

ACTIVITY 1

You will need a partner for this activity. Have your partner sit on a chair and cross his or her legs so that the lower knee fits into the hollow at the back of the upper knee. Now, using the edge of your open hand, firmly tap the soft part just below your partner's kneecap. You may have to try a couple of times to find the spot that initiates the reflex. Switch places with your partner.

ACTIVITY 2

Repeat the above activity, but this time the sitting person should try to voluntarily prevent the reflex from occurring. Can you do it?

FIGURE 4.5
Withdrawal and crossed-extensor reflex arc.

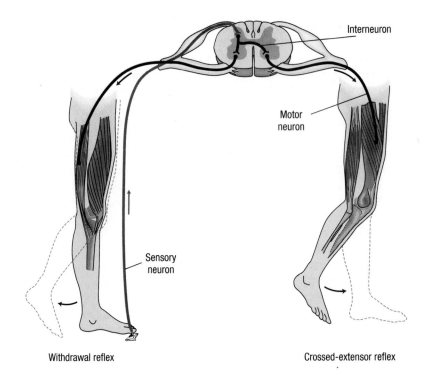

Withdrawal reflex   Crossed-extensor reflex

result will be a loss of motor functions. In Reeve's case, because the spinal cord was completely crushed, most experts predicted that he would never walk again. Recently, however, CBS News (Sept. 17, 2002) reported that Reeve has regained limited movement at most of his joints and sensation to 50-60% of his body. Doctors cite his attitude, work ethic and involvement in exercise and electrical muscle stimulation as potential contributing factors.

The Brain

The brain is composed of about 100 billion neurons and is therefore highly complex in both structure and function. It is divided into four main parts: (1) brainstem, (2) diencephalons, (3) cerebrum and (4) cerebellum (Figure 4.6). While the brainstem and diencephalons serve many vital functions, their major roles with respect to movement production and control include serving as a reflex center and relaying sensory and motor information between different parts of the brain and between the brain and the spinal cord. The cerebrum and cerebellum contribute more extensively to movement and will therefore receive greater attention here.

CEREBRUM

The cerebrum is the largest portion of the brain. It is divided into left and right cerebral hemispheres, each of which is concerned with the sensory and

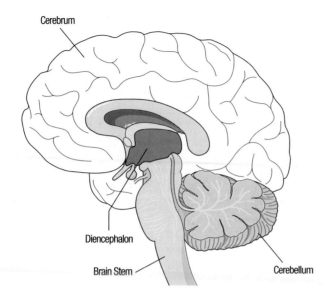

FIGURE 4.6
Parts of the brain.

Cerebrum

Diencephalon

Brain Stem

Cerebellum

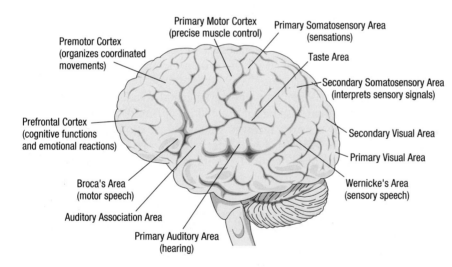

FIGURE 4.7
The functional areas of the cerebral cortex.

Premotor Cortex
(organizes coordinated movements)

Primary Motor Cortex
(precise muscle control)

Primary Somatosensory Area
(sensations)

Taste Area

Secondary Somatosensory Area
(interprets sensory signals)

Prefrontal Cortex
(cognitive functions and emotional reactions)

Secondary Visual Area

Primary Visual Area

Broca's Area
(motor speech)

Wernicke's Area
(sensory speech)

Auditory Association Area

Primary Auditory Area
(hearing)

motor functions of the opposite side of the body. The outermost layer of the cerebrum is called the **cerebral cortex**. It is here that we find the centers responsible for higher brain functions.

Functional Regions of the Cerebral Cortex The cerebral cortex can be subdivided into three functional areas: (1) sensory areas, (2) motor areas and (3) association areas. Each of these areas can be further subdivided as depicted in Figure 4.7. This discussion will focus on those areas associated with movement production and control. It should be noted that each area does

cerebral cortex: The outermost layer of the cerebrum.

not function independently and that a detailed examination is beyond the scope of this text.

Sensory Areas The sensory areas interpret information received from the various sensory receptors. The primary somatosensory area receives sensations from cutaneous receptors (touch, pressure, temperature, pain) and proprioceptors in the periphery of the body. In this area, the information is processed and an individual becomes consciously aware not only of the sensation itself but also the exact location from which the sensation arose. Primary somatosensory area damage from a stroke, for example, will therefore eliminate one's ability to consciously feel and localize touch and pressure on the skin. This in turn will impact grip and object manipulation (Leonard, 1998). In addition, a loss in joint position awareness will result, as the individual will no longer be able to accurately perceive sensory feedback associated with movement. Movements will therefore become uncoordinated.

In contrast, the secondary somatosensory area serves to integrate and interpret sensory signals. If damage were to occur in this area of the cerebral cortex, sensory information that would normally be associated with object manipulation would no longer be available and your ability to identify that your hand is feeling a golf ball vs. a racquetball, for example, would be impaired. In addition, because signals to the secondary area are partly processed in the primary somatosensory area before being relayed, similar impairments to those described for the primary somatosensory area would be manifested.

Given the role of vision in movement, the visual areas also deserve attention. The visual areas can also be subdivided into primary and secondary areas. The primary visual area receives visual information about the image formed on the retina. While this area detects light and dark spots and determines the orientation of the visual field, it is the function of the secondary visual area to interpret what one is seeing.

CEREBRAL CHALLENGE #4

Damage to the primary visual area would result in functional blindness. Speculate as to the consequence of damage to the secondary visual area.

Motor Areas The function of the motor areas is to coordinate and initiate voluntary movements of skeletal muscles. The primary motor cortex is the region responsible for initiating skilled voluntary movements, including those required for the performance of fine motor skills. Decisions made regarding how to initiate those movements are a function of the premotor cortex, which lies just anterior to the primary motor cortex. More specifically, the premotor cortex organizes learned coordinated movements that involve complex sequencing of muscles. For example, if a performer decides to take a step, decisions regarding which muscles to contract, in what order and to what degree are made in the premotor cortex (Seeley, Stephens & Tate, 1997). Impulses are then sent to the primary motor cortex, which initiates each planned movement.

Association Areas The association areas are concerned with the analysis and interpretation of sensory information. In performing this function, it appears that new sensory inputs are associated with past experiences. The prefrontal cortex's role involves emotional reactions and cognitive functions. Attentiveness, the ability to make accurate judgments and plan for future events and the motivation to practice are dependent on prefrontal cortex functioning.

A second area known as the general interpretive area plays a primary role in complex thought processing. Situations are interpreted as a result of the integration of sensory information in this region. The interpretation is then sent to the prefrontal cortex, where it is linked with emotion and a decision about how to respond is made.

Basal Ganglia The basal ganglia are a group of functionally related nuclei that lies deep within the cerebrum. Extensive communication occurs between the basal ganglia and both the cerebral cortex and the brainstem, creating a loop of information flow that is relayed through the thalamus. The basal ganglia are important in the initiation and control of subconscious gross body movements such as swinging the arms while walking (Tortora, 1997), and they play a key role in regulating the intensity (scaling) of movement parameters. The importance of scaling movement parameters is demonstrated through the functional changes that occur in two different degenerative conditions of the basal ganglia. The first, Parkinson's disease, which is characterized by slow, uncontrollable shaking (tremor) of the limbs and difficulty in initiating voluntary movements, is the result of understimulation of the basal ganglia. Huntington's disease, on the other hand, is the result of an overstimulation of the basal ganglia. An individual with this condition will display uncontrollable jerking movements of the limbs and/or facial muscles.

CEREBELLUM

The cerebellum monitors movement by comparing the intended movement that was programmed by the motor areas to what is actually taking place. In other words, it compares the sensory input it receives from proprioceptors and visual receptors to the expected sensory consequences. Consequently, it plays a key role in the detection and correction of errors and works in conjunction with the motor cortex to produce smooth, coordinated movements. The cerebellum also plays a key role in the maintenance of posture and balance.

CEREBRAL CHALLENGE #5

A patient, who was not wearing a helmet, suffered brain damage as a result of a serious biking accident. The part of the brain affected was the cerebellum. Speculate as to what behaviors this patient would display as a result of trauma to the cerebellum.

CEREBRAL CHALLENGE #6

Relate motor program and schema concepts to the neurological functions described in this chapter.

MEMORY

memory: The ability to store and recall information.

An exploration of the brain and motor skill acquisition and performance would be incomplete without a discussion about memory. **Memory** is the ability to store and recall information. That information may be a friend's telephone number or it may represent past movement experiences that help you make decisions about what motor response to make and how to make it. Several changes have to occur in the CNS in order for an experience to become represented in memory. While portions of the brain, including the association cortex of the frontal, parietal, occipital and temporal lobes, parts of the limbic system and the diencephalon, are known to be associated with memory, much about its function remains unknown.

Composition of Memory A popular model of memory offered by Atkinson and Shiffrin (1968, 1971) proposed that memory is composed of three distinct systems, each of which is defined by its storage and processing characteristics. The first stop in memory for the continuous flow of information transmitted by the body's receptors is the sensory register. Because of its large capacity, an abundant amount of information can be held here momentarily (few hundred milliseconds), with each modality (visual, kinesthetic, etc.) having a separate storage space. At this point, the information a performer selectively attends to will be further processed, while that remaining will be lost.

The selected information is then passed on to the next system, the short-term memory (STM), where we become consciously aware of it. Contrary to the sensory register, the STM has a limited capacity and can only temporarily hold seven plus or minus two items or chunks of information at a given time (Miller, 1956). In addition, the information is only retained in this temporary storage space for 20–30 seconds unless it is given further attention through processes such as repetition, association or rehearsal. This active processing is also necessary to transfer the information for more permanent storage in long-term memory. Without this transfer, effective learning is not possible.

Long-term memory (LTM) is characterized as having a seemingly limitless capacity and duration. LTM consists of three subsystems (Tulving, 1985). The first two, episodic and semantic memory, are concerned with factual information. More specifically, **episodic memory** contains information about personal experiences and events that are associated with a specific time and context. Your high school graduation date is an example of knowledge represented by episodic memory. **Semantic memory**, on the other hand, represents general knowledge that is developed by our experiences but is not associated with time. Factual knowledge, such as your school colors, and conceptual knowledge, such as your concept of success, are included in semantic memory. Episodic and semantic memory store information used to decide what to do in a given situation. This information is also termed **declarative knowledge**. The third subsystem, **procedural memory**, retains information regarding how to do something. It is therefore the memory of skills, operations and actions or **procedural knowledge** and is fundamental to our ability to achieve movement goals.

episodic memory: The memory of personal experiences and events that are associated with a specific time and context.

semantic memory: The memory of general knowledge that is developed by our experiences but is not associated with time.

declarative knowlegde: Information used to decide what to do in a given situation.

procedural memory: The memory of information regarding how to do something.

EXPLORATION ACTIVITY 4.6 Chunking

Below is a list of 21 letters. Study the letters for 15 seconds, and then close your book. Based on what you remember, write down as many letters as you can.

TRY
CHU
NKI
NGT
HEL
ETT
ERS

How did you do? What strategies did you use to remember the letters?

One strategy that you may have used is called chunking. If you look at the first three letters, they spell the word "try." By grouping the letters into a word, you now have to remember only one word instead of three individual letters. Since STM is limited in capacity to seven plus or minus two items, chunking can increase the amount of information that can be remembered. In fact, if you look closely, the letters spell out the following:

TRY CHUNKING THE LETTERS

If you noticed this trick, remembering all 21 letters was probably quite easy!

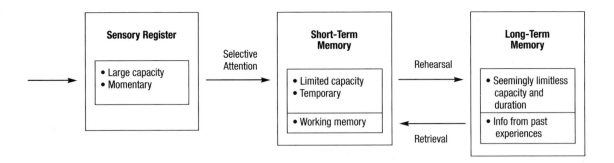

FIGURE 4.8
Schematic of memory
systems.

procedural knowledge:
Information regarding skills,
operations and actions.

proactive inhibition:
Interference that results when
old memories interfere with
the retention of new ones.

retroactive inhibition:
Interference that results when
new learning impedes the
retention of older memories.

STM and LTM: Partners in Integration There is more to memory than simply the storage of information. Short- and long-term memory work together to integrate information about the current situation and past experiences, which, in turn, enables a performer to make, execute and evaluate strategic and movement decisions. For example, a racquetball player must combine information about the current situation, such as the position of the opponent and their level of fatigue, with information retrieved from LTM about past experiences, such as the opponent's strengths and weaknesses and probable responses, in order to decide what serve to use. Furthermore, once the serve has been selected, additional information and integration are needed for its execution. These integrative processes take place in STM, which has also been labeled working memory because of its active role in information processing (Baddeley & Hitch, 1974).

Forgetting Through practice, learners can transfer increased information into LTM. However, all performers, regardless of skill level, are vulnerable to the phenomenon of forgetting. Two theories have been proposed to explain forgetting. The first, known as the decay theory, suggests that forgetting occurs as a result of the passage of time. A second theory, the interference theory, proposes that forgetting can be attributed to either proactive or retroactive inhibition. In **proactive inhibition** old memories interfere with the retention of new ones. Conversely, **retroactive inhibition** occurs when new learning interferes with the retention of older memories

CEREBRAL CHALLENGE #7

Generate a list of tips for practitioners with respect to memory. For example, because of limited capacity, keep instructions short and simple.

A Look Ahead   At this point, the complexity involved in movement production should be apparent. Numerous receptors provide information to various levels of the CNS via afferent pathways for integration. Reflexes are integrated at the spinal cord, while information requiring conscious thought travels up the spinal cord to various locations of the brain, where it is integrated and interpreted. Through the collective efforts of numerous brain structures, including the cerebral cortex, and the basal ganglia, movements are organized and signals are sent to the effectors to produce the output, which is continuously monitored by the cerebellum.

The focus of chapters 1 through 4 has been on the behavioral and neurological processes that influence performance. We will now build on this foundational knowledge of how skilled movements are produced and examine the processes involved in their acquisition and refinement. The next chapter begins this discussion by examining the characteristics of learners as they progress from novices to experts.

Summary

- The nervous system is responsible for the processes that underlie movement preparation, execution and control.
- Sensory receptors can be classified as exteroceptors, interoceptors and proprioceptors.
- Vision is the dominant sensory system. As a result, there is much interest in its role in the production of skilled movement, which has led to the development of a subdiscipline known as sport vision.
- The focal system functions to identify objects primarily located in the central region of the visual field, while the ambient system is responsible for spatial localization and orientation.
- The focal and ambient systems work in conjunction to process visual information during movement.
- Visual search is the manner by which the performer directs his or her attention while trying to locate critical regulatory cues.
- Proprioceptors provide information regarding body position and movement by detecting changes in muscle tension, joint position and equilibrium through golgi tendon organs, muscle spindles, joint kinesthetic receptors and the vestibular apparatus.
- Proprioception provides the information about initial body and limb position that serves as the basis for the programming of motor commands, evaluates ongoing movements by comparing proprioceptive feedback to the intended goal and provides response-produced feedback that can be used to make adjustments on the next trial.
- The spinal cord serves as a reflex center and a pathway for the transmission of sensory and motor information.
- The cerebral cortex plays a significant role in movement production and control through three major functional areas (sensory, motor and association) where interpretive and integrative processes occur.
- The cerebellum plays a key role in error detection and correction and in the maintenance of posture and balance.
- Learning occurs when information is moved from short- to long-term memory.

1. Compare and contrast exteroceptors, interoceptors and proprioceptors.
2. Which photoreceptor is specialized for vision in dim light? Which one is specialized for visual acuity?
3. Define visual acuity.
4. What is the significance of the optic chiasm?
5. Compare and contrast focal and ambient vision. Which one of the two deals with peripheral vision?
6. How do performers use *tau*?
7. Define fixation. How can we use fixations to infer visual attention?
8. Compare and contrast golgi tendon organs, muscle spindles, joint kinesthetic receptors and the vestibular apparatus.
9. What functional problems would be associated with damage to the dorsal column pathways? The extrapyramidal pathway?
10. What are the five components of a reflex arc? Explain why reflexes are faster than voluntary movements.
11. Speculate as to the result of damage to the general interpretive area.
12. What is Parkinson's disease?
13. What are the three memory systems? Compare each with respect to capacity and duration.
14. Explain why phone numbers are traditionally seven digits long.
15. Why is STM also referred to as working memory?
16. Two theories have been suggested as explanations for forgetting. Explain each.

References

Abernathy, B. (1996). Training the visual-perceptual skills of athletes: Insights from the study of motor expertise. *The American Journal of Sports Medicine, 24*(6), S-89–S-92.

Abernethy, B., & Wollstein, J. (1989). Improving anticipation in racquet sports. *Sports Coach, 12*(4), 15–18.

Atkinson, R.C. & Shiffrin, R.M. (1968). Human memory: A proposed system and its control processes. In K.W. Spence and J.T. Spence (eds.), *The Psychology of Learning and Motivation (Vol. 2)*. Orlando, FL: Academic Press, pp. 89–195.

Atkinson, R.C. & Shiffrin, R.M. (1971). The control of short-term memory. *Scientific American, 225*, 82–90.

Azar, B. (1998). Why can't this man feel whether or not he is standing up? *APA Monitor Online, 29*(6).

Baddeley, A.D. & Hitch, G. (1974). Working memory. In G.H. Bower (ed.), *The Psychology of Learning and Motivation: Advances in Research and Theory (Vol. 8)*. New York: Academic Press, pp. 47–89.

Cole, J. (1995). *Pride and a daily marathon*. Cambridge, MA: The MIT Press.

Danion, F., Boyadjian, A. & Marin, L. (2000). Control of locomotion in expert gymnasts in the absence of vision. *Journal of Sports Sciences, 18,* 809–814.

Fleury, M., Bard, C., Teasdale, N., Paillard, J., Cole, J., Lajoie, Y. & Lamarre, Y. (1995). Weight judgement: The discrimination capacity of a deafferented subject. *Brain 118,* 1149–1156.

Goulet, C. Bard, C. & Fleury, M. (1989). Expertise differences in preparing to return a tennis serve: A visual information processing approach. *Journal of Sport and Exercise Psychology, 11,* 382–398.

Kluka, D. A. (1999). *Motor behavior: From learning to performance.* Englewood, CO: Morton Publishing Company.

Kluka, D.A. & Knudson, D. (1997). The impact of vision training on sport performance. *Journal of Health, Physical Education, Recreation and Dance, 68*(4), 17–24.

Kreighbaum, E. & Barthels, K. (1996) *Biomechanics: A qualitative approach for studying human movement.* San Francisco, CA: Benjamin Cummings.

Lajoie, Y., Paillard, J., Teasdale, N., Bard, C., Fleury, M., Forget, R. & Lamarre, Y. (1992). Mirror drawing in a deafferented patient and normal subjects: Visuoproprioceptive conflict. *Neurology, 42,* 1104–1106.

Laskowski, E.R., Newcomer-Aney, K., & Smith, J. (1997). Refining rehabilitation with proprioception training: Expediting return to play. *The Physician and Sportsmedicine, 25*(10), 89–102.

Leach, R.E. (1982). Overall view of rehabilitation of the leg for running, in Mack, R.P. (ed.), *Symposium on the Foot and Leg in Running Sports.* St. Louis, MO: Mosby.

Lee, D.N. (1976). A theory of visual control of braking based on information about time to collision. *Perception, 5,* 437–459.

Lee, D.N. (1980). Visuo-motor coordination in space-time. In G.E. Stelmach and J. Requin (eds.), *Tutorials in Motor Behavior,* Amsterdam: North Holland Publishing Company (pp. 281–295).

Lee, D.N. & Aronson, E. (1974). Visual proprioceptive control of standing in human infants. *Perception and Psychophysics, 15,* 527–532.

Leonard, C.T. (1998). *The neuroscience of human movement.* St. Louis, MO: Mosby-Year Book.

Lephart, S.M. & Swanik, C.B. (1999). Reestablishing neuromuscular control. In Prentice, W.E. (ed.), *Rehabilitation Techniques in Sports Medicine,* 3rd ed., Dubuque, IA: WCB/McGraw-Hill.

Magill, R.A. (1998). Knowledge is more than we can talk about: Implicit learning in motor skill acquisition, *Research Quarterly for Exercise and Sport, 69*(2), 104–110.

Marieb, E.N. & Mallatt, J. (2002). *Human anatomy.* Menlo Park, CA: Benjamin Cummings.

Miller, G.A. (1956). The magical number seven, plus or minus two: Some limits on our capacity for processing information. *Psychological Review, 63,* 81–97.

Milne, C., Buckolz, E. & Cardenas, M. (1995). Relationship of eye dominance and batting performance in baseball players. *International Journal of Sports Vision 2* (1), 17–21.

Park, S. & Toole, T. (1999). Functional roles of the proprioceptive system in the control of goal-directed movement. *Perceptual and Motor Skills, 88*(2), 631–647.

Pew, R.W. (1974). Levels of analysis in motor control. *Brain Research, 71,* 393–400.

Prentice, W.E. (1999). Using therapeutic exercise in rehabilitation. In W.E. Prentice (ed.), *Rehabilitation Techniques in Sports Medicine*, 3rd ed. Boston, MA: McGraw-Hill, pp. 226–243.

Prentice, W.E. (2003). *Arnheim's principles of athletic training: A competency based approach*. St. Louis, MO: McGraw-Hill.

Seeley, R., Stephens, T., & Tate, P. (1997), *Anatomy & Physiology*, 3rd ed. St. Louis, MO: Mosby-Year Book.

Shank, M.D. & Haywood, K.M. (1987). Eye movements while viewing a baseball pitch. *Perceptual and Motor Skills, 64,* 1191–1197.

Shea, C.H., Shebilske, W.L. & Worchel, S. (1993). *Motor Learning and Control*. Englewood Cliffs, NJ: Prentice Hall.

Tortora, G.J. (1997). *Introduction to the human body: The essentials of anatomy and physiology*. Mountain View, CA: Benjamin Cummings.

Tulving, E. (1985). How many memory systems are there? *American Psychologist, 40,* 385–398.

Williams, A.M., Davids, K., Burwitz, L. & Williams, J.G. (1994). Visual search strategies in experienced and inexperienced soccer players. *Research Quarterly for Exercise and Sport, 65*(2), 127–135.

Williams, A.M. & Davids, K. (1998). Visual search strategy, selective attention, and expertise in soccer. *Research Quarterly for Exercise and Sport, 69*(2), 111–128.

CHAPTER FIVE

Stages of Learning

In 1927 Babe Ruth hit 60 home runs in a single season. That record would stand until 1961, when New York Yankee Roger Maris hit 61. On September 8, 1998, the home run record for a single season was once again being challenged. The St. Louis Cardinals were playing the Chicago Cubs on their home field, and Mark McGwire was tied with Maris, having hit 61 home runs that season. But the season wasn't over, and that day more than 43,600 fans packed the stands in anticipation of seeing history in the making. They would not leave disappointed! In the fourth inning, McGwire connected and sent the ball over the left field fence. By the end of the season, he hit 8 more.

Waiting at home plate that day was McGwire's 10-year-old son and batboy, who was immediately hoisted in the air and hugged by his record-breaking father. Will he follow in his father's footsteps and become a professional baseball player? Time will tell, but if he chooses this road, he will have a long journey. To reach the high caliber of skill obtained by his father will take countless hours of hard work and practice; practice that is grounded in the underlying principles discussed thus far that effect skill acquisition and control; practice that is also designed to accommodate the changing needs of the learner as he/she moves through the learning process.

Stages of Learning

When developing motor skill proficiency, regardless of whether it is hitting a baseball or relearning how to walk after a serious accident, learners progress through distinct stages. Several models, each examining the progression from beginner to expert from a different perspective, have been proposed. These models can assist practitioners in defining the needs of their learners throughout the learning process and, in turn, enable them to select appropriate instructional activities (Rink, 1998)

FITTS AND POSNER'S THREE-STAGE MODEL

A popular model proposed by Fitts and Posner (1967) suggests that learners pass through three distinct stages. These stages are defined by the behavioral tendencies learners display at various points throughout the learning process.

cognitive stage: The initial or beginning stage of learning in Fitts and Posner's model.

The first stage, the **cognitive stage,** is named for its high degree of cognitive activity. During this stage, the learner is first introduced to the new motor skill, and the primary task is to develop an understanding of the movement's requirements. A learner in this stage may have many questions.

EXPLORATION ACTIVITY 5.1   Juggling Reflection

Return to the juggling activity presented in Exploration Activity 1.1 on page 4. If you can consistently juggle two balls with your nondominant hand five or more times, then try to juggle four balls with both hands. Juggle for 10 minutes, and then answer the following questions:

1. What were you thinking during each juggling attempt?
2. What decisions did you make during the 10 minutes with regard to strategy? Why did you make those choices?
3. Could you determine the cause of your errors? Were you then able to make appropriate adjustments?
4. Juggle one more time, but recite the alphabet backwards while juggling. How did the recitation influence your juggling performance?
5. Think of a skill you are very familiar with that you can perform with a high degree of proficiency. Would you answer the above questions differently following a performance of your chosen skill? Explain.

Distinct differences exist between skilled and novice performers. While some of those differences may be quite obvious when comparing overt performances, others cannot be directly observed. To facilitate skill acquisition, practitioners must understand what is happening during the learning process from the learner's perspective. Yet this perspective can be elusive, since most practitioners have reached a high level of proficiency in the motor skills they are teaching.

Think back to your experience with juggling. Questions such as how do I hold onto the balls, how and when do I let go, how high do I throw them, what is the pattern of movement and countless others likely came to mind. In an attempt to discover the solutions to these questions, learners will often attempt numerous techniques and strategies through a trial-and-error approach. In addition, past movement experiences will be reformulated in an effort to solve the current movement problem. The resulting movements lack synchronization and appear choppy and deliberate. In addition, the attentional demands throughout this process are high and fairly limited to movement production. Consequently, difficulties will be apparent when learners are required to time their movements in conjunction with an external object or event. Performance at this stage is therefore inconsistent and characterized by the production of numerous errors, which are typically gross in nature.

Through effective verbal instructions and demonstrations, practitioners can facilitate a learner's progression through this stage. Practitioners should also take into account the fact that learners can more easily reformulate past movement experiences into new patterns if the similarities and differences between them are pointed out. Furthermore, while a trained observer may easily recognize the errors being made, the learner lacks the capability to determine the specific cause of an error and may be unable to make the necessary adjustments. Practitioners therefore play a key role not only in the detection and correction of errors but in the development of the learner's capability to do the same.

The second stage, or the **associative stage,** is characterized by marked performance improvements. Having attempted numerous possible movement strategies, a learner at this stage becomes committed to refining one particular movement pattern. Performance becomes more consistent, with fewer, less gross errors. The ability to time movements with external objects and events also improves as the attentional demands of performing the movement itself decrease, allowing learners to begin attending to other things. This also results in a gain in the ability to make adjustments in movement in accordance with various environmental conditions. In this stage, the learner becomes increasingly capable of not only detecting the cause of his or her errors but also of developing appropriate strategies to eliminate them.

associative stage: The intermediate stage of learning in Fitts and Posner's model.

Given the changing characteristics of the learner, the practitioner's role at this stage shifts from one of predominantly providing instruction to that of designing constructive practice experiences. The provision of information regarding errors remains important for both the refinement of the skill and to further the development of the learner's error detection and correction capabilities.

Transition to the final stage in Fitts and Posner's model, the **autonomous stage,** requires countless hours of practice. In fact, this final stage is one that not all learners will reach. In the autonomous stage, performance reaches the highest level of proficiency and has become automated. Learners' attention

autonomous stage: The advanced or final stage of learning in Fitts and Posner's model.

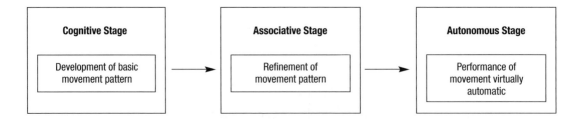

FIGURE 5.1
Fitts and Posner's three-stage model of learning.

during this stage is reallocated to strategic decision making. In addition, multiple tasks can be performed simultaneously. Finally, learners in this stage are consistent, feel confident, make few errors and can generally detect and correct those errors that do occur.

One might falsely assume that when a learner has reached this stage the role of the practitioner is minimal at best. It is important to remember that while skill proficiency has reached the highest levels, there remains room for improvement. Practice design and error detection and correction therefore remain responsibilities of the practitioner. Performance improvements are difficult to obtain at this level, and advances occur so gradually that learners can become discouraged and lose the motivation necessary to strive to obtain them, so practitioners must serve in the capacity of motivator to assist learners in reaching their potential.

CEREBRAL CHALLENGE #1

Using the following format, choose a skill or task and generate a list of practical tips practitioners could follow based on Fitts and Posner's description of the behavioral characteristics of the learner for their three-stage model.

Cognitive	Associative	Autonomous

EXPLORATION ACTIVITY 5.2   Stage of Learning Analysis

Observe a youth sport competition or practice session in a skill of your choice. Choose five individuals to watch closely. Based on your observations, determine which stage of learning each is in using Fitts and Posner's model. Discuss specific behavioral characteristics observed to justify your answers.

GENTILE'S TWO-STAGE MODEL

Rather than simply describing the characteristics of the learner in each phase of the learning process, Gentile (1972, 1987) approached the identification of stages of learning from the learners' perspective. More specifically, Gentile's model emphasizes the goal of the learner and the influence of task and environmental characteristics on obtaining that goal.

The first stage of learning in Gentile's model is termed "**getting the idea of the movement.**" According to Gentile, the goal of the learner introduced to a new motor skill is to develop an understanding of the movement requirements necessary to meet the demands imposed by the characteristics of the task and the environment in which the task is to be performed and to subsequently organize a corresponding movement. Paramount to the learner's success in achieving this goal is his or her ability to discriminate between regulatory conditions and nonregulatory conditions. As you will recall from Chapter 1, regulatory conditions are environmental conditions that specify the movement characteristics necessary to successfully perform the task. In contrast, nonregulatory conditions are those factors that are not inherently related to producing the appropriate motor response. To produce a movement pattern that meets the demands imposed by task and environmental conditions, the learner must be able to selectively attend to relevant information while ignoring irrelevant information.

Once a general idea of the requisite movement pattern is acquired, the learner advances to the second and final stage, **fixation/diversification.** During this stage, the learner's goal is one of refinement. The nature of that refinement is a function of the predictability of the environment in which the skill is to be performed. Consequently, the learner's objective for closed vs. open skills will be different. Closed skills, such as taping an ankle, performing a balance beam routine or playing a musical instrument, are performed in a fixed, stable environment. Successful performance of such skills requires that the learner be able to consistently and accurately replicate the movement pattern. Open skills, on the other hand, are performed in an unpredictable, ever-changing environment. Accordingly, the performer must

getting the idea of the movement: The first stage of learning in Gentile's model, characterized by the learner trying to develop an understanding of a movement's requirements.

fixation/diversification: Second and final stage of learning of Gentile's model; involves matching the new movement pattern to the particular environment in which it is to be performed. Fixation emphasizes consistency of movement and is the objective for closed skills. If the environment is variable, the diversification of the movement pattern is emphasized to promote flexible behavior.

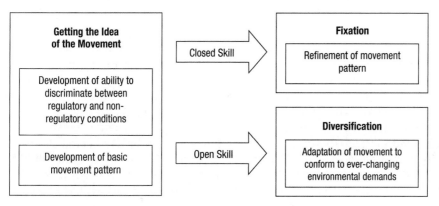

FIGURE 5.2
Gentile's two-stage model of learning.

be able to continually adapt his or her responses to conform to these ever-changing demands. With open skills, the objective of the learner is to diversify the movement pattern. An individual confined to a wheel chair, for example, must be able to change directions, traverse various surfaces and inclinations and negotiate obstacles. Similarly, a hockey player must be able to shoot the puck from countless angles, distances and positions, as well as negotiate around the movements of teammates and defenders.

CEREBRAL CHALLENGE # 2

Determine which strategy, fixation or diversification, would be most appropriate for practicing each of the following skills:

a. Free throw
b. Guarding (soccer, basketball, etc.)
c. Patient moving from sitting to standing position

d. Floor routine in gymnastics
e. Stair ascent and descent
f. Diving

Given the inclusion of task and environmental influences on the learning process, Gentile's model provides the practitioner with additional instructional direction. Instruction and practice during the initial stage of learning should facilitate the learner's development of a basic movement pattern. To accomplish this, the practitioner must clearly communicate to the learner the goal of the task through verbal instructions and demonstrations. In addition, practitioners must point out those features of the environment that are regulatory and those that are nonregulatory and direct the learner's attention and visual search towards those stimuli that are relevant.

Once the learner has acquired the basic movement pattern, the instructional strategies employed will be dependent on whether the skill is categorized as open or closed. Regardless of the type of skill, learners should practice under the same conditions in which the skill will be performed. For closed skills, such as the free throw, where the regulatory conditions remain fixed during each successive performance attempt, practice should reflect these fixed conditions (basket is same height, shot taken from behind free throw line, etc.), while also subjecting the learner to the variety of nonregulatory cues that would normally be present in the applied setting (performer's level of fatigue, crowd noise and importance of the shot). If the regulatory conditions change across trials, as is the case in golf, learners should practice under the various regulatory conditions that may be presented in the criterion condition (e.g., putts from various locations and distances on the green including different slopes). This is also true of practice for open skills. Because learners performing open skills must be able to respond proficiently under ever-changing and often unpredictable environmental conditions, variations in regulatory conditions that simulate possible criterion conditions should also be systematically introduced in practice.

This approach not only assists the learner to acquire a larger repertoire of movement possibilities but also aids in the development of vital decision-making skills. Because decision making is dependent on the learner's ability to detect regulatory cues and ignore nonregulatory stimuli, practitioners should continue to highlight those features of the environment that are regulatory and nonregulatory and direct the learner's attention and visual search towards those stimuli that are relevant.

CEREBRAL CHALLENGE # 3

Using the following format, choose a skill or task and generate a list of practical tips practitioners could follow based on Gentile's two-stage model of learning.

Getting the idea of the movement	Fixation	Diversification

Inferring Progress: Learner and Performance Changes

Given that learning is not directly observable, it would be difficult to determine with any certainty the exact moment that a learner makes a transition to another stage. How, then, can we tell that learning has occurred? One of the most common methods of assessing an individual's progress is by noting changes in observable motor behavior over time. The following section discusses a number of performance indicators that have been identified through the study of novice vs. expert performers and can provide clues for the practitioner as to the progress of the learner.

MOVEMENT PRODUCTION

It would not be difficult to distinguish between the swing of an expert, such as Mark McGwire, and that of a novice hitter. While both may be able to achieve the goal of the task, hitting the ball, the movement pattern produced to do so will be quite different. As the novice hitter's skill level improves, however, these differences will diminish.

Coordination and Control While a learner's progression in skill acquisition characteristically results in several changes related to movement production, perhaps those most notable are changes in coordination and control. The organization of a movement pattern that will effectively achieve the goal of the task requires that the learner coordinate and control numerous independent elements or degrees of freedom. In the early stages of skill acquisition, the learner accomplishes this by freezing or fixing the possible movements of a joint so that the limb(s) will function as a single unit or segment. In other words, novices will reduce the available degrees of freedom into a more manageable quantity in order to accomplish the goal of the task. This strategy, termed **freezing the degrees of freedom** (Bernstein, 1967; Whiting, 1984), results in the production of stiff, rigid, inefficiently timed movements. As learners progress in skill development, those degrees of freedom once constrained will be gradually released and collectively reorganized into a new movement pattern that is smoother and faster and that more closely resembles the correct movement.

Comparisons of the swing pattern produced by a novice hitter and that of Mark McGwire will reveal significant differences indicative of skill level, as the novice will attempt to control the swing by restricting the movement that occurs at each joint. A straight-arm swing, where the bat is simply treated as a rigid extension of the arm, is often the initial swing the novice makes. Furthermore, it is likely that the lower body will remain inactive. The pattern of coordination exhibited by McGwire, on the other hand, will incorporate multiple and sequential joint action (both upper and lower body) and, because of its biomechanical efficiency, the movement will be significantly faster. Support for this resulting increase in velocity as well as the notion of freezing and then gradually releasing or unfreezing the available degrees of freedom has been found in studies investigating the acquisition of the forehand shot in racquetball (Southard and Higgins, 1987), kicking (Anderson and Sidaway, 1994) and learning a slalom skill on an indoor ski apparatus (Vereijken, van Emmerik, Whiting, and Newell, 1992).

freezing the degrees of freedom: Strategy whereby the learner freezes or fixes the movement possibilities of a joint, causing the limb(s) to function as a single unit or segment in order to accomplish the goal of the task.

RESEARCH NOTE

Using the soccer in-step kick, Anderson and Sidaway (1994) examined changes in coordination as a result of practice. Six novices enrolled in a beginning soccer class were given an initial demonstration of the skill. They then performed 15–20 shots for each of 20 practice sessions. Performance was videotaped before and after the practice period, and hip and knee peak angular velocities, timing variables and joint range of motion were analyzed along with maximum linear velocity of the foot using motion analysis software. Results of the kinematic analysis revealed a change in the fundamental pattern of coordination for the skill as a result of practice. A corresponding increase in the maximum resultant linear velocity of the foot was also found.

Muscle Activity Accompanying the reorganization of the system to produce a new pattern of coordination is a change in muscular activity. As the learner becomes more proficient, the number of muscles activated to produce a

Movements of experts appear effortless.

movement will be reduced to only those fundamental to correct performance. In addition, the timing and sequence with which the muscles are activated will be altered. Skilled movement is the result of cooperative actions of muscle groups (Hall, 1999). Early in the learning process, however, the cycle of muscle activation is mistimed. This has been found to be the case in both sport skills (e.g., Jaegars, Peterson, Dantuma, Hillen, Geuze & Schellekens, 1989) and rapid arm movement tasks (Gabriel & Boucher, 1998; Schneider, Zernicke, Schmidt & Hart, 1989). With practice, correct activation patterns are achieved and movements become more fluid.

Energy Expenditure Unlike experts, whose movements appear effortless, beginners are mechanically inefficient. This can be readily seen with beginning swimmers who are learning to flutter kick. Because of poor mechanics, many beginners will initially lack forward progress, and some will even move backwards in the water! Puzzled by their lack of movement across the pool, they will quite often kick harder, but to no avail. Fatigue will eventually set in, and the learner will have to rest before attempting the skill again.

Understandably, beginning swimmers will expend a great deal of energy (and frustration) through their efforts. We know, however, that with practice comes improved coordination, the use of only those muscles necessary and the increased accuracy of muscle activation. In other words, through practice, movements become more efficient and the amount of energy needed to perform them will be reduced. Eventually, this decreased energy expenditure will enable our once frustrated swimmer to travel greater distances with less frequent rest periods.

Consistency Another means of assessing a learners' progress is through changes in performance consistency. Recall from Chapter 1 that learning is defined as a relatively permanent change in a person's capability to execute a motor skill, as a result of practice or experience. Indicative of a relatively permanent change is increased consistency. It should be noted, however, that although a learner may be able to reproduce an action consistently, it does not necessarily mean that the skill is being performed correctly. Practitioners should therefore take into consideration several performance variables prior to making a judgment about learning.

While increased consistency can be a sign of learning, practitioners can also look at the onset of inconsistent performance for clues about skill acquisition. As suggested above, you may encounter a learner who has developed a consistent movement pattern that is fundamentally flawed. Unless the movement is corrected, future progress will be impeded. To change a fundamentally flawed movement, the learner must learn new invariant characteristics, which translates to learning a new motor program. Or, as described by the dynamic systems theory, the learner must move from one state of stability to a new state of stability (phase shift). This transition, regardless of what theory is used to describe it, will first be characterized by increased inconsistency as the learner tries to abandon the old movement and adopt the new coordination pattern. Eventually, with practice, the learner will begin to produce the new movement, and with continued practice, it will become consistent.

EXPLORATION ACTIVITY 5.3 Observation: Novice vs. Expert Swimmers

For this Exploration Activity you will need to go to a local swimming pool.

a. Watch a beginning swimmer (performing freestyle) for several minutes. Describe his or her technique. List the muscles that are involved in accomplishing this technique. Now watch an individual who is more proficient at the freestyle stroke. Describe his or her technique. Again, analyze the muscles involved in the performance.

b. What physical differences did you observe between the two learners' execution of the swimming stroke?

ATTENTION

Changes in both the amount of conscious attention focused on movement execution and the allocation of visual attention accompany skill development. These changes subsequently lead to quicker and more accurate movement preparation and a corresponding reduction in response times.

Attention and Skill Execution Initially, learners concentrate on how to perform each technical component of a skill, and their undivided attention is focused solely on the skill's execution. As skill proficiency develops, however, the need to consciously attend to each aspect of the movement is reduced, and eventually (after a great amount of practice) performance becomes virtually automatic. Conscious thought is no longer required to perform the movement. Throughout this transition, overt performance shifts from being hesitant with a robotic appearance to being smooth and free flowing and appearing effortless.

Once a learner has reached the point at which the skill can be performed with little or no conscious control, two consequences emerge. First, the learner can reallocate his or her attentional resources to other factors of performance. For example, in the volleyball spike, rather than concentrating on the technique that will successfully result in ball contact, the learner can focus on game strategy, such as where to place the ball in the opponent's court. The learner will be better able to focus on and evaluate the environmental context in which he or she is performing and as a result will be able to respond more quickly and accurately to performance conditions presented.

EXPLORATION ACTIVITY 5.4 Automatic Behaviors

EXERCISE 1

Count how many times you breathe in 15 seconds.

EXERCISE 2

Everyone has a walking pace that is natural for him or her. Determine your natural pace by walking down a hallway several times.

QUESTIONS

1. Describe what happened when you tried to count how many times you breathed in 15 seconds.
2. Describe what happened when you tried to determine your natural walking pace.
3. When a practitioner asks a patient to walk naturally across the clinic in order to evaluate his or her gait, would you expect to see results similar to those in exercise #2? Provide suggestions that would ensure an accurate assessment.

CEREBRAL CHALLENGE # 4

Having just introduced a beginning soccer class to dribbling, a teacher designs a drill where the learners are paired up and must dribble to the other end of the field while avoiding the other person, who is trying to take away the ball. Will this be an effective drill? Justify your answer.

A second consequence of automaticity is that once it is achieved, conscious control of the movement can actually be detrimental to performance. By consciously focusing on the specifics of a well-learned skill that is normally performed automatically, the processing of information needed to coordinate a muscle pattern is slowed (Byers, 2000). The resulting performance becomes hesitant and choppy. Adopting a nonawareness strategy where the performer simply "lets the movement happen" is therefore recommended.

Visual Attention As we saw in Chapter 4, differences exist between experts and novices with respect to where their visual attention is allocated. Recall the study by Shank and Haywood (1987) that showed that expert hitters not only direct their visual attention towards information-rich areas but also were able to ignore nonregulatory cues. Beginners, on the other hand, pay attention to too many things and have difficulty discriminating between environmental cues that are relevant and those that are irrelevant to performance. The superior visual attention allocation strategy, combined with extensive knowledge of their sport enables highly skilled performers to recognize, predict and respond to performance situations more accurately and rapidly than their less skilled counterparts (Abernathy, 1997).

Knowledge and Memory It stands to reason that changes in a learner's knowledge base regarding the activity would accompany performance changes. Quite simply, accomplished performers know more about the skill than do their less proficient counterparts. They have higher levels of both declarative knowledge (e.g., rules) and procedural knowledge (e.g., what to do in a given situation), giving them a larger knowledge base from which to draw (Thomas & Thomas, 1994).

Patients may change how they walk when undergoing gait analysis.

CEREBRAL CHALLENGE # 5

Generate a list of examples of declarative and procedural knowledge for a skill of your choice.

The structure of that knowledge base (specific to the activity) has also been found to be more complex and organized in a manner that facilitates pattern recognition and recall. This was demonstrated by Allard, Graham and Paarsalu (1980), who found expert basketball players to be superior to novices in a recall study. Participants were shown two sets of slides that depicted basketball game situations. The difference between the two was that one set displayed structured situations while the other unstructured. At the end of a four-second viewing period, participants were asked to recreate the slide using magnets representing players on a magnet board that simulated half of a basketball court. The study authors found the experts to be superior to the novices at recalling the structured situations only. Since the experts' superiority was only evident in the game condition, it appears that experts are able to build a better representation of the problem because of their ability to organize or chunk the information presented into meaningful units (Allard, 1982). This along with a larger knowledge base enables them to access information more efficiently, focus on higher-level concepts, make more connections between concepts, and therefore solve problems more quickly and with fewer errors (McPherson & Thomas, 1989; Thomas, French & Humphries, 1986). Similar results have been found in chess (Chase & Simon, 1973), snooker (Abernathy, Neal & Koning, 1994) and dance (Smyth & Pendleton, 1994).

ERROR DETECTION AND CORRECTION

Another indicator of skill development is the increased ability of the learner to detect and correct his or her performance errors. With practice, learners develop the capability to monitor and interpret the exteroceptive and proprioceptive feedback provided by the various sensory receptors. This information can then be used to either make corrections during a movement (time permitting) or to direct future attempts.

As error detection and correction capabilities improve, learners will become less dependent on practitioners. There will be a reduction in questions such as, "What did I do that time?" In addition, the type of questions asked will become more specific. Learners will also display behaviors that will indicate they know they have made an error. For example, when performing the tennis serve, if the ball toss is off, less skilled learners will likely attempt to hit it anyway, jeopardizing the outcome, but more proficient learners will be able to recognize a bad ball toss and will let the ball drop so they may re-toss it.

SELF-CONFIDENCE

As your learners become more skilled, you will notice that their confidence in their ability to perform the skill will increase. With increased confidence comes increased motivation to improve further. Consequently, when designing learning experiences, practitioners should ensure that each learner experiences some degree of success each practice period.

Measuring Progress

In addition to subjectively evaluating an individual's progress by observing variations in performance over time, a number of objective assessment measures can be used to evaluate the effectiveness of training or instructional strategies. These techniques allow the practitioner to document changes in proficiency by quantifying learning based on skilled performance indicators such as time, distance and frequency.

PERFORMANCE CURVES

Performance curves are obtained by systematically plotting the results from repeated measurements of a specific performance variable across time. The resulting graph offers the practitioner two pieces of information. First, the general direction of the curve is indicative of improvement. Second, by examining successive trials, consistency can be inferred.

To construct a performance curve, the practitioner must first select a performance variable to evaluate that is an appropriate indicator of skill. For example, the Functional Reach Test (Duncan, Weiner, & Chandler, 1990) is one measure that can be used to evaluate the impact of a rehabilitation program designed to assist a patient regain postural control. To perform the test, patients stand with feet shoulder width apart and their shoulders flexed to 90 degrees so that the arms are parallel to the floor. They then reach as far forward as possible while maintaining their balance. The distance reached is measured and recorded. In our example, the patient was tested once a week for a period of twelve weeks. On the graph, the distance reached is plotted on the y-axis, while the number of weeks forms the x-axis. The resulting hypothetical performance curve is shown in Figure 5.3.

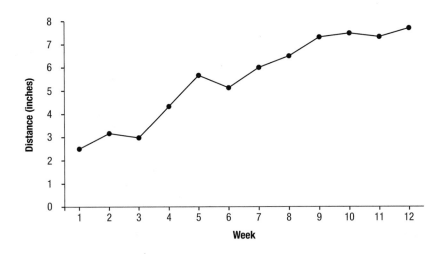

FIGURE 5.3
Hypothetical performance curve for the Functional Reach Test.

Types of Performance Curves   Performance curves generally follow one of four patterns (see Figure 5.4). The most common performance curve is the negatively accelerating curve. This curve reflects the **power law of practice,** which states that when learning a new skill, there tends to be a large initial improvement in performance, and the rate of improvement slows later in practice. The second type is the positively accelerating curve, which is characterized by little initial improvement with larger gains occurring later. The linear curve reflects a direct relationship between performance and time. Finally, the S-shaped curve is a combination of both the negatively and positively accelerating curves.

When reading performance curves it should also be noted that the nature of the curve is dependent on what is being measured. For example, if the performance variable being measured was time and decreasing the time

power law of practice: Law that states that when learning a new skill, there tends to be a large initial improvement in performance, which slows later in practice.

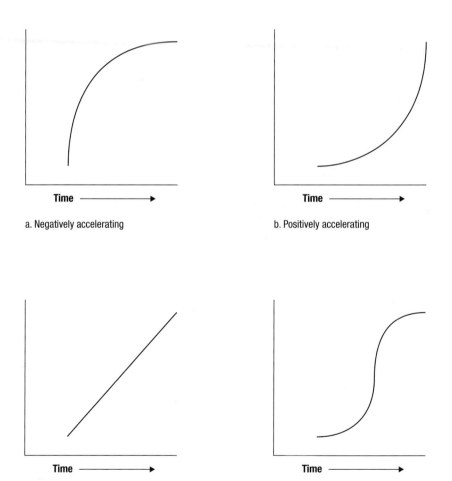

a. Negatively accelerating

b. Positively accelerating

c. Linear

d. S-shaped

FIGURE 5.4
Types of performance curves.

required to execute the skill indicated improved performance, then the curve would be reversed.

Limitations of Performance Curves Although a popular method of documenting progress, performance curves do present several limitations. To understand the first limitation, we must review the distinguishing characteristics between performance and learning. Recall that learning results in a relatively permanent change in a person's capability to execute a motor skill, whereas performance is simply the act of executing a skill. Because the measures for performance curves are taken during the practicing of a skill, they represent temporary effects and therefore cannot establish relative permanence.

A second limitation is that the measurements used to construct the curve are often obtained by extrapolating the mean of several trials for a particular session. Consequently, it is possible that by looking only at the average, valuable information regarding the learning process is lost.

PERFORMANCE PLATEAUS

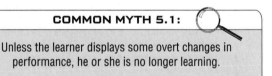

COMMON MYTH 5.1:

Unless the learner displays some overt changes in performance, he or she is no longer learning.

performance plateau: A period of time during the learning process in which no overt changes in performance occur.

Practitioners must be careful not to falsely assume that learning has ceased when performance improvement subsides. It may be that the learner is experiencing a performance plateau. A **performance plateau** is a period of time during the learning process in which no overt changes in performance occur. Again, it is important that practitioners be able to distinguish between temporary changes in performance and relatively permanent changes, which are indicative of learning.

Remember that learning is not directly observable. We can't see what someone perceives, we can't see what someone is thinking and we can't see changes in underlying behavioral and neurological processes. Thomas and Thomas (1994) remind us that "knowing when and how is not synonymous with the execution of the activity" (p. 296). Plateaus often represent transitional periods in the learning process where the integration of task components (and perhaps strategy) is being resolved. Consequently, performance plateaus do not always indicate that the learner has stopped learning but are instead a normal part of the learning process. A second reason for the occurrence of performance plateaus is that performance can temporarily be impacted by variables such as fatigue, anxiety or a lack of motivation. Finally, plateaus can be the result of limitations in the performance measurement used. Ceiling and floor effects occur when there exist a maximum or minimum achievable score on a task. For example, if a learner's average number of successful free throws out of 10 attempts was plotted on a performance

FIGURE 5.5
Retention test time line.

curve, as he or she approached the ceiling (10), the performance curve would begin to plateau.

RETENTION TESTS

One method of inferring that a relatively permanent change in a performance has occurred is through a retention test. A **retention test** measures the persistence of improved skill performance. Unlike a **posttest,** which is administered directly following the practice period (which could be one session or multiple sessions) and is therefore used to find out what a learner can do after practicing a skill, a retention test is given following a period of no practice (see Figure 5.5). The resulting performance level is then compared to the initial performance level of that same skill (before practice). If the comparison indicates a high degree of improvement, you can infer that learning has occurred.

For example, at the beginning of a handball unit, the Tyson thirty-second volley test (1970) could be administered to establish a baseline of the learner's skill proficiency prior to the practice period. To perform this particular skills test, the learner stands behind the short line of the court. When the signal is given, the student tosses the handball against the front wall and volleys it as many times as possible in 30 seconds. For a volley to be counted, it has to be made from behind the short line.

A common practice is to then retest learners following the completion of the unit or to give a posttest. A posttest is not a true indicator of learning, however, as it does not measure performance persistency. Instead, learners should be given a retention test where they are retested following a period of no practice, such as one week after the completion of the handball unit.

TRANSFER TESTS

A second type of assessment that can be used to distinguish between temporary and permanent performance changes is a transfer test. A **transfer test** measures the degree to which the learner can adapt the practiced skill to a different performance situation. Variations in the skill itself or the environment in which it is performed can serve to test adaptability and infer learning. For example, a transfer test for a patient learning to execute a sit to stand movement might involve a novel chair height or surface (e.g., firm vs. padded). Using the handball skill presented earlier, a transfer test for volleying might require learners to strike the ball after it bounces off of the back wall instead of the front wall.

retention test: Skill performance test given following a period of no practice that measures the persistence of improved skill performance.

post test: Skill performance test administered directly following a practice period that is used to find out what a learner can do after practicing a skill.

transfer test: Measurement of the adaptability of a response determined by testing a learner's ability to use a skill in a novel context or manner.

A Look Ahead

Learners progress through distinct stages of learning as they acquire skill. Each stage is characterized by both behavioral changes and alterations in the goal of the learner. In addition a number of learner and performance indicators have been identified to assist practitioners' inference of skill development. Understanding the characteristics of each stage in addition to being able to assess a learner's proficiency level can guide a practitioner's decision making with respect to the delivery of instructions, practice design and experiences and the provision of feedback. The next chapter begins our discussion of how to design appropriate learning environments by examining pre-instructional considerations that influence communication.

Summary

- According to Fitts and Posner, learners pass through three distinct stages:
  - Cognitive stage: Development of basic movement pattern
  - Associative: Refinement of movement pattern
  - Autonomous: Performance of movement virtually automatic
- Gentile's two-stage model emphasizes the goal of the learner and the influence of task and environmental characteristics on that goal.
  - Stage 1: Getting the idea of the movement
  - Stage 2: Fixation (closed skills) / Diversification (Open skills)
    - Want to accommodate regulatory conditions
- Numerous performance changes can be assessed to infer learning, including changes in coordination and control, muscle activity, energy expenditure, consistency, attentional focus, knowledge and memory, error detection and correction and self-confidence.
- Progress can also be assessed through performance curves, retention tests and transfer tests.
- Retention tests measure the persistence of improved skill performance.
- Transfer tests measure the degree to which the learner can adapt the practiced skill to a different performance situation.
- A performance plateau is a period of time during the learning process in which no overt changes in performance occur. Plateaus often represent transitional periods in the learning process where the integration of task components (and perhaps strategy) is being resolved and are not necessarily indicative of a cessation in the learning process.

Review Questions

1. What are the names of each stage of learning in Fitts and Posner's model? How do the names reflect the corresponding stage?
2. Explain how the role of the instructor shifts as a learner progresses through Fitts and Posner's three stages of learning.

3. How does Gentile's model differ from that of Fitts and Posner?
4. Define fixation and diversification, and explain their relationship to closed and open skills.
5. Explain how the role of the instructor shifts as a learner progresses through Gentile's two-stage model of learning.
6. List five performance characteristics that can help you infer learning has occurred.
7. What does the term "freezing the degrees of freedom" mean?
8. What are the two consequences of automaticity?
9. Explain how experts are able to build a better representation of the movement problem.
10. What can you look for to determine whether a learner's error detection and correction capabilities have improved? Do you have any suggestions beyond those listed in the chapter?
11. Why might it be a false assumption that someone is no longer learning if they do not display any performance improvements?
12. Compare and contrast retention and transfer tests.

References

Abernathy, B. (1997). Motor control adaptations to training. In B. Abernathy, V. Kippers, L.T. Mackinnon, R.J. Neal & S. Hanrahan (eds.), *The Biophyscial Foundations of Human Movement*. Champaign, IL: Human Kinetics Publishers, pp. 334–353.

Abernathy, B., Neal, R.J. & Koning, P. (1994). Visual-perceptual and cognitive differences between expert, intermediate and novice snooker players. *Applied Cognitive Psychology, 8*, 185–211.

Allard, F. (1982). Cognition, expert performance and sport. In J.H. Salmela, J.T. Partington, & T. Orlick (eds.), *New paths of sport learning and excellence*, Ottawa, ON: Sport in Perspectives Inc., pp. 22–27.

Allard, F., Graham, S. & Paarsalu, M.F. (1980). Perception in sport: Basketball. *Journal of Sport Psychology, 2*, 14–21.

Anderson, D.I. & Sidaway, B. (1994). Coordination changes associated with practice of a soccer kick. *Research Quarterly for Exercise and Sport, 65*(2), 93–99.

Bernstein, N. (1967). *The coordination and regulation of movements*. Oxford, England: Pergamon Press.

Byers, B.B. (2000). "Just do it"—Commercial slogan or movement principle? *JOPERD, 71*(9), 16–19.

Chase, W.G. & Simon, H.A. (1973). Perception in chess. *Cognitive Psychology, 4*, 55–81.

Duncan, P.W., Weiner, D.K. & Chandler, J. (1990). Functional reach: A new clinical measure of balance. *Journal of Gerontology, 45*, 192–195

Fitts, P. M. & Posner, M.I. (1967). *Human performance*. Belmont, CA: Brooks/Cole.

Gabriel, D.A. & Boucher, J.P. (1998). Practice effects on the timing and magnitude of agonist activity during ballistic elbow flexion to a target. *Research Quarterly for Exercise and Sport, 69*, 30–37.

Gentile, A.M. (1972). A working model of skill acquisition with application to teaching. *Quest*, Monograph 17:3–23.

Gentile, A.M. (1987). Skill acquisition: Action, movement, and the neuromotor processes. In J.H. Carr, R.B. Shepard, J. Gordon, A.M. Gentile & J.M. Hind (eds.), *Movement Science: Foundations for Physical Therapy in Rehabilitation*. Rockville, MD: Aspen, pp. 93–154.

Hall, S.J. (1999). *Basic biomechanics.* New York: McGraw-Hill.

Jaegars, S.M.H.J., Peterson, R.F., Dantuma, R., Hillen, B., Geuze, R. & Schellekens, J. (1989). Kinesiologic aspects of motor learning in dart throwing. *Journal of Human Movement Studies, 16*, 161–171.

McPherson, S.L. & Thomas, J.R. (1989). Relation of knowledge and performance in boys' tennis: Age and expertise. *Journal of Experimental Child Psychology, 48*, 190–211.

Rink, J.E. (1998). Motor learning. In B.S. Mohnsen (ed.), *Concepts of Physical Education: What Every Student Needs to Know*. Reston, VA: NASPE, pp.15–37.

Schneider, K., Zernicke, R.F., Schmidt, R.A. & Hart, T.J. (1989). Changes in limb dynamics during the practice of rapid arm movement. *Journal of Biomechanics, 22*, 805–817.

Shank, M.D. & Haywood, K.M. (1987). Eye movements while viewing a baseball pitch. *Perceptual and Motor Skills, 64*, 1191–1197.

Smyth, M.M. & Pendleton, L.R. (1994). Memory for movement in professional ballet dancers. *International Journal of Sport Psychology,* 25:282–294.

Southard, D. & Higgins, T. (1987). Changing movement patterns: Effects of demonstrations and practice. *Research Quarterly for Exercise and Sport, 58,* 77–80.

Thomas, J.R., French, K.E. & Humphries, C.A. (1986). Knowledge development and sport performance: Directions for motor behavior research. *Journal of Sport Psychology, 8,* 259–272.

Thomas, K.T. & Thomas, J.R. (1994). Developing expertise in sport: The relation of knowledge and performance. *International Journal of Sport Psychology, 25*, 295–311.

Tyson, K.W. (1970). *A handball skills test for college men.* Unpublished Master's thesis, University of Florida, Gainesville, FL.

Vereijken, B., van Emmerik R.E.A., Whiting, H.T.A. & Newell, K.M. (1992). Free(z)ing degrees of freedom in skill acquisition, *Journal of Motor Behavior, 24*(1), 133–142.

Whiting, H.T.A. (1984). *Human motor actions: Bernstein reassessed.* Amsterdam: North-Holland.

CHAPTER SIX

The Learner: Pre-Instruction Considerations

Perhaps the single greatest factor that impacts a learner's ability to understand new concepts and achieve movement proficiency is communication. Effective communication occurs when messages are clear, concise and match the level of the receiver. However, all learners are different in how they receive new information and attempt to make sense of it. Recognizing the influence of individual differences such as learning style, past experiences and level of motivation on how learners receive information enables the teacher, coach or therapist to provide instruction and design experiences that are meaningful for each learner.

FIGURE 6.1.
Messages must match the level of the receiver. (Reprinted by permission of Johnny Hart Creators Syndicate, Inc.)

CEREBRAL CHALLENGE #1

Discuss the importance of effective communication for teachers, coaches and therapists. Include in your discussion those with whom you will have to communicate and when communication will be used throughout the learning process.

Learning Styles

While coaching at a college track meet, I noticed another coach talking with a long jumper after she had performed a warm-up jump. The coach was giving her verbal instructions to assist her in correcting a technical flaw. When he was finished with his explanation, he asked the athlete if she understood what he had said. She replied that she did and returned to the end of the runway. When she got there, she turned to one of her teammates and said, "Can you show me what he was saying?" Once the technique was demonstrated, she understood perfectly.

learning style: Individual preference for receiving and processing new information.

All learners have unique preferences for receiving and processing new information. These preferences constitute one's individual **learning style.** Research has shown that when instructional style and learning style match, learners are able to process information more effectively, resulting in greater learning (Brunner & Hill, 1992; Cano, Garton & Raven, 1992; Dunn, Beaudry & Klavis 1989; Dunn & Dunn, 1975; Murray, 1979; Onwuegbuzie & Daley, 1998; Price, Dunn & Sanders, 1981; Ross, Drysdale & Shultz, 1999). Since no two individuals possess identical learning styles, the incorporation of instructional strategies that accommodate each learner is an important consideration when designing the learning environment. The athlete in the scenario just described, for example, better understood her error when shown a demonstration than she did after hearing verbal instructions. Had her coach known of and accommodated her preference for visual information, the need for the athlete to turn to another source would have been eliminated.

Among the many learning style models, including Gardner's multiple intelligences (1993), Kolb's learning styles inventory (1986) and Gregorc's mind styles model (1985), the Learning Styles Inventory of Dunn, Dunn, and Price (1989) has been informally used in a motor skill acquisition setting. Dunn and Dunn (1993, 1992, 1975) contend that an individual's learning style is an integrative collection of multiple levels and can be determined through the assessment of five areas: (1) instructional environment preferences with regard to sound, light, temperature and class design; (2) emotionality preferences including motivation, persistence, responsibility and structure; (3) sociological preferences for individual, pair, peer, team, adult or varied relations; (4) physiological preferences regarding perception, intake, time and mobility and (5) psychological preferences derived from analytic mode, hemisphericity and action.

Not only do each of the individual elements of the five areas identified need to be considered when designing the learning environment, but many have been found to correlate with two learning profiles that are based on processing preferences, that is, whether someone is considered a global learner, an analytical learner or a combination of both (Dunn, Bruno, Sklar, Zenhausern & Beaudry, 1990; Dunn, Cavanaugh, Eberle, & Zenhausern, 1982). Global learners learn more easily when they are first presented with the big picture and are then asked to concentrate on details. Humor, anecdotes and graphics are helpful when being introduced to new information. Analytical learners, on the other hand, prefer to have new information

EXPLORATION ACTIVITY 6.1 Exploring Your Learning Preferences

Several elements from Dunn and Dunn's learning style model are presented below. For each element, circle the description that best suits your preference when learning new information.

Element	Option A	Option B
Sound	Work best in silence	Work best when there is background noise or music
Lighting	Prefer room to be well-illuminated	Prefer soft lighting
Design	Prefer to work at a desk, table, etc.	Prefer to work in an easy chair, on bed, etc.
Persistence	Need to finish a task once started	Need frequent breaks; prefer to work on several tasks simultaneously
Structure	Prefer guidelines, specifications, procedures, rules, etc.	Prefer less structure, which allows for creativity
Social	Prefer to learn alone or with a practitioner	Prefer to learn with peers
Intake	Rarely eat, drink, smoke or have other distracters while learning	Prefer to eat, drink, smoke or have other distracters while learning

Analytical learners will have a tendency to select the responses under Option A, while global learners are more inclined to choose the responses provided in Option B. Remember that all learners are different, and some people may have a combined profile.

presented in a step-by-step, sequential manner that builds towards the main concept. Rules, guidelines and procedures are helpful for analytical learners. Interestingly, those individuals in scientifically based professions, such as medical personnel, tend to fall within the analytical profile, while most patients do not (Samelson, 1997). Complete Exploration Activity 6-1 to gain a better understanding of your learning preferences.

While some of the elements of Dunn and Dunn's model are not directly related to a skill acquisition setting, such as intake, others can easily be accommodated. Brunner and Hill (1992) altered their coaching strategies and redesigned the practice area used by a varsity high school wrestling team in order to accommodate individual preferences for two of the elements from Dunn and Dunn's model, perceptual mode and sociological inclination. In addition to opportunities to physically attempt new skills, videotapes, handouts, charts and verbal presentations were provided according to perceptual preference. The wrestling room was also redesigned to accommodate sociological preferences by providing areas where wrestlers could work alone, in pairs or in groups. Although their program was not examined through a formal research study, Brunner and Hill reported positive changes in wrestlers' athletic skill, academic achievement and self-esteem as a result of matching instructional style with individual wrestler's learning styles.

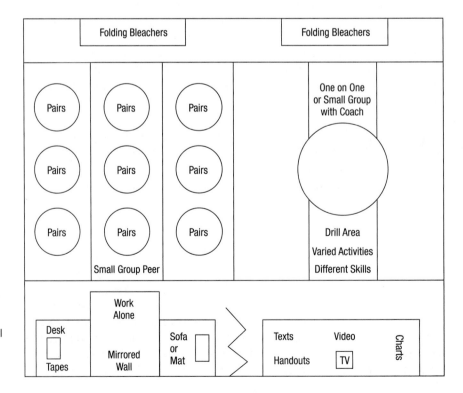

FIGURE 6.2.
Wrestling room layout accommodating sociological and perceptual preferences (Reprinted with permission of JOPERD).

PERCEPTUAL MODE

Although one's learning style consists of many variables, perhaps the easiest to accommodate for motor skill learning is the preferred perceptual mode. Perceptual mode is the way information is received and processed. Learners preferentially take in and process information in different ways. This preferred mode is referred to as our **modal strength.** Four perceptual modes should be considered when giving instructions and designing practice environments: visual, kinesthetic, analytical and auditory.

Visual learners understand new concepts better when visual cue words such as "watch," "see" and "look" are incorporated in explanations. Demonstrations, videotapes, pictures, models and the use of mirrors are all effective methods used to accommodate learners whose modal strength is visual. Kinesthetic learners strive to understand what the desired movement feels like. Once they achieve this understanding, they use it as a frame of reference with which to compare future attempts. Instructional strategies such as simulations, guidance, repeated practice and incorporating cue words such as "feel," "move" and "experience" all assist the kinesthetic learner to develop a sense of what the correct movement feels like. Analytical learners approach the desired movement in a problem-solving fashion. Scientific concepts and principles and cue words such as "analyze," "investigate" and "why" assist the analytical learner in solving the impending movement problem. Sounds and rhythms are the preference of auditory learners. Cue words such as "hear," "pace" and "tempo" should therefore be incorporated to assist in learning the movement pattern. Auditory learners are also more likely to benefit from verbal descriptions such as the one given by the coach in the beginning story. Finally, some individuals have more than one modal preference. To accommodate these learners, combine strategies to target each of the preferred modes.

modal strength: The preferred perceptual mode through which a learner takes in and processes information.

CEREBRAL CHALLENGE #2

Go back to the long jump story at the beginning of the chapter. What was the athlete's preferred perceptual mode? Suggest alternative strategies that the coach could use to better accommodate his athlete's learning style.

ACCOMMODATING YOUR LEARNERS

How can you find out each individual's learning style? Formal testing instruments are available, such as Kolb's Learning Style Inventory (1986) or Dunn, Dunn and Price's Learning Style Inventory (1989). Caution must be taken when using such instruments, however, as they were designed for traditional classroom settings, and it has recently been found that learning style shifts depending on whether the nature of the task is predominantly a cognitive or motor one (Coker, 1995). As a result, if formal testing instruments are used, respondents must be instructed to answer the questions as they apply to a motor setting.

Informal assessment is also possible, and it can be a powerful and reliable technique. Learners provide clues about their learning preference. Listen to the descriptive words they use to assess their performance and the questions they ask. Do the words consistently fall into one of the four perceptual mode categories? Also, do they ask for clarification through a different mode? The athlete in the opening story was a visual learner. When the coach verbally explained the athlete's mistakes (auditory mode) and how to fix them, the athlete did not completely understand. As a result, she sought out an alternative way to get the information through her modal strength, vision. The demonstration her teammate gave her was all she needed to understand what the coach was trying to explain to her.

Utilizing only one presentation style denies learners comparable opportunities to understand the information presented. Rearrange the learning environment as suggested by Dunn and Dunn (1993, 1992, 1975). Get to know your instructional tendencies, and make an effort to expand your repertoire to incorporate all learning styles. Research suggests that one's learning style preference influences one's teaching style. As a result, practitioners will tend to focus almost exclusively on their preferred style when giving instructions, but a practitioner's natural instructional tendencies may not match the needs of the learner (Heikkinnen, Pettigrew & Zakrajsek, 1985; MacNeil, 1980; McDaniel, 1986). In mismatched situations, practitioners must make a conscious effort to utilize alternate strategies that are compatible with the learner's preferences. When working one on one with an individual, provide instruction and feedback through the individual's preferred perceptual mode so as to capitalize on their strengths (see Table 6-1 for ideas). In situations that involve large groups, however, providing instruction and feedback through each individual's preferred mode is not feasible. When working with groups, practitioners should instead use an eclectic approach whereby the mode through which information is presented is constantly varied so that all modes are used. Recognizing and accommodating learning styles will result in more meaningful communication and will translate to enhanced learning.

EXPLORATION ACTIVITY 6.2 Self-Analysis

Videotape yourself teaching a 10-minute lesson on a skill of your choice. While reviewing your video, tabulate the number of cue words and strategies you use in each of the four perceptual mode categories: visual, kinesthetic, auditory and analytical. Do you have a tendency to teach the way you prefer to learn, as research suggests? Do you incorporate all four modes of presentation, or do you have a tendency to use only one mode? Suggest areas on the tape where you could have used a different mode. Give a specific example of an alternative cue word or strategy for each area suggested.

TABLE 6.1
Examples of Cue Words and Strategies Used to Target Each Perceptual Mode

	Visual	Kinesthetic	Analytical	Auditory
Sample Cue Words to Use	See	Feel	Analyze	Hear
	Look	Touch	Think	Listen
	Watch	Sense	Examine	Detect
	Observe	Move	Compare	Tempo
Sample Teaching Strategies to Use	Demonstrations	Simulations	Use principles	Clapping
	Pictures	Guidance	Test	Music
	Video	Trial and error	Investigate	Sound

TABLE 6.2
Example of Eclectic Approach Using the Basketball Set Shot

Preparation	Action
• Toes and shoulders face basket	• Knees bend slightly until tension felt in quads
• Eyes focused on front of rim	• Smooth sequential rhythm begins from knees and ends at fingers
• Feel weight distributed evenly over both feet	• Force for shot comes from legs (discuss why generating force with legs is more effective)
• Ball positioned between shoulders and eye level	• Should see arm extend through the ball

CEREBRAL CHALLENGE #3

Using a motor skill of your choice, develop a more extensive list of cue words and strategies that could be used to accommodate each of the four modal strengths.

Transfer of Learning

Another individual difference that should be considered by the practitioner to enhance communication and design optimal learning experiences is the learner's past experience. Throughout our lifespan, our experience with movement accumulates. The sum of our past experiences influences our

transfer: When the learning of a new skill or its performance under novel conditions is influenced by past experience with another skill or skills.

positive transfer: When the learning of a new skill or its performance under novel conditions is positively influenced by past experience with another skill or skills.

negative transfer: When the learning of a new skill or its performance under novel conditions is negatively influenced by past experience with another skill or skills.

zero transfer: When past experience with another skill or skills has no influence on the learning of a new skill or its performance under novel conditions.

ability to learn new skills in both positive and negative ways. This phenomenon, where the learning of a new skill or its performance under novel conditions can be influenced by past experience with another skill or skills, is known as **transfer.**

TYPES OF TRANSFER

Three types of transfer exist: positive, negative and zero. **Positive transfer** occurs when a learner's past experience with one skill facilitates the learning of a new skill or the use of a skill in a different context. The zone defense used in football and basketball, for example, share many commonalities. In this instance, learners' past experience with a zone defense in football will likely accelerate the rate at which they learn the zone defense in basketball. **Negative transfer,** on the other hand, occurs when a learner's past experience with one skill hinders or obstructs the learning of a new skill or the performance of a skill under novel conditions. Despite the fact that swinging a bat in softball and in baseball share similar movement characteristics, the task of tracking the oncoming pitch differs significantly in the two sports. In baseball, the pitcher uses an overarm throwing motion, causing the ball's trajectory to move from high to low. In softball, however, the pitcher uses an underhand throwing motion, and the ball rises as it approaches the plate. Previous experience in baseball could therefore temporarily interfere with hitting performance in softball. Finally, when two skills are completely unrelated, such as swimming the butterfly stroke and goaltending in water polo, **zero transfer** occurs, because experience with the first skill has no influence on the second.

While practitioners want to capitalize on positive transfer, negative transfer can occur and is often the result of having to learn a new response to a well-learned stimulus. A classic example of negative transfer occurs when a skilled badminton player decides to learn tennis. In badminton, the forehand drive requires a wrist snap. This is not the case in tennis, where there is minimal contribution of the wrist. Initially, the badminton player may attempt to incorporate a wrist snap in the tennis forehand. Fortunately, most negative transfer effects are temporary and can be overcome with practice.

 CEREBRAL CHALLENGE #4

Generate a list of examples of positive, negative and zero transfer from your own experience.

THEORIES OF TRANSFER

Understanding the theoretical underpinnings of transfer will assist the teacher, coach or therapist in designing learning experiences that foster positive transfer. This understanding will also help you account for difficulties that individuals display during initial attempts as a result of negative transfer. The author of the identical elements theory originally hypothesized that transfer was based on the number of common elements shared by two skills (Thorndike, 1914). It was thought that the more identical elements shared by two skills, the greater the positive transfer from one to the other. Accordingly, positive transfer would be anticipated to occur between picking up buttons and picking up coins, while the amount of transfer between putting and an instep kick in soccer would be negligible.

The identical elements theory was amended by Osgoode (1949), who specified that similarities between the stimulus and response conditions of the two tasks were fundamental rather than identical elements. Consequently, a high degree of positive transfer would be expected when stimulus and response conditions for the previously acquired task were the same as for the task being learned.

When two skills have opposite stimulus response requirements, learning difficulties can arise. For example, negative transfer would be predicted when the skill being introduced has an identical stimulus as that of a previously learned skill but now requires a new response. An individual who purchases a new mountain bike, for example, will experience some temporary frustration if the gear shifting mechanism is different from that of the previously owned bike.

The identical elements theory does not, however, account for all possible transfer conditions. Strategic and conceptual aspects of games or tasks can also transfer. As a result, the transfer appropriate processing theory was proposed to account for cognitive processing similarities that occur between practice conditions and the performance criterion (Bransford, Franks, Morris & Stein, 1979; Lee, 1988; Morris, Bransford & Franks, 1977). According to the transfer appropriate processing theory, positive transfer would be expected when practice conditions require learners to engage in problem-solving processes similar to those experienced during the criterion task.

In volleyball, when a spike is hit around a block, one of three main defensive skills can be used: the dig (forearm pass), the roll or the sprawl. The technique chosen by the defensive player is dependent on a number of factors that have to be assessed instantaneously. To facilitate the player's ability to not only choose the appropriate skill but to execute it correctly, proponents of transfer appropriate processing would recommend practicing all three skills during the same practice period, but in a random order, rather than practicing each skill independently (a concept known as contextual interference). Furthermore, continuously changing the direction, speed, position and trajectory of the oncoming ball would increase the likelihood of maximum positive transfer. This practice strategy, known as variable practice, forces the learner to engage in realistic cognitive processing, since the learner will never be in exactly the same situation twice. Both contextual interference and variable practice will be discussed in more detail in Chapter 9.

TRANSFER AND INSTRUCTIONAL DESIGN

Many instructional decisions regarding presentation sequence and the use of instructional aids are based on the principles of transfer. For example,

Skill progressions are based on the assumption that experience with simplified versions will positively transfer to the actual movement.

simplified versions of skills, drills and games are developed to serve as precursors to more complex forms that will be introduced in the future. Skill progressions, such as that of diving into a swimming pool, where learners are first taught to dive from a kneeling position and then advance to a crouched position, a stride position and finally a standing position, are based on the assumption that experience with simplified versions will positively transfer to the actual movement, thereby facilitating its acquisition. Similarly, lead-up games, such as T-ball, sideline soccer, five hundred in softball or baseball, keep-away in basketball and three-hit volleyball, have been adopted to assist the leaner.

Other modifications are made when the skill involves a potential risk of injury, when practicing the skill is expensive, when there is a lack of practice facilities or when practice in a real-life setting is not possible. Gymnasts first learn complex and potentially dangerous skills with some type of instructional aid, such as a harness, to minimize the risk of injury. Bicycles are equipped with training wheels. Fighter pilots train on flight simulators that allow countless practice trials with minimal risk and expense. Astronauts train underwater, as it simulates the weightless environment they will be exposed to in space. In the clinical environment, the BTE Work Simulation device allows patients to simulate activities such as prosthetic driving, turning a key, pulling a knob and applying brakes, and the Resusci Annie mannequin (Laerdal Medical) is used to learn rescue breathing and CPR. Numerous examples exist, all of which attempt to capitalize on positive transfer.

CEREBRAL CHALLENGE #5

Develop a list of examples from your own experience of skill modifications that may foster positive transfer.

FOSTERING POSITIVE TRANSFER

Considerable efforts are made to design instructional methodology that capitalizes on the notion of positive transfer. The following guidelines, based on the theories of transfer, provide a starting point for practitioners.

1. **Analyze the skill.** Given that transfer is based on degree of similarity, the ability to analyze skills effectively becomes indispensable for designing instructional strategies that will facilitate learning. Four subcomponents of skill can be examined to determine the degree of similarity and assess the potential for positive transfer.

   1) *The fundamental movement pattern.* The last three steps of the lay-up, for example, are comparable to those of the high jump. Someone who is

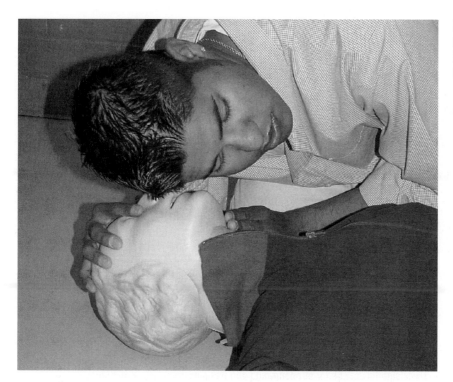

Resusci Annie
mannequins allow
learners to simulate
CPR.

proficient at the lay-up will have an advantage in learning the high
jump if the practitioner were to associate the two during instruction.

2) *The strategic and conceptual aspects of the game or task.* The "give and go"
strategy, for example, is used in a variety of sports. If a learner has
performed a "give and go" previously in one sport, pointing out the
similarities to a "give and go" in a different sport should facilitate
learning. Similarly, practitioners could point out similarities in the use
of a pelvic tilt in numerous therapeutic and fitness activities, or the influence of head position on balance.

3) *Perceptual elements.* White-water kayaking and white-water rafting
may lack similarity with respect to required physical skills, but
both activities require knowledge of how to read the water to choose
the best route. The skill's regulatory cues as well as the visual search
strategies used for their detection would be quite similar in both
skills.

4) *Temporal and spatial elements.* Ensuring that an implement meets with
an object at both the ideal time and location is required of many skills,
including the racket sports of squash, tennis and racquetball.

Prior to providing instruction, then, practitioners should become
familiar with their learners' past experience with various motor
skills. Those skills should then be analyzed to determine if there are

similarities in fundamental movement pattern, strategic and/or conceptual aspects, perceptual elements and temporal and spatial elements between the skill being taught and those with which the learner is familiar. Comparisons can then be made throughout the instructional process to facilitate understanding.

RESEARCH NOTE

An experiment by Coldwells and Hare (1994) was conducted to determine if short tennis skills positively transferred to lawn tennis. Short tennis is a modified version of tennis designed for children. The rackets are smaller and made of plastic, making them lighter and easier to swing. The ball, made of foam, bounces lower and slower. The court is smaller, with a lower net, and the rules are simplified.

Sixteen subjects were divided into two groups. The experimental group received 10 hours of short tennis instruction and 10 hours of lawn tennis instruction. The control group received 20 hours of lawn tennis instruction only. A pre- and posttest using the Dyer backboard test was administered and videotaped. Three experienced coaches then analyzed the videotape, judging each subject's backswing, follow-through, ball placement and positioning (the position of the player relative to the bounce of the ball). Results revealed no significant difference between groups on the test but found that the experimental group improved significantly with practice. In addition, the video analysis indicated that the experimental group performed significantly better on the backswing and the follow-through, while the control group was significantly better at positioning and ball placement. A second study, limited to 8 hours of total instruction and focusing only on ground strokes, revealed no significant differences between groups for the test but found the experimental group to be significantly better on the backswing, follow-through and placement, while the control group was better at positioning. The authors concluded that because the experimental group was superior in the backswing and follow-through in both experiments, positive transfer of those actions occurred. They further concluded that the positioning superiority of the control group was probably due to the greater experience with the bounce of a tennis ball. Consequently, negative transfer for reading ball bounce likely resulted between the use of the foam ball in short tennis and the use of the tennis ball.

Question:

How could this study be redesigned to test the authors' hypothesis regarding the control group's superiority with positioning?

 CEREBRAL CHALLENGE # 6

Analyze the following pairs of skills to determine their similarities and differences. Be sure to compare the fundamental movement pattern, strategic and conceptual aspects, perceptual elements and temporal and spatial elements. Based on your analysis, assess the potential for transfer, either positive or negative, for each pairing. Justify your answer.

a. Cane walking and using a walker   **c.** Kickball and baseball
b. Downhill skiing and water skiing   **d.** Mountain biking and white-water kayaking

a.

b.

FIGURE 6.3.
There is a high degree of similarity between the hand position for catching a football above the waist and that for setting a volleyball.

2. **Determine the cost benefit trade-off.** Lead-up games, the use of simulators and breaking down skills into parts should be evaluated for cost effectiveness prior to their use. The volleyball drill that requires teammates to form a circle and bump the ball to the next person in a clockwise direction will transfer poorly to a game situation and may in fact teach players the bad habit of swinging their arms to the side versus facing their target. Unless there is a high degree of similarity between the designed experience and the criterion, the implementation of some preliminary activities and drills may not be warranted. In addition, it should also be noted that even when a high degree of similarity exists, transfer has generally been found to be relatively small. Accordingly, efforts made to design instructional methodology that capitalizes on positive transfer are not always worthwhile.

EXPLORATION ACTIVITY 6.3 Observation: Transfer

For this Exploration Activity you will have to do an observation at a local rehabilitation or physical therapy clinic.

1. How many examples of equipment, instructions, exercises and activities can you find that are designed to elicit positive transfer? List them.
2. For each example on your list, determine which component(s) of the skill will probably transfer (fundamental movement pattern, strategic and conceptual aspects, perceptual elements or temporal and spatial elements).

3. **Get to know the learner.** All learners have past experiences that can influence their ability to acquire new skills. Get to know your learners. Find out what types of experiences they have had that might be used as a comparison with the skill you are introducing. In rehabilitation, for example, patients will see greater success if clinical practice conditions closely match the real-world functional activities in which the patient will be engaged (Stevens & Hall, 1998). Determining the real-world demands imposed on each patient is therefore prerequisite to designing an effective rehab program.

4. **Point out similarities and differences.** Having determined the similarities between the skills already learned and the skill about to be learned, point them out to the learner. Learners are not always able to make connections between skills unless their attention is drawn to these connections. Stating that rollerblading and ice-skating are similar is insufficient. You must point out specifically which aspects of the two skills are similar and which are dissimilar. For example, the push off to start in both rollerblading and ice-skating is comparable, but stopping is very different. With rollerblades, the "brake" is located at the back of the boot, and it must be forced in front of the participant to engage. In ice-skating, stopping may be performed several ways, depending on your experience. If you learned how to skate in hockey skates, you probably stop by turning to the side with your feet parallel. If you learned how to skate using figure skates, however, you may have learned to simply dig the pick into the ice and drag it. Consequently, blanket statements are misleading and may impede initial performance rather than facilitate it.

5. **Make sure that the skills you refer to have been well learned.** Any time you attempt to capitalize on the use of transfer, it is important to be sure that the skill or concept you refer to has been well learned. Although shoveling snow and scooping up a ball in lacrosse share a similar movement pattern, if you live in the southwest, your experience with shoveling snow may be limited. Another example is comparing the overhead throwing motion to the volleyball serve. If the individual has an immature throwing pattern to begin with, this strategy may backfire. Unless the skills you refer to are well learned, the example will not be meaningful and the idea you are trying to convey will not be communicated effectively.

6. **Use analogies.** Another technique employed to elicit positive transfer is the use of analogies. Learners create a mental image of how a skill is to be executed based on an instructor's explanation. New concepts can be simplified by relating the new information with a familiar model. For example, when teaching the correct grip in tennis, instructors often ask students to "shake hands" with the racquet. This analogy relates the grip to something familiar, a handshake, enhancing the learner's mental picture of the task.

Using a variety of skills of your choice, generate a list of 10 analogies that could be used to assist a learner in creating a mental picture of the corresponding skill.

7. **Maximize similarities between practice and performance/ competition.** When teaching for positive transfer, provide practice opportunities that have a high degree of similarity to the actual performance context. The movement required to step up stairs is one that is used in a variety of situations. A patient learning this stepping-up motion will use it not only to climb stairs of differing heights but also to step over curbs, step into the bath tub and step onto an escalator. Similarly, a second baseman needs to be able to accurately throw to first, second, third and home from a variety of fielding positions. Providing opportunities to use newly learned skills in a variety of situations and designing drills that simulate actual performance will foster maximum positive transfer.
8. **Consider the skill level of the learner.** Transfer is more beneficial for beginning learners than for those who are intermediate or advanced. Comparing aspects of an overhand volleyball serve to a tennis serve can assist beginners to create a mental image that enables them to generate initial attempts. Once learners have demonstrated an idea of the desired movement, however, they must focus on skill-specific cues to improve.

Motivation to Learn

COMMON MYTH

All learners are motivated to learn the skills presented to them.

Motivation is an internal condition that incites and directs action or behavior. Motivation influences how receptive learners are to instruction. Learners who are motivated will explore, practice, think and have a strong desire to master the task. Practitioners should recognize that although some individuals are excited to learn, others may be apprehensive, have misconceptions about the skill being introduced or simply not see the relevancy for learning it. Regardless of the reason, lack of motivation hinders learning.

motivation: An internal condition that incites and directs action or behavior.

CEREBRAL CHALLENGE # 8

Think back to the last time you had to learn something that you weren't interested in. Why were you not motivated to learn? How much effort did you put into learning the task? Can you think of any other consequences that occurred throughout the learning process due to your lack of motivation?

The introduction of a new skill should captivate learners' interest, and simply explaining the objective of the skill is not always enough to do this. Learners must be given a reason why it is important to learn that particular skill, which may be to develop a good foundation from which to build future skills, to gain an edge in competition or to regain the use of a limb that has been injured. Learners' interest in the skill can also be increased by exposure to elite role models and performances through the use of videotape or live demonstrations. Finally, creating a learning environment that is positive, supportive, challenging but realistic and provides opportunities for success can reduce apprehensions and increase motivation.

CEREBRAL CHALLENGE #9

1. How might you motivate an injured athlete to complete his or her rehabilitation program? How would your suggestions differ if the scenario involved a physical education class who perceived volleyball as boring?
2. Generate a more extensive list of reasons students, athletes or patients may not be motivated to learn, and then develop a number of specific strategies that could stimulate their interest.

A Look Ahead

The learning process is highly dependent on quality practitioner-learner interactions. Recognizing the influence of individual differences such as learning style, past experiences and level of motivation on how learners receive information enables the teacher, coach or therapist to provide instruction and design experiences that are meaningful for each learner. The application of this information will continue as we explore methods for presenting novel skills in the next chapter.

Summary

- All learners have unique preferences for receiving and processing new information, which defines their learning style.
- Greater learning gains have been shown when instructional style is matched to an individual's learning style.
- Four perceptual modes should be considered when giving instructions and designing practice environments: visual, kinesthetic, analytical and auditory.
- When the learning of a new skill or its performance under novel conditions is influenced by past experience with another skill or skills, transfer is said to occur.
- While practitioners want to capitalize on positive transfer, negative transfer can occur and is often the result of having to learn a new response to a well-learned stimulus.

- To determine the similarity between two skills and assess the potential for positive transfer, four factors should be compared: fundamental movement pattern, strategic and conceptual aspects of the game or task, perceptual elements and temporal and spatial elements.
- Considerations for fostering positive transfer include determining the cost benefit trade-off of its implementation, understanding the past experiences of your learners, determining and highlighting the similarities and differences between skills already learned and those being learned, ensuring that the skills being referred to have been well learned, using analogies, maximizing similarities between practice and performance/competition and the skill level of the learner.
- Motivation is an internal condition that incites and directs action or behavior.
- In order to learn, an individual must be motivated to do so.

Review Questions

1. What are the characteristics of effective communication?
2. Define learning style.
3. What is the significance of matching presentation style and learning style?
4. Two major theories have been proposed to account for transfer. Compare and contrast them.
5. What four subcomponents of a skill would you assess to determine the similarities and differences between two skills?
6. Explain why it is important to point out both the similarities and differences when comparing two skills for the purpose of transfer.
7. What is motivation, and why is it a pre-instruction consideration?

References

Bransford, J.D., Franks, J.J., Morris, C.D. & Stein, B.S. (1979). Some general constraints on learning and memory research. In L.S. Cermak & F.I.M. Craik (eds.), *Levels of Processing in Human Memory*. Hillsdale, NJ: Erlbaum, pp. 331–354.

Brunner, R. & Hill, D. (1992). Using learning styles research in coaching. *Journal of Physical Education, Recreation and Dance, 63*(4), 26–28.

Cano, J. Garton, B.L. & Raven, M.R. (1992). The relationship between learning and teaching styles and student performance in a methods of teaching agriculture course. *Journal of Agricultural Education, 33*(3), 16–22.

Coldwells, A. & Hare, M.E. (1994). The transfer of skill from short tennis to lawn tennis. *Ergonomics, 37*(1), 17–21.

Coker, C.A. (1995). Learning style consistency across cognitive and motor settings. *Perceptual and Motor Skills, 81,*1023–1026.

Dunn, R., Beaudry, J.S. & Klavis, A. (1989). Survey of research on learning styles. *Educational Leadership, 46*(6), 50–58.

Dunn, R, Bruno, J., Sklar, R. Zenhausern, R. & Beaudry, J. (1990). Effects of matching and mismatching minority developmental college students hemispheric preferences on mathematics scores. *Journal of Educational Research, 83*(5), 283–288.

Dunn, R., Cavanaugh, D., Eberle, B. & Zenhausern, R. (1982). Hemispheric preference: The newest element of learning style. *The American Biology Teacher, 44*(5), 291–294.

Dunn, R, & Dunn, K. (1975). *Educator's self-teaching guide to individualizing instructional programs.* Nyack, NY: Parker Publishing Company, Division of Prentice Hall.

Dunn, R., & Dunn, K. (1992). *Teaching elementary students through their individual learning styles.* Boston: Allyn and Bacon.

Dunn, R., & Dunn, K. (1993). *Teaching secondary students through their individual learning styles.* Boston: Allyn and Bacon.

Dunn, R., Dunn, K. & Price, G. (1989). *Learning styles inventory.* Lawrence, KS: Price Systems.

Gardner, H. (1993). *Frames of mind: A theory of multiple intelligences.* New York: Basic.

Gregorc, A.F. (1985). *Inside styles: Beyond the basics.* Maynard, MA: Gabriel Systems.

Heikkinen, M. Pettigrew, F. & Zakrajsek, D. (1985). Learning styles vs. teaching styles—Studying the relationship. *NASSP Bulletin, 69*(478), 80–85.

Kolb, D. (1986). *Learning styles inventory.* Boston, MA: McBer & Company.

Lee, T.D. (1988). Transfer appropriate processing: A framework for conceptualizing practice effects in motor learning. In O.G. Meijer & K. Roth (eds.), *Complex Motor Behavior: The Motor Action Controversy.* Amsterdam: Elsevier Science, pp.201–215.

MacNeil, R.D. (1980). The relationship of cognitive style and instructional style to the learning performance of undergraduate students. *Journal of Educational Research, 22,* 354–359.

McDaniel, T.R. (1986). A primer on classroom discipline: Principles old and new. *Phi Delta Kappan, 66*(1), 63–67.

Morris, C.D., Bransford, J. D., & Franks, J.J (1977). Levels of processing versus transfer appropriate processing. *Journal of Verbal Learning and Verbal Behavior, 16,* 519–533.

Murray, M. (1979). Matched preferred cognitive mode with teaching methodology in learning a novel motor skill. *Research Quarterly, 50,* 80–87.

Onwuegbuzie, A.J. & Daley, C. (1998). Similarity of learning styles of students and a teacher in achievement in a research methods course. *Psychological Reports, 82,* 163–168.

Osgoode, C.E. (1949). The similarity paradox in human learning: A resolution. *Psychological Review, 56,* 132–143.

Price, G., Dunn, R. & Sanders, W. (1981). Reading achievement and learning style characteristics. *The Clearing House, 54,* 223–226.

Ross, J. L., Drysdale, M. T. B. & Schulz, R.A. (1999). Learning style in the classroom: Towards quality instruction in kinesiology. *Avante, 5*(3), 31–42.

Samelson, T.C. (1997). Getting information across to patients. *Medical Economics, 74*(3),105–108.

Stevens, J., & Hall, K.G. (1998). Motor skill acquisition strategies for rehabilitation of low back pain. *Journal of Orthopaedic Sports Physical Therapy, 28*(3): 165–167.

Thorndike, E.L. (1914). *Educational psychology.* New York: Columbia University.

CHAPTER SEVEN

Skill Presentation

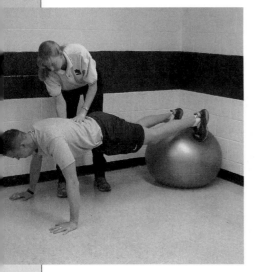

A 42-year-old patient has been referred for physical therapy following surgery to repair a torn anterior cruciate ligament (ACL). A component of the rehabilitation program prescribed for this patient is core stability training using a therapeutic ball. Since the patient is unfamiliar with therapeutic ball exercises, the therapist will have to introduce them. But how is that best accomplished? Should the therapist use verbal instructions to introduce the exercises? Should she demonstrate them? And what considerations must be made to ensure the skills are presented most effectively?

When introduced to a new skill or task, the learner utilizes the information provided from instructions and/or demonstrations to develop an idea of the movement's requirements. The idea developed helps the learner formulate a movement plan that serves as a guide during initial attempts at the skill or task. The development of an accurate movement plan is dependent on the instructor's ability to analyze a skill, determine which information to convey, organize that information and effectively communicate it (Rink, 1998). Facilitating the learner's understanding of a newly introduced skill is the focus of this chapter.

Learner Preparation

Regardless of the method used to present a skill, two factors that will directly influence learning must be considered before instruction begins. First, it is critical to capture the learner's undivided attention before skill instruction begins. Practitioners can accomplish this by arranging learners in a location that is free of background distractions. In addition, a formation that allows all to clearly see and hear the instructor should be used, and if outside, the learners should be positioned with their backs to the sun. Finally, direct learners to place equipment such as balls, hand weights, surgical tubing and rackets away from the gathering area to eliminate any temptation to play with them. A lack of attention, even for just a moment, can result in missing important information needed for successful skill development (Abernathy, 1993).

Once the learners are settled in the appropriate environment, the skill should be introduced in a manner that stimulates interest. As discussed in the previous chapter, motivated learners are more receptive to instruction. Enthusiasm is contagious: practitioners should present the skill dynamically and emphasize its importance.

CEREBRAL CHALLENGE #1

For a motor skill that you teach, or will teach, in your professional field, develop a list of variables that might compete for your learners' attention. Then, develop a number of suggestions that could be implemented to avoid the corresponding attention problems.

Verbal Instructions

Have you ever tried to teach a child how to tie his or her shoelaces? You probably didn't think it would be that difficult. After all, you have been tying your own shoelaces for years. In fact, you could probably be considered an expert at tying shoelaces. But the ability to provide effective instructions requires more than a thorough understanding of the skill. You have to be able to convey that knowledge to the learner. Suddenly, a seemingly simple skill like tying your shoelaces becomes incredibly complex to describe!

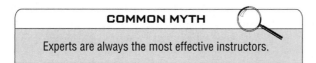

COMMON MYTH

Experts are always the most effective instructors.

Familiarity with the skill being taught is an obvious asset. A thorough understanding of the skill enables practitioners to determine what information is important to convey to the learner. That same skill familiarity can, however, negatively influence how that information is conveyed. Practitioners can unknowingly provide excessive descriptions, use confusing technical terminology or leave out important details. The result is a frustrated learner who ultimately loses interest. Effective instructions send clear messages to the learner. This can only be accomplished if individual differences are considered in their design.

CEREBRAL CHALLENGE #2

Thus far we have focused our attention on characteristics of the learner. Understanding the learner enables us to make more effective decisions regarding instructional design. Based on your understanding of the learner up to this point,

EXPLORATION ACTIVITY 7.1 Verbal Instructions

ACTIVITY 1

Find a partner whose shoes have shoelaces and who is willing to temporarily forget how to tie them. Using verbal descriptions alone, provide instructions for your partner to assist him or her in tying a shoelace.

ACTIVITY 2

For this experience you will need a partner, a piece of paper and a pencil. Your partner should sit facing away from you with the paper and pencil. Your task is to describe the following diagram so that your partner can replicate it. Throughout the exercise, you should not look at what your partner is drawing, and your partner should not look at the diagram. Your partner may ask you questions but cannot use gestures to augment those questions. Once you have completed your description and your partner has finished his or her interpretation of what you described, compare diagrams.

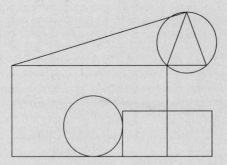

Perform the exercise again using the following diagram and switching roles. This time the "drawer" is not permitted to ask any questions and must

list the characteristics of effective instructions. Support your answer by explaining how your suggestions will accommodate the learner. Remember, there may be more than one supporting point for each suggestion. Read the next section to see how well you did.

Example:

Prediction: Instructions should be brief.
Rationale: Limited capacity of short-term memory.

ROLE OF TASK INSTRUCTIONS

Task instructions serve two distinct roles. First, they are used to introduce a learner to a new skill. In this capacity, instructions must communicate a general idea of the goal of the skill or strategy and make the learners aware of

replicate the diagram solely based on the verbal description. Once again, compare diagrams when you are finished.

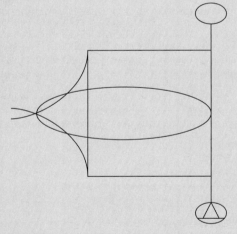

QUESTIONS:

1. How accurate was your partner's reproduction of the diagrams you described? Do the differences give you any hints about how you communicate?
2. What type of clarification questions did your partner ask? Do these questions give you any hints about how you communicate?
3. How did you feel during the second reproduction when questions were not permitted? Can you generalize any of that information to other learning situations?
4. What changes, if any, could you make to improve your communication effectiveness in the future?

major technical features or critical elements (Siedentop & Tannehill, 2000). Once this general idea of the movement has been conveyed, the focus of instructions shifts and skill refinement becomes the goal. Instructions in this capacity serve to develop the learners' skill level so they can perform the skill under criterion conditions.

AMOUNT OF INFORMATION

Keep explanations short and simple. Long, detailed instructions challenge the learners' attentional capacity and short-term memory, which, as discussed in Chapter 4, has a limited capacity. Moreover, after capturing the learners' interest with your introduction, take advantage of it! Learners will be eager to try the skill. Supply only the key elements of the skill. While an explanation about how to grip the bat is appropriate for a first lesson, specific techniques to elicit an optimal hip turn for the generation of maximum force is not. Those specifics should be addressed later when the learner strives to refine the movement pattern.

PRECISION

When giving instructions, be sure to provide the learner with enough information to relay the concept while using developmentally appropriate terminology. Telling an individual who is learning how to do empty can exercises for rotator cuff rehabilitation to "raise your arm" vs. "raise your arm to the point where your upper arm is parallel with the floor" will elicit different actions. The phrase "choke up on the bat" may be common terminology to some learners, but to a beginner with limited sporting experience, the statement makes little sense. Choose your words carefully. By using developmentally appropriate terminology that matches the skill level of the learner, the likelihood that the instructions will be clearly understood increases significantly.

LOCUS OF ATTENTION: INITIAL INSTRUCTIONS

When providing initial instructions, focus the learners' attention on critical elements of the motor skill being learned (Rink, 1998; Siedentop & Tannehill, 2000). Beginners have difficulty discriminating between relevant and non-relevant stimuli. For example, the juggling activity presented in Chapter 1 provided little direction on how to juggle. If you had not tried juggling before, you probably had a seemingly unlimited number of questions about how to perform the task, including, How high do I throw the balls? When do I let go? and What type of rhythm should be used? Because the key points of the juggling task were not pointed out to you, you probably discovered later, through trial and error, that many of the elements you chose to attend to really had no bearing on learning the task. By drawing the learner's attention to the critical elements of the skill, the learner is not left guessing what to focus on, as was the case when you were juggling.

CEREBRAL CHALLENGE #3

Reflect on your juggling experience. What variables did you choose to attend to that fall into the category of irrelevant stimuli? Which were relevant stimuli? Now choose a motor skill with which you have a high degree of familiarity. Again, determine what variables could be classified as relevant and irrelevant.

LOCUS OF ATTENTION: SKILL REFINEMENT

An emerging question with respect to instructions is, where should learners' conscious attention be directed when they perform the skill? Research exploring this concept has uncovered two instances where traditional instructional strategies have been found to hinder the learning process rather than facilitate it.

Internal vs. External Focus Recently, the common practice of instructing learners to focus their conscious attention on their own body movements has been questioned. Wulf and Weigelt (1997) demonstrated that instructions that prompted learners to adopt an **internal focus** of attention by directing them to concentrate on a specific body movement while learning a slalom-type movement on a ski simulator degraded performance compared to when no instructions were given at all. These results suggest that in addition to degrading the execution of automated skills, allocating conscious attention to one's own body movements may also have a negative impact on the acquisition and refinement of new skills.

internal focus: Focusing one's attention on a specific body movement.

Given the negative impact on learning found when adopting an internal focus, Wulf, Hoβ, and Prinz (1998) questioned the effectiveness of using an external focus. In their experiment, instructions that directed learners' attention to the effects of their actions on the environment (**external focus**) were compared to those that prompted an internal focus. Using a ski simulator task, they found that instructions focusing learners' attention on the force they exerted on the simulator's platform wheels (external focus) were more effective than the internal focus where learners' locus of attention was on their feet, which exerted the force. Similar findings were documented for the learning and performance of pitch shots in golf (Wulf, Lauterbach & Toole, 1999).

external focus: Focusing one's attention on the effects of his or her actions on the environment

Given these findings, it appears that the instructions given to the learner as to how to focus their attention can impact motor skill acquisition and performance. Rather than instructing a patient to focus on the heel strike in the gait cycle, for example, having patients imagine kicking a ball during the swing phase may be a viable strategy (McNevin, Wulf & Carlson, 2000). Additional research is needed to fully understand which contexts would most benefit from the adoption of an external focus.

RESEARCH NOTE

To provide further insights into how instructions influence motor skill learning, Wulf, McNevin, Fuchs, Ritter and Toole (2000) conducted a study to compare the relative effectiveness of two effect-related (external) attentional focus conditions. Two groups of 13 subjects hit golf balls with a 9 iron toward a target. The club group was instructed to focus on the movement of the club, while the target group was instructed to direct their attention to the ball's trajectory and the target. More specifically, the club group was asked to concentrate on allowing the club to perform a pendulum motion, and the target group was asked to anticipate the arc of the ball and its outcome relative to the target. While both groups became more accurate during the 80-shot practice phase, the club group significantly outperformed the target group. This superior performance was also seen in the retention test. The authors concluded that instructions that focus the learner's attention on technique-related effects were more effective for both learning and performance compared to attentional focus instructions that were related to the outcome of the action.

Awareness of Regulatory Conditions In open skills, the early detection of task-relevant information can reduce response delays and enhance performance. As a result, instructions are commonly given that direct the learner's attention towards such information in an attempt to facilitate learning. For example, a learner may be instructed to look for certain hand positions when a pitcher releases the ball in order to identify/predict the oncoming pitch. Preliminary research indicates, however, that this strategy may not only be unnecessary but may in fact hinder learning.

Using a computer-simulated catching task, Green and Flowers (1991) found that participants were able to determine the predictive relationship of ball flight without the benefit of being made aware of it through explicit verbal instructions. Moreover, this implicit learning group showed greater performance improvement than did those in the explicit learning group who were instructed about the underlying rules of the relationship. The authors attributed the poorer performance of the group that received instructions to an overloading of the available attentional resources as a result of trying to remember the rule and its application and the demands of performing the movement itself.

Additional support for the notion that conscious awareness might not be necessary for acquisition of knowledge about the environmental regulatory features of a motor skill has been provided by Magill (1998). In a tracking study, participants once again were able to exploit an embedded relationship without being aware of it through verbal instructions. Magill suggests that learners' attention should be directed at information-rich areas such as where the ball is released rather than instructing learners to look for specific cues, such as how the ball leaves the pitcher's hand. In addition, learners should be exposed to a variety of performance situations that contain the critical environmental regulatory cues to facilitate their acquisition.

FRAME OF REFERENCE

Tell learners what to expect or what they will experience when they perform a given action. For example, when punting, they should feel a little pressure in the shoelace area of the foot when they contact the ball. Or, when using crutches, they should feel weight on their hands and not in their armpits. This information provides learners with a frame of reference with which they can compare the correctness of their actions.

LEARNING STYLES

Recall that all learners are unique in how they prefer to receive new information, and instructions are more meaningful if delivered through the learner's preferred mode. "See your fingers point to the floor after you release the ball" and "Feel the tension in your wrist after you release the ball" both describe what the learner should experience if the follow-through in the free throw is performed correctly. The first statement appeals to a visual learner, while the second is more meaningful to a kinesthetic learner. Providing explanations that accommodate learning preferences enables learners to process information more effectively, resulting in greater learning gains (e.g., Ross, Drysdale, & Shulz, 1999).

PREVIOUSLY LEARNED SKILLS

According to the principles of transfer, when a skill is introduced, the learner will derive greater meaning from the explanation if it relates to some previous experience. For example, for an individual with extensive volleyball experience, understanding the arm position at contact for a tennis serve would be easier if a comparison was made to that of the volleyball serve. Such a connection simplifies the new concept for the learner and accelerates the development of an accurate movement plan.

VERBAL CUES

A **verbal cue** is a word or concise phrase that focuses the learner's attention or prompts a movement or movement sequence. For example, "Feet shoulder width apart" focuses the learner's attention on a key element of the skill, and "Free ball," used in volleyball, directs the learner's attention to specific environmental stimuli, which in turn prepares the defense. The cue "Step" prompts a movement, and the cue "Right, right, left, together" prompts a movement sequence, the series of foot contacts that occur in the triple jump.

Practitioners frequently use verbal cues to facilitate learning. Learners also develop and use cues to guide themselves through an action or a movement sequence. This technique is referred to as **self-talk** or verbal rehearsal because the learners essentially talk to themselves while performing a task.

verbal cue: A word or concise phrase that focuses the learner's attention or prompts a movement or movement sequence.

self-talk: Development and use of cues by learners to help guide themselves through an action or a movement sequence.

Saying "right, right, left, together" to cue the steps in the triple jump is a good example.

Four guidelines can help you develop effective practitioner and self-directed cues. First, the cues must be concise. Self-talk cues are most effective if they contain only one or two words (Ziegler, 1987). With respect to practitioner-directed cues, phrases should ideally be no longer than four words (Masser, 1993).

Second, the cues must be accurate. Unless cues clearly represent skill components, they will be ineffective. To develop critical cues that accurately represent key movement components, you need to be familiar with the skill.

Third, the number of cues should be limited. Too many cues will not only increase the chances of forgetting but could also interfere with the natural rhythm of the skill. Remember that cues are used to focus the learner's attention. If a skill is broken down into too many components in an effort to simplify it for the learner, the overall timing of the skill can be negatively impacted. Learning to drive a car with a manual transmission is a good example. If the cues "Push in the clutch," "Shift," "Let out the clutch" and "Step on the accelerator" are attended to as separate steps, the learner may be surprised when the car stalls or leaps forward!

Finally, use the same cues repeatedly. Repetition assists the learner in developing a strong association between the cue and the task. This association will, in turn, have a positive effect on retention.

CEREBRAL CHALLENGE #4

One method to develop cues is to analyze the skill, determine the key points and then reduce those key points to cues. Choose a motor skill with which you have a high degree of familiarity to perform this process. How will you perform this same task for a skill that you are not familiar with? What resources might you refer to?

CHECK FOR UNDERSTANDING

Instructions can elicit the desired response only if they are understood. Rather than waiting until learners attempt to carry out the instructions to assess their understanding of them, provide an opportunity for learners to ask questions following the skill presentation. Asking learners to restate the key elements of the skill can further assess their comprehension of the instructions. A quick check for understanding may help the practitioner from having to reassemble the learners to repeat or clarify instructions.

CEREBRAL CHALLENGE #5

Generate a list of behaviors or mannerisms that suggest the learner may not have understood the instructions given.

Demonstrations

Let's revisit the experience of teaching an individual how to tie his or her shoelaces. It probably didn't take too long before you realized that verbally describing the subtleties of shoelace tying in a meaningful way would not only require a great amount of detail but would involve a rather lengthy explanation, neither of which facilitates learning. In fact, your first instinct, when presented with this challenge, most likely involved showing the learner how to do it. Certainly, because a demonstration will quickly provide the learner with a meaningful visual picture of the skill, it is a preferred instructional tool.

THEORIES OF OBSERVATIONAL LEARNING

Demonstrations, which are also referred to as modeling or observational learning, rely on the ability of the learner to acquire information through observation of another individual or model performing the movement. The predominant theory explaining how a demonstration facilitates skill acquisition is the social cognitive theory of observational learning (Bandura, 1986). Bandura suggests that when a learner observes another individual perform a movement, the learner processes the information conveyed by the model and transforms it into a cognitive memory representation of the activity. This cognitive representation, formed by symbolic coding and cognitive rehearsal, not only serves to guide the learner's subsequent movement attempts but also provides a frame of reference for error detection and correction.

The dynamic interpretation of modeling (Scully & Newell, 1985) presents an alternative perspective about how observational learning facilitates skill acquisition. This perspective proposes that the key information the learner acquires from a demonstration is the relative features of the movement pattern or, in other words, the pattern of coordination of the limbs relative to one another. This information is directly perceived and enables the learner to coordinate body movements to reproduce the observed relative motion. The coordinated motion is further scaled according to individual specifications. Consequently, the need to create a cognitive representation of the skill, as suggested by Bandura, is disputed.

Although the dynamic theory offers an intriguing alternative perspective, currently the social cognitive theory is widely accepted and has been the theory of focus in the literature. Further research is needed to determine whether either perspective or a combination of the two most accurately explains how demonstrations facilitate learning.

DESIGNING EFFECTIVE DEMONSTRATIONS

If a demonstration is to effectively convey information that will assist the learner with subsequent movement attempts, the practitioner must make five decisions regarding its design: (1) What should be demonstrated? (2) Who should demonstrate? (3) How should the demonstration be organized?

(4) When should the demonstration occur? and (5) How often should the demonstration occur?

Content (What?) While it is obvious that the demonstration should focus on the skill in question, several additional considerations are important. The specific content of the demonstration is therefore the first decision facing the practitioner.

Coordination vs. control Although demonstrations are one of the most popular techniques for presenting skills, learners seem to benefit most from those that focus on the acquisition of a new pattern of coordination, such as the technique used to cradle a lacrosse ball (Magill & Schoenfelder-Zohdi, 1996). When demonstrations emphasize the acquisition of variables, such as speed and force, which control well-learned patterns of movement, they are no more effective than other forms of instruction (Magill, 1998).

Entire vs. partial Since the purpose of the initial demonstration is to provide the learner with a general idea of the movement's requirements, the skill should be performed in its entirety, as it would be in a competitive or criterion situation. Seeing the whole skill not only gives the learner an idea of the movement and its intended outcome but also shows the interrelationship between its component parts. The content of subsequent demonstrations depend on the skill's complexity and the ease with which it can be broken down into components. Following a demonstration of the breaststroke, for example, a swimming instructor may then want to focus learners' attention on how to execute the whip kick, and perform a subsequent demonstration isolating the kick.

Real time vs. slow motion Slow motion is often used to direct the learner's attention to a particular aspect of a skill. However, its use should be limited, because viewing the skill in real time is important for the development of a frame of reference for the skill (Williams, 1986), and it provides the learner with an appreciation of the natural timing of the movement. Two recommendations are that, first, the initial demonstration of the skill should occur in real time, and second, that once the learner comprehends the concept emphasized using slow motion, the demonstration should be shown again at the correct speed.

Characteristics of the Model (Who?) The second decision the practitioner must make regarding the demonstration is who should perform it, because the characteristics of the model affect demonstration effectiveness.

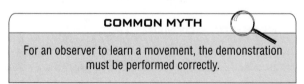

COMMON MYTH

For an observer to learn a movement, the demonstration must be performed correctly.

Expert vs. learning model Learners create a cognitive representation, or "perceptual blueprint" (Lee, Swinnen & Serrien, 1994), of the skill to be performed based on their observation of a demonstration. Since this representation serves to guide the learner's subsequent movement attempts and error detection and correction, it stands to reason that the model should perform the skill correctly. The more the learner sees the skill performed correctly, the stronger the blueprint. The stronger the blueprint, the greater the ability to replicate the skill.

Surprisingly, increasing evidence has challenged the exclusive use of an expert model. An equally, if not more, effective strategy is the use of a learning model, or an unskilled model who is learning the same skill as the observer. The key to this technique is that the observer not only views another learner practicing the skill, but she or he also benefits from listening to the corresponding instructor feedback and watching the individual attempt to correct the errors that are identified (Hebert & Landin, 1994).

Comparisons of expert vs. learning models suggest a significant difference in the degree to which the learner is actively engaged in the learning process. The use of an expert model may encourage the learner to emphasize movement imitation over movement exploration. On the other hand, learners are required to generate personal movement solutions following the observation of a learning model. This not only encourages self-discovery through the exploration of a variety of possible task solutions but also increases the learner's cognitive effort. Furthermore, observers may be able to better identify with the learning model. Expert and learning models are compared in Table 7.1.

Model-observer similarity What influence do variables such as model status, age, gender and similarity have on how well a movement pattern or skill is ultimately learned? Several studies have revealed that when participants viewed models they perceived as similar to themselves, they performed better than when they viewed models they perceived as dissimilar (Gould &

TABLE 7.1
Model Characteristics of Expert vs. Learning Demonstrations (Darden, 1997).

	Expert	**Learning**
Model Characteristics	• High skill proficiency • High status	• Level of skill proficiency slightly above that of observer • Similar status to observer
Content of Demonstration	• Skill performed correctly • Verbal cues accompany demonstration • Learner's attention directed to correctness of performance	• Performance may include both correct and incorrect aspects • Verbal cues plus instructor feedback accompany demonstration • Learner's attention directed at both correct and incorrect aspects of performance
Outcome	• Passive engagement of observer • Encourages movement imitation	• Active engagement of observer • Encourages movement exploration

Weiss, 1981; McCullagh, 1987). In addition, when participants view an unfamiliar model, the skill level rather than the status of the model may be more significant (Lirgg & Feltz, 1991).

These results may be attributed to increased self-efficacy beliefs (Gould & Weiss, 1981; McAuley, 1985; Schunk & Hanson, 1985). Essentially, when observers view a model similar to themselves successfully perform the skill, their perception that they, too, will be able to successfully reproduce the skill increases. Consequently, the improvements found in performance may be the result of increases in observer attention and/or motivation. Care must be taken when interpreting these results, however. Note that the increases found were in performance. To date, little direct evidence exists that supports the influence of model characteristics on learning.

Alternative mediums Live models are not the only kind of model available to demonstrate concepts and movements. Due to advances in technology, videotape demonstrations have become popular. They not only free up the instructor but they also permit the learner to view the movement and specific aspects of a skill repeatedly, from numerous angles (some of which may be difficult to see during a live demonstration) and at various speeds. On the other hand, drawbacks to using video demonstrations are that not everyone in a large group may be able to clearly hear and see the screen, and that commercial videotapes may not show all of the pertinent elements and angles.

Another effective way to demonstrate concepts and movements is to supplement a live or video model with drawings or still photos. Relationships between performers and implements or opponents can be shown, key positions can be isolated, and hard-to-see aspects of the skill or formation can be highlighted with still pictures such as those in Figure 7.1.

Finally, sound can sometimes be used. Many sport skills have consequent sounds. For example, a different sound results when a softball is caught in the pocket than when it is caught in the palm of a glove. A demonstration of consequent sounds can provide the learner with a frame of reference. Sound can also emphasize the internal rhythm of a skill. The last five steps in the javelin run-up, for instance, generally have the rhythm: medium, medium, long . . . , short, short. Although a live model could reproduce the step pattern for the observer, clapping the pattern to isolate the rhythm can increase understanding, especially for an auditory learner.

Mechanics of Effective Demonstrations (How?) Determining how the demonstration will be organized is the third decision the practitioner must make when designing a demonstration. He or she must ensure that all learners have a good viewing angle and focus on the key elements of the demonstration.

Formations and viewing considerations All learners must be able to clearly see and hear the demonstration. Some formations lend themselves quite well to this objective, while others are problematic. An example of a problematic

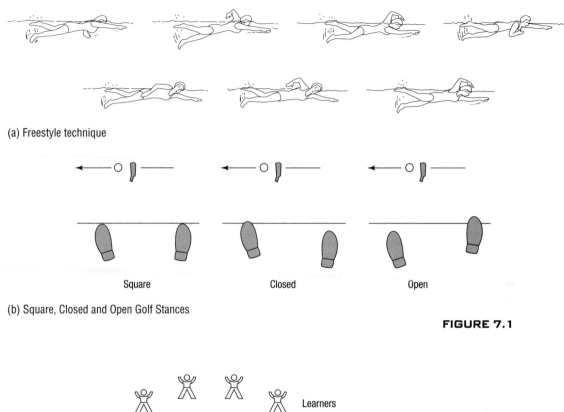

(a) Freestyle technique

Square   Closed   Open

(b) Square, Closed and Open Golf Stances

FIGURE 7.1

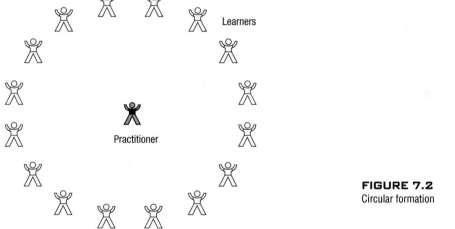

Learners

Practitioner

FIGURE 7.2
Circular formation

formation is a circle with the model in the center, as displayed in Figure 7.2. The ability of the learner to attend to the key elements of the skill when positioned to the left of a right-handed model will obviously be hindered. Likewise, the learner positioned behind the model will have a difficult time hearing any cues or instructions. The other problem with a circle is that all learners cannot view the demonstration from the same perspective. Some learners will see it from the front, others from the rear, and still others from the side. Alternative formations designed to resolve these concerns are illustrated in Figure 7.3 a. The demonstrator must not position himself or herself too close to the learners, or the learners at the ends of the formation will have a different viewing angle from those in the center (see Figure 7.3 b).

(a) Examples of effective formations.

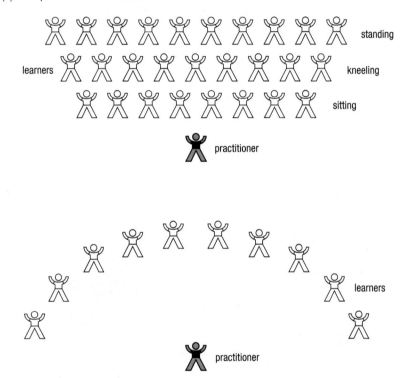

(b) Potential viewing angle problems as a result of the demonstrator standing too close to the formation.

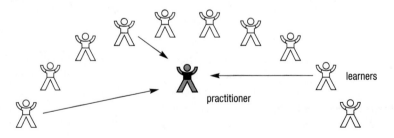

FIGURE 7.3

Demonstrating the skill from a number of different viewpoints is another way to enhance learners' understanding of movement requirements. Different viewpoints highlight different aspects of the skill. For example, a patient learning to use a walker can see the overall movement pattern from the front, while a side view provides information regarding the placement of the walker in relation to the body prior to stepping. Similarly, a side view of the gliding action in the shot put enables learners to focus on the movement of the legs, while a rear view highlights the position of the shoulders. The opportunity to see the demonstration from multiple viewing angles presents a more complete picture of the skill.

Sometimes viewing a skill from the front is problematic, however. Learning the grapevine in an aerobics class is a good example. If a model demonstrates this skill while facing the group, the learners are required to move in the opposite direction to perform the steps using the same limbs, which can be quite confusing. In this situation, viewing the model from behind will ease the learners' ability to imitate the movement. An alternative strategy would be to present a mirror image by facing the group but performing the skill in the same direction that the group is moving.

Multiple viewing angles present a more complete picture of the skill.

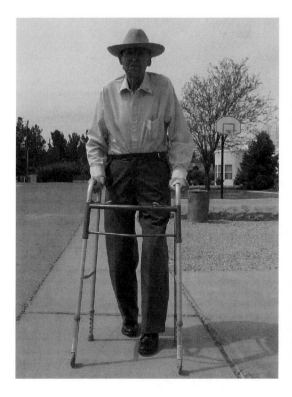 

Explain how the demonstration will proceed and what to watch for It has been stressed repeatedly throughout this chapter that unless the learner's attention is directed to the relevant features of the movement, instructions are likely to be worthless. Avoid using the phrases "like this" and "like that" in conjunction with the demonstration. These phrases are not specific enough to direct the learner's attention. Instead, when performing a demonstration, tell the learners how the demonstration will proceed and what to specifically watch for. For example, the initial demonstration of a new skill should encompass the whole skill, as it would be performed in competitive or criterion situations. Since the intent here is to give the learner a general idea of the movement's requirements, instructions to simply watch the skill in its entirety are justified. However, in subsequent demonstrations of either the whole skill or part of the skill, learners should be pre-cued to direct their attention to specific aspects of the movement.

Avoid product options Although the initial demonstration of a new skill should encompass the whole skill, as it would be performed in competitive or criterion situations, subsequent presentations should be designed to avoid product options. In other words, design the demonstration so that the outcome is eliminated. As humans, we are very curious creatures. We want to know if the ball went in, how far the javelin flew, and whether or not the catch was made. Unfortunately, this curiosity often overrides our ability to maintain focus on the key aspects of the movement that produced the outcome (the process). By removing the outcome, throwing a modified javelin into a net for example, learners are less likely to track the implement and more likely to focus on the key elements of the movement.

Demonstrate for both right and left limb dominance If demonstrating to a group, be aware of the composition of that group with respect to limb dominance. If all learners are right-handed, demonstrating the tennis serve with the left hand may not be necessary. However, if both limb preferences are represented in the group, demonstrate the skill both ways. Telling the left-handed learners to simply switch everything you said to the other side increases the complexity of the task.

Distribution and Frequency (When and How Often?) The final two decisions the practitioner must make are when and how often to demonstrate. An understanding of both the learner and task complexity will assist the practitioner in making these decisions.

When to demonstrate The use of a demonstration to complement instruction when introducing a new skill is obvious; however, other occasions exist when a demonstration would benefit the learner. When interspersed throughout the practice session, additional demonstrations give learners an opportunity to answer questions that arise from their performance attempts. Furthermore, instructors, having had an opportunity to evaluate initial attempts, can use

What	Who	How	When	How Often
New pattern of coordination	Expert vs. learning model	Formations and viewing angle	Introduction of skill	Complexity of skill
Whole vs. part	Observer-model similarity	Limb preference	Throughout practice	Extent of learners' understanding
Real time vs. slow motion	Video, still pictures, audio	Direction of movement	Conclusion of practice period	
		Avoid product options		

TABLE 7.2
Demonstration Considerations

additional demonstrations to address problems that surface. When used at the conclusion of the practice session, demonstrations leave learners with a mental image of the skill, which helps to reinforce concepts and strengthen memory. Finally, demonstrations can serve as useful reminders of skill requirements when shown at the beginning of practice the following day.

How often Both the complexity of the skill and the extent to which the learner understands the information presented should be considered when determining how often a skill is demonstrated. In general, the more complex

EXPLORATION ACTIVITY 7.2 Evaluating Skill Presentation Effectiveness

ACTIVITY 1

Using the information presented in this chapter, design an evaluation checklist that could be used to determine skill presentation effectiveness.

Examples:
1. Did the practitioner use a clear signal to call the learners together?
2. Did the practitioner demonstrate the skill for both right and left limb dominant learners?

ACTIVITY 2

Observe a teacher, coach or therapist presenting a new skill. Using the checklist designed in part A, evaluate the effectiveness of the skill presentation.

ACTIVITY 3

Videotape yourself presenting a new skill. Review the tape using the checklist from part A to evaluate your performance. How might you improve your demonstration effectiveness?

the skill, the more demonstrations required. This applies not only to the whole skill but to its component parts as well.

Discovery Learning

discovery learning: Teaching strategy where a learning environment is created that engages the learner in attempts to solve a movement problem through exploration.

An effective alternative to the "show and tell" approach to presenting skills is **discovery learning** (Mosston & Ashworth, 1994; van Emmerik, den Brinker, Vereijken & Whiting, 1989; Vereijken, Whiting & Beek, 1992; Wulf & Weigelt, 1997). In discovery learning, the practitioner creates a learning environment where the learner attempts to solve the movement problem through the exploration of a variety of possible task solutions. This approach redefines the practitioner's role into that of a facilitator rather than an information provider who, through verbal instructions and/or demonstrations, dictates the correct movement response. A corresponding change in the role of the learner from passive observer to active problem solver is likely to follow.

Wulf & Weigelt (1997) suggest that learning might be more effective if learners have a chance to discover the movement's requirements on their own when the task being learned requires whole body movements or the coordination of many degrees of freedom. Learning to ice-skate in a forward direction without losing one's balance is a good example of a task that could benefit from discovery learning. Rather than providing specific instructions on how to skate, the practitioner simply introduces the movement problem and goal to be achieved. The learner is then encouraged to discover the ideal solution to the movement problem through trial and error. In this example, once a basic solution has been generated, the practitioner can then use instructions, demonstrations and the like for skill refinement.

Ice-skating is an example of a task that could benefit from discovery learning.

CEREBRAL CHALLENGE #6

Generate a list of motor skills for which the use of discovery techniques would be well suited, for example, walking on a treadmill.

CEREBRAL CHALLENGE #7

If you were the therapist in the opening story, what technique would you use to teach the patient the therapeutic ball exercises? Or, would you use a combination of techniques? Explain your answer.

GUIDED DISCOVERY

In some cases, discovery learning can be too general, allowing the learner to discover a coordination mode that might initially work but potentially inhibiting progress beyond a certain point. In these instances, a variation of discovery learning known as guided discovery may be more effective. In **guided discovery,** the practitioner designs a sequence of questions, each of which elicits a single correct response discovered by the learner (Mosston & Ashworth, 1994). This step-by-step process leads to the eventual discovery of the intended concept or principle.

guided discovery: Discovery learning technique where the practitioner designs a sequence of questions, each of which elicits a single correct response discovered by the learner.

To implement this technique, the practitioner must design a series of questions or clues regarding the movement or concept of interest. The first question is then delivered as designed, and the learner is given the opportunity to answer. Once the learner responds, the practitioner either reinforces the response or redirects the learner. Once the correct answer has been discovered, the next question in the sequence is asked. For example, in introducing the skill of dribbling a soccer ball, the learner might be asked about the goal of the defenders. Once the learner identifies the goal of the defender as stealing the ball, subsequent questions leading to the learner's discovery of kicking the ball softly and with the side of the foot as opposed to the toe would follow. Gradually, the learner will not only learn the technique but also develop an understanding of why that technique is used.

CEREBRAL CHALLENGE #8

Using a motor skill or concept of your choice, outline the sequence of questions you might use if implementing the guided discovery technique.

A Look Ahead

The initial goal of the instructor when presenting a new skill is to convey to the learners the information they need to develop a basic understanding of the movement's requirements in order to formulate an initial movement plan. Once this is accomplished, the focus shifts to one of skill refinement. Three techniques, instructions, demonstrations and discovery learning, have been presented that can facilitate both initial skill understanding and skill refinement. However, motor skill acquisition also requires that learners be provided with ample opportunities to practice the skills that have been presented. Issues related to designing optimal practice opportunities are therefore the focus of the next chapter.

Summary

- When giving instructions:
  - Keep explanations short and simple.
  - Use developmentally appropriate terminology.

- Direct learners' attention to critical elements of the skill during initial instructions.
- Provide learners with a frame of reference for correctness.
- Incorporate learners' learning style and previous experiences.
- Instructions focusing learners' conscious attention on specific body movements have been shown to negatively influence learning.
- Verbal cues are used to focus the learners' attention or prompt a movement or movement sequence and should be concise, accurate, limited in number and used repeatedly throughout the learning process.
- When planning a demonstration, its content, the characteristics of the model, how the demonstration will be organized and its distribution and frequency must all be considered.
- When providing an initial demonstration, the whole skill in real time should be performed to give learners an idea of the movement.
- Learners benefit from demonstrations that focus on the acquisition of a new pattern of coordination.
- The use of a learning model encourages movement exploration and active involvement in the learning process.
- An effective demonstration ensures that all learners have a good viewing angle and are focused on the key elements being demonstrated.
- The complexity of the skill and the extent to which the learner understands the information will dictate when and how often a demonstration should be provided.
- In discovery learning the practitioner acts as a facilitator while the learner is given the opportunity to explore a variety of possible solutions to a given movement problem.
- Guided discovery also provides the opportunity to explore possible movement solutions but is more structured in that the practitioner designs a sequence of questions, each of which elicits a single correct response to be discovered by the learner.

Review Questions

1. Why is it critical to capture the learners' attention before skill instruction begins?
2. Explain why practitioners who are highly familiar with their subject matter are not always the most effective instructors.
3. What is the function of a verbal cue?
4. Compare and contrast instructor-directed verbal cues and self-talk.
5. What guidelines should be followed to optimize the use of cues?
6. Compare and contrast the social cognitive theory of observational learning and the dynamic interpretation of modeling.
7. Which of the four subprocesses in Bandura's observational learning theory might be influenced by model characteristics? Justify your answer.

8. What is a learning model? What are some advantages of using a learning model?

9. Using a motor skill of your choice, explain what decisions you will make regarding the mechanics of its demonstration. Justify your answers.

10. Compare and contrast demonstrations and discovery learning.

References

Abernathy, B. (1993). Attention. In R.N. Singer, M. Murphy & L.K. Tennent (eds.), *Handbook of Research on Sport Psychology.* New York: MacMillan, pp. 127–170.

Bandura, A. (1986). *Social foundations of thought and action: A social cognitive theory.* Englewood Cliffs, NJ: Prentice Hall.

Darden, G.F. (1997). Demonstrating motor skills—Rethinking that expert demonstration. *JOPERD, 68* (6), 31–35.

Gould, D. & Weiss, M.R. (1981). The effects of model similarity and model talk on self-efficacy and muscular endurance. *Journal of Sport Psychology, 3,* 17–29.

Green, T.D. & Flowers, J.H. (1991). Implicit vs. explicit learning processes in a probabilistic, continuous fine motor catching task. *Journal of Motor Behavior, 23,* 239–300.

Hebert, E.P. & Landin, D. (1994). Effects of a learning model and augmented feedback on tennis skill acquisition. *Research Quarterly for Exercise and Sport, 65*(3), 250–257.

Lee, T.D., Swinnen, S.P. & Serrien, D.J. (1994). Cognitive effort in learning. *Quest, 46*(32), 328–344.

Lirgg, C.D. & Feltz, D.L. (1991). Teacher vs. peer models revisited: Effects on motor performance and self-efficacy. *Research Quarterly for Exercise and Sport, 62*(2), 217–224.

McAuley, E. (1985). Modeling and self-efficacy. A test of Bandura's model. *Journal of Sport Psychology, 6,* 283–295.

McCullagh, P. (1987). Model similarity effects on motor performance. *Journal of Sport Psychology, 9,* 249–260.

McNevin, N.H., Wulf, G. & Carlson, C. (2000). Effects of attentional focus, self-control and dyad training on motor learning: Implications for physical rehabilitation. *Physical Therapy, 80*(4), 373–385.

Magill, R.A. (1998). Knowledge is more than we can talk about: Implicit learning in motor skill acquisition. *Research Quarterly for Exercise and Sport, 69*(2), 104–110.

Magill, R.A. & Schoenfelder-Zohdi, B. (1996). A visual model and knowledge of performance as sources of information for learning a rhythmic gymnastics skill. *International Journal of Sport Psychology, 27,* 7–22.

Masser, L.S. (1993). Critical cues help first grade students' achievement in handstands and forward rolls. *Journal of Teaching Physical Education, 11,* 301–312.

Mosston, M. & Ashworth, S. (1994). *Teaching physical education* (4th edition). New York: MacMillan.

Rink, J.E. (1998). *Teaching physical education for learning.* St. Louis, MO: Mosby.

Ross, J.L. Drysdale, M.T.B. & Schulz, R.A. (1999). Learning style in the classroom: Towards quality instruction in kinesiology. *Avante, 5*(3), 31–42.

Schunk, D.H. & Hanson, A.R. (1985). Peer models: Influence on children's self-efficacy and achievement. *Journal of Educational Psychology, 77,* 313–322.

Scully, D.M. & Newell, K.M. (1985). Observational learning and the acquisition of motor skills: Towards a visual perception perspective. *Journal of Human Movement Studies, 11,* 169–186.

Siedentop, D. & Tannehill, D. (2000). *Developing teaching skills in physical education.* Mountain View, CA: Mayfield.

van Emmerik, R.E.A., den Brinker, B.P.L.M., Vereijken, B. & Whiting, H.T.A. (1989). Preferred tempo in the learning of a gross cyclical action. *The Quarterly Journal of Experimental Psychology, 41,* 251–262.

Vereijken, B., Whiting, H.T.A. & Beek, W.J. (1992). A dynamical systems approach to skill acquisition. *The Quarterly Journal of Experimental Psychology, 45A*(2), 323–344.

Williams, J.G. (1986). Perceiving human movement: Review of research with implications for the use of demonstrations during motor learning. *Physical Education Review, 9*(1), 53–58.

Wulf, G., Hofl, M. & Prinz, W. (1998). Instructions for motor learning: Differential effects of internal vs. external focus of attention. *Journal of Motor Behavior, 30,* 169–179.

Wulf, G., Lauterbach, B. & Toole, T. (1999). The learning advantages of an external focus of attention in golf. *Research Quarterly for Exercise and Sport, 70*(2), 120–126.

Wulf, G., McNevin, N., Fuchs, T., Ritter, F. & Toole, T. (2000). Attentional focus on complex skill learning. *Research Quarterly for Exercise and Sport, 71*(3), 229–239.

Wulf, G. & Weigelt, C. (1997). Instructions about physical principles in learning a complex motor skill: To tell or not to tell. *Research Quarterly for Exercise and Sport, 68*(4), 363–367.

Ziegler, S.G. (1987). Effects of stimulus cueing on the acquisition of groundstrokes by beginning tennis players. *Journal of Applied Behavioral Analysis, 20,* 405–411.

CHAPTER EIGHT

Practice Design Factors

Although it would be two more hours before the sun would peak over the horizon, the alarm clock was beeping. It was the dead of winter, and Mike had 30 minutes before he would have to be on the deck of the pool warming up for morning practice. As a boy, Mike had watched as Greg Louganis won gold in both the 10-m platform and 3-m springboard diving competitions at the 1988 Seoul Olympics. Since then he had dreamed of being an Olympic diver, but this morning that dream was a distant one. He hadn't been diving well recently, and he didn't feel like practicing. He hit the snooze button and fell back asleep. Five minutes later, his father poked his head in and said encouragingly, "Come on son, practice makes perfect!"

While several misconceptions regarding skill acquisition and control have been interspersed throughout this book, perhaps the most widespread is the old adage "Practice makes perfect." In reality, practice does not guarantee that a learner will become more proficient. Only when practice is designed that carefully considers how the learner, the task and the environment influence the learning process can optimal gains in skill proficiency be realized. This chapter will focus on several variables that contribute to effective practice design, including skill progressions, sequencing and psychological strategies.

Breaking Down Skills: Progressions and Sequencing

In designing effective practices and rehabilitative experiences, practitioners are faced with several decisions regarding the breakdown of skills. More specifically, when should a skill be broken down into parts and when should it be practiced as a whole, how do speed and accuracy influence skill acquisition and how are skills that must be performed with equal proficiency on both the dominant and nondominant side best learned?

WHOLE VS. PART PRACTICE

Learning a novel motor skill can be a daunting task. Part practice has become a commonly used technique to simplify the learning process. The **part practice method** generally involves breaking the skill down into natural parts or segments, practicing those parts separately until they are learned and then integrating them to perform the skill in its entirety. While this strategy is advantageous in that it (1) simplifies the skill, (2) allows learners to experience early success leading to increased motivation and (3) permits practice on problematic components without wasting time on those already mastered, separating the skill into parts might not be the most efficient method to employ in all cases. In fact, under certain conditions, the whole method approach, where the complete skill is practiced, is favored.

part practice method:
Teaching strategy that involves breaking the skill down into natural parts or segments, practicing those parts separately until they are learned and then integrating them to perform the skill in its entirety.

The decision to use whole or part practice depends on which method is more likely to result in the greatest amount of positive transfer to the performance of the whole skill (Wightman & Lintern, 1985). That judgment is dependent upon careful assessment of the nature of the skill and the capability of the learner.

Nature of the Skill As we have seen repeatedly, the nature of the skill influences the learning process. Recognizing this, Naylor and Briggs (1963) hypothesized that the effectiveness of part and whole practice was dependent on two inherent features of the skill. The first, *task complexity*, is directly correlated with the number of subcomponents that make up the skill. It is also a function of the information-processing demands imposed by the task. Consequently, the more components and/or the greater the attention, memory and decision-making requirements, the more complex the task is considered to be. Given this description, it may seem warranted to utilize the part practice method to simplify highly complex skills for the learner; however, this judgment would be premature without taking into account a second variable, *task organization*.

Task organization refers to the degree to which the subcomponents of the skill are interdependent. In other words, how dependent is the performance of

TASK COMPLEXITY

	Low	High
Low	Clapping your hands	Tying a figure 8 knot
High	Putting a golf ball	Executing a jump serve in volleyball

TASK ORGANIZATION

FIGURE 8.1
Examples of skills classified according to their task complexity and organization.

each part on the component that precedes it? If the answer is very dependent, as is the case in a cartwheel, the task is considered to be high in organization. In this situation, breaking the skill down into parts would not be effective, as it would change its natural rhythm. Similarly, in gait training using parallel bars or when running hurdles, adjustments must continuously be made according to the positioning of the previous part. Specifically, if an athlete clears the hurdle too high or hits it, adjustments in the step pattern must be made if he or she is to successfully negotiate the next hurdle. This ability can only be acquired if the athlete practices over several hurdles. Finally, in actions characterized by rapid loading of the muscles, such as a slap shot in hockey, breaking the skill into parts can eliminate the stretch reflex inherent to the task and therefore change its underlying dynamics (Schmidt & Young, 1987). Conversely, the freestyle, where the kick and arm action are relatively independent, or low in organization, would lend itself quite well to part practice.

CEREBRAL CHALLENGE #1

Analyze each of the following skills and identify whether they are low or high in task complexity and organization:

Fielding a ground ball	Heading a soccer ball
Slalom ski racing	Playing the piano
Transferring from a chair to a wheel chair	Performing a balance beam routine
Doing the grapevine (aerobics)	Walking with crutches
Making a layup	Performing CPR

Breaking down skills that are high in task organization can change their underlying dynamics.

So, how do task complexity and organization interact to provide direction as to which technique, the whole or part practice method, will be most effective for a given skill? Generally, skills that are high in organization and low in complexity are best served through whole practice, while part practice is the preferred technique for those low in organization and high in complexity (Naylor & Briggs, 1963). Of course, this guideline does not account for all possible combinations of complexity and organization. For example, it does not suggest the optimal method to employ when a skill is assessed as both high in complexity and organization. In these situations, remember that the objective is to maximize learning. Judgments should therefore be based on which technique will be most efficient in achieving the desired outcome.

CEREBRAL CHALLENGE #2

1. Reexamine each skill presented in Cerebral Challenge #1, and indicate whether it would best be served by whole or part practice. Justify your answer.
2. What generalizations, if any, can be made about the use of whole or part practice for skills considered (a) discrete, (b) serial and (c) continuous?

Capability of the Learner Although the assessment of the skill may warrant the use of either whole or part practice, practitioners should also take the capability of the learner into consideration before making a final decision about which method to employ. Learners with limited movement experiences, for example, may be overwhelmed by the demands imposed by the task if presented in its entirety. Likewise, if the cognitive or attentional requirements of the task exceed the capacity of the learner, the use of the whole method could hinder skill acquisition and leave the learner frustrated. That frustration, a result of lower success rates, could, in turn, lead to a loss of motivation. In these instances, breaking the skill down into more manageable units will be more effective for its acquisition. Conversely, gains in skill acquisition can be achieved through the whole method when learners are highly motivated and have had a variety of movement experiences.

Part Practice Techniques When conditions dictate the use of part practice, the practitioner has several variations from which to choose. Wightman and Lintern (1985) categorized these variations as segmentation, simplification and fractionization. Regardless of which method is selected, it is important to remember that when using part practice, learners must also be taught how the parts being practiced are associated with the whole skill. Failure to do so may decrease the amount of transfer to the whole skill, as demonstrated in an experiment by Newell, Carlton, Fisher and Rutter (1989), who found that providing learners with part practice in addition to information regarding the goal of the skill resulted in greater learning gains than that gained by part practice only.

Segmentation **Segmentation** is a commonly used part practice technique that separates the skill into parts according to spatial or temporal elements. The specific structure of this type of practice can take on several forms. In the part-whole method, each part is practiced separately until a given level of proficiency is demonstrated, and then the parts are combined and the skill is practiced in its entirety. Using the football punt to illustrate this method, the catch, approach, drop and kick would each first be practiced separately. All parts would then be combined and practiced as a unit until the punt is mastered.

> **segmentation:** Part practice technique that separates the skill into parts according to spatial or temporal elements.

In addition to simplifying the skill, an alternative approach, the progressive part method, provides the learner with the opportunity to better understand its underlying timing and integration. The learner begins by practicing two parts separately. When the criterion level has been achieved, the parts are combined and practiced together. Once mastered, the third part is introduced and practiced separately. This separate component is then combined with the other two once the learner has performed it proficiently. This pattern continues until the whole skill is being performed. So, for the football punt, an example would be to have learners practice the catch and approach separately, then combine them, then practice the drop separately, combine it with the other two and so on.

A variation of this method is the repetitive part method, where rather than the new component being practiced independently, it is directly added to the previous part and they are practiced together. Using this method, the catch would be practiced first and then combined with the approach. Once that combination is acquired, the drop would be added and so on.

When a skill is broken down using segmentation, the practitioner can also choose to use forward or backward chaining. In **forward chaining**, the parts are presented and practiced in a sequence that progresses from the first to the final part of the skill. The examples given thus far using the football punt have employed forward chaining. The sequence in **backward chaining**, on the other hand, progresses in reverse order from the final segment to the initial one. In the football punt then, the kick would be practiced, then the drop, the approach and finally the catch.

forward chaining: Part practice technique whereby the parts of a skill are presented and practiced in a sequence that progresses from the initial skill component to the final one.

backward chaining: Part practice technique whereby the parts of a skill are presented and practiced in a sequence that progresses from the final skill component to the initial one.

 CEREBRAL CHALLENGE #3

Select a skill for which segmentation would be effective. Outline how you would employ each of the following methods to practice that skill: (a) progressive part, (b) repetitive part and (c) backward chaining. Support your answer.

fractionization: Part practice technique where skill components that are normally performed simultaneously are partitioned and practiced independently.

Fractionization In **fractionization,** skill components that are normally performed simultaneously are partitioned and practiced independently. For example, tacking (changing direction by turning into the wind) on a windsurfer requires simultaneous movements with both the arms and legs. These movements would be separated and practiced in isolation and once mastered would be rejoined so the learner can perform the whole skill. Another example would be to practice the movements of each hand separately in keyboarding or drumming. The effectiveness of this particular part practice technique remains in question, however. For rhythmic skills that require bimanual coordination (simultaneous use of the arms) or upper and lower limb coordination (simultaneous use of arms and legs), such as playing a musical instrument, fractionization appears to transfer poorly to the whole skill (Klapp, Nelson & Jagacinski, 1998; Lee, Chamberlin & Hodges, 2001). Such tasks are high in organization, and whole practice is recommended. However, when the spatial or temporal characteristics of each limb are different, this part practice method may be a viable technique. Further research is needed to determine its effectiveness in such situations.

simplification: Part practice technique that reduces the level of difficulty of the task or some aspect of the task for the learner.

Simplification The third part practice technique, **simplification,** reduces the level of difficulty of the task or some aspect of the task for the learner. Practitioners can implement this strategy in several ways. For example, modified equipment can be utilized to simplify the skill, including oversized striking implements, larger, softer balls for catching, and training stairs or parallel bars. Another option is to reduce the coordination requirements of the task. For instance, simple to complex progressions are used in teaching Swiss ball exercises. Initially, basic positioning is practiced, with exercises becoming more difficult by progressively decreasing the areas of support, increasing the lever arm length on the ball and increasing the range of motion with which the exercise is performed (Hoglblum, 2001). The overall speed or force at which the skill is executed is another variable that can be manipulated through simplification. Slowing down the tempo at which one swings a golf club or serving a volleyball from half court instead of the baseline are examples. When using this particular strategy, it is important that the relative timing or force of the skill remain intact.

The complexity of the environment can also be reduced to decrease the attentional demands imposed by the task. This can be accomplished by changing the environmental characteristics of an open skill to make it more closed. For example, hitting in baseball/softball can be initially taught as a closed skill, with the ball stationary (placed on a batting tee). Once the basic striking pattern has been acquired, the skill can be made progressively more open by using a pitching machine that consistently delivers the ball to a specific location and then using a live pitcher who delivers a variety of pitches. Similarly, patients may first learn to reach and grasp for a can that is directly in front of them and eventually have to perform the skill at shoulder height in addition to selecting a particular can from many. Finally, skill building games or lead up games such as one bounce volleyball, five hundred in softball and baseball and twenty-one in basketball are another form of simplification.

 CEREBRAL CHALLENGE #4

1. Under what circumstances would you want to use simplification instead of either fractionization or segmentation? Give an example.
2. Using the World Wide Web or product catalogs, survey the equipment manufacturing companies in physical education/rehab and generate a list of products specifically designed for simplification.
3. Rearrange the following progression for the overhead pass into a simple to complex sequence. What part practice technique(s) is being employed in this example?

   • Randomly toss the ball so that the learner is forced to move forwards, backwards and side to side. The learner should set the ball back to the individual who tossed it.
   • Toss the ball to a stationary learner. The learner should catch the ball above the head in the correct position and be facing the individual who tossed it.
   • Set the ball continuously with a partner.
   • The learner assumes the correct ready position for the set.
   • Toss the ball so that the learner is forced to move forwards, backwards and side to side. The learner should catch the ball in the correct setting position and be facing the individual who tossed it. Indicate to the learner the direction that the ball will be tossed prior to tossing it.
   • Toss the ball to a stationary learner. The learner should set the ball back to the individual who tossed it.
   • Toss the ball to the learner who then must set it to a spiker.

> - Toss the ball so that the learner is forced to move forwards, backwards and side to side. The learner should set the ball back to the individual who tossed it. Indicate to the learner the direction that the ball will be tossed prior to tossing it.
> - The learner assumes the correct ready position for the set with the ball placed in the hands just above the head. The learner then pushes the ball away using the correct setting motion.

RESEARCH NOTE

To gain a greater understanding of the influence of task progressions Hebert, Landin and Solmon (2000) examined their influence on students' practice quality and task-related cognition. Eighty-one students enrolled in university beginning tennis classes learned and practiced the serve under one of three conditions. The Criterion group practiced the criterion task, serving using the complete motion from behind the baseline. The remaining two conditions, Part to Whole and Extension, practiced using a simple to complex four-step progression that ended with the criterion task. Within this progression, the Part to Whole group practiced using segmentation, where the skill was broken down into the toss, tossing and hitting from the back scratch position, tossing and hitting from the hip and performing the full serve. Learners in the Extension group, on the other hand, were engaged in a simplification practice strategy. Here, the full serve was performed from four different distances on the court, starting at the net and ending at the baseline. Although performance changes were not measured, data revealed that those instructional conditions that involved easy to difficult progressions (the Part to Whole and Extension groups) resulted in more successful and appropriate practice trials and enhanced student self-efficacy and motivation.

---

attention cueing: A practice technique where the learner directs his or her attention to a specific aspect of the skill during its performance as a whole.

Attention Cueing Another practice option that combines the benefits of both part and whole practice is attention cueing. **Attention cueing** is a practice technique where the learner directs his or her attention to a specific aspect of the skill during its performance as a whole. Focusing on a high elbow recovery while swimming the freestyle or on the placement of an assisted walking device while traversing across a room are examples. This strategy allows the learner to concentrate on one particular task component or movement problem without disrupting the underlying temporal and spatial characteristics inherent to the skill.

SPEED-ACCURACY TRADEOFF

speed-accuracy tradeoff: A tradeoff that exists between speed and accuracy such that an emphasis on speed negatively impacts accuracy and vice versa.

Many movements call for both speed and accuracy in their execution and are governed by a basic motor behavior tenet known as the **speed-accuracy tradeoff**. As is implied, a tradeoff exists between speed and accuracy such that an emphasis on speed negatively impacts accuracy and vice versa. More specifically, through a series of experiments using a rapid aiming task, Fitts (1954) found that performers had to slow their movements as the distance to be moved increased or the size of the target decreased, if they were to perform the task accurately.

While spatial accuracy is governed by the speed-accuracy tradeoff, it appears that temporal accuracy is not. Temporal accuracy, or timing accuracy, is concerned with when a movement should be executed. For example, a tennis player must decide when to swing in order to intercept the ball. Interestingly, when temporal accuracy is a determinant of successful skill performance, research has found that increasing movement speed decreases timing errors (Schmidt, Zelaznik, Hawkins, Frank & Quinn, 1979). In other words, timing accuracy improves when the performer swings faster, thus

EXPLORATION ACTIVITY 8.1 Speed-Accuracy Tradeoff

EQUIPMENT:

Piece of paper
Pen
Watch with second hand or timer
Someone to keep time

PROCEDURE:

On a piece of paper, draw a circle about the size of a half dollar coin two inches from the top edge and a second circle of the same size two inches from the bottom edge of the paper. Draw a second set of circles, but this time the circles should be about the size of a dime. Your paper should look like this:

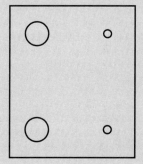

Now, place the tip of your pen in the large top circle. Your objective is to move the pen back and forth between the two large circles as fast as possible for 10 seconds, placing a dot in each one with each pass (*Note:* lift the pen off of the paper during the movement). Repeat the exercise, keeping in mind the objective of moving as fast as possible, using the smaller circles.

What changes did you note between the two tasks? Did your results support that there is a speed-accuracy tradeoff?

violating the speed-accuracy tradeoff. Similar results have been found for the production of very forceful movements (Schmidt & Sherwood, 1982).

At this point, the speed-accuracy tradeoff offers several implications for motor skill performance. First, if spatial accuracy is the goal of the task, such as when a patient reaches for an object or when the computer mouse is moved to click on an icon on the screen, accuracy will be compromised if the task is attempted with too much velocity. If, on the other hand, the goal of the skill is temporal accuracy or the production of very forceful movements, such as a smash in table tennis, speed should be emphasized.

While these guidelines are useful, they are somewhat limited for the practitioner. First, they are the product of experiments that employed laboratory tasks. In reality, complex motor skills usually involve a combination of spatial and temporal accuracy in addition to the production of forceful movements (Belkin & Eliot, 1997). Second, these experiments examined issues of control rather than skill acquisition. Several studies have been conducted to examine the influence of the speed-accuracy tradeoff on the development of complex motor skills, however (Belkin & Eliot, 1997; Southard, 1989). What the study authors found was that an emphasis on accuracy during the initial stages of skill acquisition may impede the development of efficient motor patterns. When learners sacrificed velocity in order to increase accuracy, a constrained movement pattern emerged. Conversely, an emphasis on speed had a facilitating effect on skill development.

These results suggest that during the initial stages of skill acquisition, accuracy should be de-emphasized, but many traditional practice techniques are not structured this way. For example, a technique often used to practice the in-step kick in soccer is to split the group into sets of partners who kick

EXPLORATION ACTIVITY 8.2 Speed-Accuracy Tradeoff II

EQUIPMENT:

2 friends
1 tennis ball

PROCEDURE:

Position the two friends so that they are facing one another at a distance of approximately five feet. Have them throw the tennis ball back and forth 10 times. Using the characteristics of a mature throwing pattern listed below, assess the throwing technique used. Next, have the friends repeat the task from a distance of 25 feet. Again, observe and assess the technique used to accomplish the task. Finally, assess the throwing technique used when one of the two friends performs hard throws into an open field.

Reflect on the technique assessments you made for the three different situations. Which situation led to the use of a technique that most resembled the ball back and forth to one another. Rather than focusing on technique, the goal of the learner is to get the ball to the partner. Because this accuracy goal has indirectly been established by the practice strategy employed, learners may choose to adopt a less efficient kicking pattern in order to successfully get the ball to their partner. Instead, practitioners should eliminate targets, or make them much larger and instruct learners to emphasize speed. Some examples include throwing a ball as far across the gymnasium as possible, throwing lacrosse balls into a soccer goal instead of a lacrosse goal and hitting tennis balls against a backstop rather than into the tennis court (Ciapponi, 2001).

CEREBRAL CHALLENGE #5

How does the speed-accuracy tradeoff influence the use of your computer? How might you redesign the desktop to maximize efficiency?

BILATERAL TRANSFER

The ability to use both limbs with equal proficiency is advantageous in many sport and daily living skills. The question facing the practitioner is how to design practice to best achieve this proficiency. The answer lies in the understanding of a phenomenon known as **bilateral transfer**. In Chapter 6 we examined the transfer of learning between tasks. Transfer can also occur between limbs when practice with one limb enhances the rate of skill acquisition with the opposite limb on the same task.

bilateral transfer: When practice with one limb enhances the rate of skill acquisition with the opposite limb on the same task.

that of a mature throwing pattern? What influence did the speed-accuracy tradeoff have in each condition? Based on your observations, speculate as to the optimal practice conditions to elicit a mature throwing pattern. How might you apply this information when teaching a class of 25 students?

CHARACTERISTICS OF A MATURE THROWING PATTERN

1. Addresses target with non-throwing side of the body.
2. Throwing arm is positioned behind the head in the windup.
3. Steps towards the target with the leg opposite the throwing arm.
4. Rotates the trunk to face the target.
5. Elbow leads the throw followed by forearm extension and finally snapping of the wrist.
6. Follows through in the direction of the target finishing down and across the body.

Two explanations have been offered to explain the occurrence of bilateral transfer. The first explanation is derived from a motor control perspective. Theoretically, the nonpracticed limb would utilize the same generalized motor program as the practiced limb because the specification of muscles and/or limbs to perform the movement is considered a parameter (see Chapter 3 for a review). In addition, when a movement is performed with one limb, EMG evidence indicates the presence of subthreshold electrical activity in the nonperforming limb (Hicks, Gaultieri & Schroeder, 1983).

The second proposal suggests that when the skill is practiced with the first limb, important cognitive information about the movement problem, such as the goal of the skill and how to achieve it, are acquired. When the learner later practices the same skill with the untrained limb, these same cognitive elements apply and are immediately incorporated, and performance with the previously unpracticed limb is enhanced as a result. Support for this cognitive explanation has been provided by Kohl and Roenker (1983), who found that the degree of bilateral transfer was about the same regardless of whether practice was performed physically or mentally. The interpretation offered by Kohl and Roenker is that an interaction between both motor and cognitive components likely accounts for the bilateral transfer phenomenon (Chamberlin & Lee, 1993).

Practicing Bilateral Skills Since the training of one limb has been shown to enhance the rate of skill acquisition on the opposite limb, the question of optimal practice sequencing is relevant for the practitioner. The general consensus according to Magill (2001) is that a greater degree of transfer occurs from the preferred to the nonpreferred limb. Consequently, to achieve maximum transfer effects when training bilateral manipulative skills or teaching a volleyball player to spike with both hands, for example, the skill should first be practiced with the dominant limb. Once the task can be skillfully performed it should then be introduced to the nonpreferred limb. Bilateral transfer can be further capitalized upon when learners have sustained an injury to their dominant limb. In this situation, practicing with the nondominant limb can facilitate performance with the injured limb following its rehabilitation (Christina & Corcos, 1988).

 CEREBRAL CHALLENGE #6

Generate a list of sport and daily living skills that might lend themselves to bilateral transfer.

Psychological Strategies

Physical rehearsal is not the only method by which skills can be practiced; learners can also mentally rehearse skills. Remember that neither physical nor mental practice will be effective unless the learner is motivated, so the following section will discuss motivation and introduce various psychological strategies that can be incorporated in practice to maximize skill acquisition and performance.

MOTIVATION AND PRACTICE

Motivation is a powerful entity. Learners who are motivated not only devote time and energy to practice, but do so with great effort. Those who lack motivation, however, may never realize their potential, and even individuals who have great aspirations such as Mike, the diver in the opening story who dreamed of one day being an Olympian, can become inflicted with sagging motivation.

Two factors that can lead to a loss of motivation are boredom and frustration. Countless repetitions of a task or its components are often needed in order to become proficient, and at higher levels, change comes slowly. By making practices fun, and introducing variety, the monotony of this repetition can be reduced. In addition, each practice period should be designed to provide each learner with the opportunity to experience some degree of success. This will lead to feelings of achievement that will further motivate the learner to practice. That is not to say that mistakes will not be made, regardless of the amount of practice. Since mistakes are an integral part of the learning process, a positive practice environment should be established whereby learners are not afraid to make them (Stratton, 1996). The provision of reinforcement to the learner plays a major role in creating such an environment, and it will be discussed in detail in Chapter 11.

CEREBRAL CHALLENGE #7

Generate a list of possible reasons for Mike's lack of motivation, and provide suggestions as to how to refocus him.

GOAL SETTING

Perhaps one of the most powerful motivational techniques is goal setting. Goals help to focus learners' attention and encourage learners to develop new skills and strategies to improve performance (Stratton, 1997). They also provide a means of monitoring progress or success (Harris & Harris, 1984), and research as to their effectiveness in enhancing performance is abundant (see Gould, 2001 for additional information on goal setting).

Types of Goals Three types of goals, defined by the nature of the performer's objective, have been identified. These include (1) outcome goals, (2) performance goals and (3) process goals.

Outcome goals are concerned with the final result of a competition relative to one's opponent. Beating the defending champion and performing a

outcome goals: Goals that are concerned with the final result of a competition relative to one's opponent.

skill before a fellow patient performs it are examples. Remember, though, that the use of such goals can be problematic. First, the performance of the opposition cannot be controlled. Consequently, a learner can achieve peak performance but still lose a contest and fail to accomplish his or her goal. Second, a learner can perform poorly yet still be victorious.

Performance goals are concerned with self-improvement. They focus on improvements in performance based on one's own previous results, such as increasing one's distance in the long jump or the number of steps that can be taken unassisted. Performance goals tend to be favored over outcome goals because they focus on self-improvement, which is in the direct control of the performer.

The third type, **process goals**, direct the performer's focus to achieving some technical element during skill execution. Maintaining a pelvic tilt position throughout an exercise or pulling the arms in quickly when performing a triple axel are examples. Like performance goals, process goals are favored over outcome goals, as their self-improvement nature tends to enhance motivation. However, research has shown that employing multiple strategies (a combination of outcome, performance and process goals) leads to superior performance (Filby, Maynard & Graydon, 1999).

performance goals: Goals that are concerned with self-improvement.

process goals: Goals that direct the performer's focus to achieving some technical element during skill execution.

CEREBRAL CHALLENGE #8

Generate an example of an outcome goal, a performance goal and a process goal for a skill of your choice.

Elements of a Well-Constructed Goal The benefits of goal setting can only be realized if goals are carefully constructed in accordance to several criteria. First, goals must be challenging yet realistic. Unless set at an appropriate level of difficulty, one that requires the learner to strive for their attainment, goals will have little value. Caution must be taken not to exceed learners' capabilities. This will only result in failure, which will negatively impact learning and performance. A good rule of thumb is that the goal should be set at a level slightly beyond the learner's reach based on his or her current level of performance. By basing goals on a learner's existing level of performance, they can be adjusted according to current conditions. For example, if a learner progresses faster than expected, goals can be raised. Similarly, when an athlete returns to play following an injury, goals may have to be lowered to be realistic.

It is also important to set specific, measurable goals that specify a target date for their completion. For example, "The patient will increase the range of motion for right knee extension by 10% within two weeks." This more precisely directs behavior than does simply telling the patient to do her best. While "best" may be defined in this situation as within normal limits, in other situations like driving a golf ball or pitching, the concept is somewhat elusive as it has yet to be achieved. Also, when goals are specific, learners will be able to evaluate their progress towards achieving them.

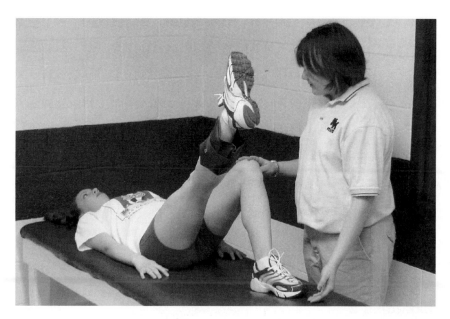

Goal setting can motivate a patient to use correct technique when performing rehabilitative exercises.

CEREBRAL CHALLENGE #9

Rewrite the outcome, performance and process goals that you wrote in Cerebral Challenge #8 incorporating the elements of a well-constructed goal.

Goal-Setting Guidelines Several additional factors should be considered when setting goals. First, a combination of short- and long-term goals should be identified. While long-term goals may identify what the ultimate objective is, such as winning a certain championship, their temporal distance makes them less effective. That is not to say that they are inappropriate, but they should be used in conjunction with short-term goals. Short-term goals, because they are more immediate, increase motivation, as they allow learners to see performance improvements and serve as the stepping-stones for long-term goal achievement.

Goals should also be set that account for individual differences. This will make them more meaningful for the learner. Their meaningfulness will also increase if learners are involved in the goal-setting process and encouraged to frequently evaluate their progress. Finally, practitioners should support their learners throughout the process by providing positive reinforcement.

MENTAL PRACTICE

In addition to physical practice, skill acquisition and performance can benefit from mental practice. One technique in particular has received much attention and boasts a variety of applications. That technique, known as

imagery: Technique involving the visualization or cognitive rehearsal of a movement in the absence of any physical execution.

imagery, involves the visualization or cognitive rehearsal of a movement in the absence of any physical execution, and repeated demonstrations of its effectiveness make it a worthy performance enhancement strategy.

Applications and Evidence While not a substitute for physical practice, mental practice has been shown to be more effective than no practice at all (Feltz & Landers, 1983; Hird, Landers, Thomas & Horan, 1991). Furthermore, the

EXPLORATION ACTIVITY 8.3 Mental imagery

EXERCISE 1

Select any object in the room for this exercise. Look at its shape and color. Examine it thoroughly, concentrating on its every detail. Close your eyes and visualize the object, and then open your eyes and compare your image to the actual object.

EXERCISE 2

Close your eyes and imagine that you are in your living room and your roommate is cooking dinner in the kitchen. Can you see your furniture? What color is it? Is the television on? Can you hear it? Are there any other noises? What can you smell? What other details do you notice? (Modified from Weinberg & Gould, 1995; p. 288)

EXERCISE 3

Close your eyes and recreate your journey to school today. Did you walk, ride your bike, drive or take the bus? See and feel yourself performing the movements associated with your mode of transportation. Visualize the people, environment and scenery. Are you hot or cold? What are you thinking about? What smells are there?

When you performed this exercise, did you see the image through your own eyes or vantage point, or did it seem as if you were watching a movie of yourself? If you answered the former, then you were using internal imagery. If, on the other hand, your perspective was that of an observer, you were using external imagery. The preference for perspective, internal vs. external, will vary among individuals, and many people will switch back and forth depending on the situation. Try Exercise #3 again, but this time use the other perspective.

While everyone has the capacity to perform imagery, not everyone will be equally proficient in its use. Initially, learners may have difficulty in creating vivid, controlled images that incorporate all of their senses. Practice is needed to develop one's imagery capability, and it is recommended that you start with objects or situations that are familiar to you, as was done in Exercises 1–3.

combination of physical practice and imagery has been found to be superior to physical practice alone. The implication of these findings for practitioners is that imagery should be included in the practice routine to assist in the learning or relearning of a skill or part of a skill. Imagery may also be a useful strategy to employ in cases where learners are fatigued or injured.

Imagery can be further implemented as a preparatory strategy to enhance performance (Vealey & Greenleaf, 2001). Athletes commonly mentally rehearse their performance prior to actually executing it. For example, a figure skater might rehearse a routine just before taking the ice, or a golfer might visualize the successful performance of a strategically placed shot prior to actually hitting the ball. Research has also shown that imagery can assist in reducing or controlling precompetitve anxiety (Ryska, 1998; Savoy, 1997), increasing self-confidence (Garza & Feltz, 1998) and enhancing motivation (Beauchamp, Halliwell, Fournier, & Koestner, 1996).

CEREBRAL CHALLENGE #10

Generate a list of examples of when the following professionals might use imagery:

a. Physical education teacher
b. Physical therapist
c. Personal fitness trainer
d. Aerobic instructor
e. Coach
f. Dance teacher
g. Athletic trainer
h. Athlete

For Example:

Physical education teacher: Have students use imagery to mentally rehearse a skill while waiting in line for their turn to practice.

Theoretical Explanations Two major explanations have been offered to account for the performance-enhancing effects of mental imagery. The first, the neuromuscular theory postulates that the act of visualizing oneself executing a movement results in the activation of the same motor pathways as would have been activated had the movement been physically performed, yet at a subthreshold level. Evidence supporting this notion has shown that muscle activity during imagery, as measured by electromyography (EMG), was indeed comparable to that during the actual movement, though at a lesser magnitude (Harris & Robinson, 1986; Jacobson, 1931; Jowdy & Harris, 1990; Suinn, 1980). It appears that by rehearsing a skill through imagery one can strengthen the neural pathways used to perform the actual movement.

The second explanation for imagery's effectiveness is the cognitive theory. This explanation suggests that imagery facilitates the acquisition of the cognitive elements of a skill by allowing learners to develop an understanding of a movement's requirements, test solutions to movement problems and develop performance strategies (Hird et al., 1991; Sackett, 1934). Its efficiency lies in the fact that the learner can practice a skill repeatedly without the risk of injury or becoming physically fatigued.

Imagery Guidelines Several guidelines have been suggested to maximize imagery's effectiveness. First, good imagery skills must be developed. Consequently, learners should practice imagery each day. For those new to the technique, that practice should occur in a distraction-free setting and should focus on familiar situations and skills. As learners become more proficient, they should strive to generate positive, vivid and controllable images of the skill or parts of a skill they wish to refine. This rehearsal should be done in real time and focus on successful performance and goal attainment. Finally, learners should try to incorporate all of their senses when using imagery, in an attempt to replicate the actual situation/environment: smell the freshly cut grass, hear the roar of the crowd when you score, focus on how the movement feels. For additional suggestions in designing an effective imagery-training program, practitioners should refer to Martens (1987), Vealey and Greenleaf (2001) or Weinberg and Gould (1995).

A Look Ahead

Skill acquisition and performance enhancement are the result of carefully designed practice opportunities. In this chapter, we have examined several variables, including sequencing and psychological strategies that practitioners can manipulate to optimize gains in skill proficiency. We will continue to focus on those variables that influence practice effectiveness in the next chapter as we turn our attention to practice organization and scheduling.

EXPLORATION ACTIVITY 8.4 Mental Imagery II

EQUIPMENT:

10-inch piece of string
1 key

PROCEDURE:

Attach the key to the end of the string. Next, place your elbow on a table while holding the other end of the string between you forefinger and thumb such that the key hangs freely. Once the string is still, focus on the key at its end, and visualize it moving back and forth like a pendulum. (Modified from Vealey and Greenleaf, 2001; p. 258.)

Were you able to move the object? How do explain this result?

Summary

- Skills that are high in task complexity and low in task organization are generally best served through part practice, while whole practice is preferred for those skills low in complexity and high in organization.
- Several part practice methods are available to the practitioner:
  - Segmentation separates the skill into parts according to spatial or temporal elements and can be implemented through the part-whole, progressive part or repetitive part methods, with the parts progressing either from the first to final part of the skill (forward chaining) or in reverse order (backward chaining).
  - Fractionization is a part practice technique where skill components that are normally performed simultaneously are partitioned and practiced independently.
  - Simplification reduces the level of difficulty of a task or some aspect of a task for the learner. This can be accomplished by modifying equipment, reducing the coordination requirements of a task, making open skills more closed or using lead-up games.
- Attention cueing directs a learner's attention to a specific aspect of the skill during its performance as a whole, allowing him or her to concentrate on one particular task component or movement problem without disrupting the underlying temporal and spatial characteristics inherent to the skill.
- Spatial accuracy is governed by the speed-accuracy tradeoff, where an emphasis on speed negatively impacts accuracy and vice versa.
- Bilateral transfer can occur when practice on one limb enhances the rate of skill acquisition with the opposite limb performing the same task.
- A combination of outcome goals, performance goals and process goals leads to superior performance.
- A well-constructed goal is challenging yet realistic, specific, measurable and includes a target date for its obtainment.
- The combination of physical practice and imagery, which involves the visualization or cognitive rehearsal of a movement, has been found to be superior to physical practice alone.

Review Questions

1. What two task characteristics must be considered when deciding whether or not to break a skill into parts?
2. Explain the difference between segmentation and fractionization. Illustrate your explanation with an example using a skill of your choice.
3. What advantage do the progressive part and repetitive part practice techniques provide over the part-whole method?
4. Give an example of backward and forward chaining with a skill of your choice.

5. Define simplification. List and explain three different simplification strategies for skills of your choice.
6. What is attention cueing? Why is it included in a discussion regarding whole vs. part practice?
7. What condition violates the speed-accuracy tradeoff principle?
8. What is bilateral transfer? Explain how an athlete who is injured might be able to capitalize on bilateral transfer.
9. List and explain the three types of goals presented in this chapter.
10. Define imagery. How could imagery be incorporated into a rehabilitation program?

References

Anderson, A. (1997). Learning strategies in physical education: Self-talk, imagery and goal setting. *Journal of Physical Education, Recreation and Dance, 68*(1), 30–35.

Beauchamp, P.H., Halliwell, W.R., Fournier, J.F. & Koestner, R. (1996). Effects of cognitive-behavioral psychological skills training on the motivation, preparation and putting performance of novice golfers. *The Sport Psychologist, 10*, 157–170.

Belkin, D.S. & Eliot, J.F. (1997). Motor skill acquisition and the speed-accuracy tradeoff in a field based task. *Journal of Sport Behavior, 20*(1), 16–28.

Chamberlin, C. J. & Lee, T.D. (1993). Arranging practice conditions and designing instruction. In R.N. Singer, M. Murphy, & L.K. Tennant (eds.), *Handbook of Research on Sport Psychology*. New York: MacMillan, pp. 213–241.

Christina, R.W. & Corcos, D. M. (1988). *Coaches guide to teaching sport skills*. Champaign, IL: Human Kinetics.

Ciapponi, T. (2001, April). *Speed-accuracy tradeoff in sport skills*. Paper presented at the meeting of the American Alliance for Health, Physical Education, Recreation and Dance, Cincinnati, OH.

Feltz, D.L. & Landers, D.M. (1983). The effects of mental practice on motor skill learning and performance: A meta analysis. *Journal of Sport Psychology, 5*, 1–8.

Filby, W.C.D., Maynard, I.W. & Graydon, J.K. (1999). The effect of multiple-goal strategies on performance outcomes in training and competing. *Journal of Applied Sport Psychology, 11*, 230–246.

Fitts, P.M. (1954). The information capacity of the human motor system in controlling the amplitude of movement. *Journal of Experimental Psychology, 47*, 381–391.

Garza, D.L. & Feltz, D.L. (1998). Effects of selected mental practice on performance, self-efficacy and competitive confidence of figure skaters. *The Sport Psychologist, 12*, 1–15.

Gould, D. (2001). Goal setting for peak performance. In J. Williams (ed.), *Applied Sport Psychology*. Mountain View, CA: Mayfield pp. 190–205.

Harris, D.V. & Harris, B.L. (1984). The athlete's guide to sport psychology: Mental skills for physical people. Champaign, IL: Human Kinetics.

Harris, D.V. & Robinson, W.J. (1986). The effects of skill level on EMG activity during internal and external imagery. *Journal of Sport Psychology, 8*, 105–111.

Hebert, E.P., Landin, D. & Solmon, M.A. (2000). The impact of task progressions on students' practice quality and task-related thoughts. *Journal of Teaching in Physical Education, 19*, 338–354.

Hicks, R.E., Gaultieri, C.T. & Schroeder, S.R. (1983). Cognitive and motor components of bilateral transfer. *American Journal of Psychology, 96*, 223–228.

Hird, J.S., Landers, D.M., Thomas, J.R. & Horan, J.J. (1991). Physical practice is superior to mental practice in enhancing cognitive and motor task performance. *Journal of Sport and Exercise Psychology, 13*, 281–293.

Hoglblum, P. (2001). *Therapeutic exercise for athletic injuries*. Champaign, IL: Human Kinetics.

Jacobson, E. (1931). Electrical measurements of neuromuscular states during mental activities. *American Journal of Physiology, 96*, 115–121.

Jowdy, D.P. & Harris, D.V. (1990). Muscular responses during mental imagery as a function of motor skill level. *Journal of Sport and Exercise Psychology, 12*, 191–201.

Klapp, S.T., Nelson, J.M. & Jagacinski, R.J. (1998). Can people tap concurrent bimanual rhythms independently? *Journal of Motor Behavior, 30*, 301–322.

Kohl, R.M. & Roenker, D.L. (1983). Mechanism involvement during skill imagery. *Journal of Motor Behavior, 15*, 197–206.

Lee, T.D., Chamberlin, C.J. & Hodges, N.J. (2001). Practice. In R.N. Singer, H. A. Hausenblas, & C.M. Janelle (eds.), *Handbook of Sport Psychology*. New York: MacMillan, pp. 115–143.

Magill, R.A. (2001). *Motor learning: concepts and applications* (6th ed.). New York: McGraw-Hill.

Martens, R. (1987). *Coaches Guide to Sport Psychology*. Champaign, IL: Human Kinetics Publishers.

Naylor, J.C. & Briggs, G.E. (1963). Effects of task complexity and task organization on the relative efficiency of part and whole training methods. *Journal of Experimental Psychology, 65*, 217–224.

Newell, K.M., Carlton, M.J., Fisher, A.T. & Rutter, B.G. (1989). Whole-part training strategies for learning the response dynamics of microprocessor driven simulators. *Acta Psychologica, 71*, 197–216.

Ryska, T.A.(1998). Cognitive-behavioral strategies and precompetitive anxiety among recreational athletes. *Psychological Record, 48*, 697–708.

Sackett, R.S. (1934). The influences of symbolic rehearsal upon the retention of a maze habit. *Journal of General Psychology, 13*, 113–128.

Savoy, C. (1997). Two individual mental training programs for a team sport. *International Journal of Sport Psychology, 28*, 259–270.

Schmidt, R.A. & Sherwood, D.E. (1982). An inverted-U relation between spatial error and force requirements in rapid limb movements: Further evidence for the impulse variability model. *Journal of Experimental Psychology: Human Perception and Performance, 8*, 158–170.

Schmidt, R.A. & Young, D.E. (1987). Transfer of motor control in motor skill learning. In S.M. Cormier & J.D. Hagman (Eds.), *Transfer of Learning*. Orlando, FL: Academic Press, pp. 47–79.

Schmidt, R.A., Zelaznik, H.N., Hawkins, B., Frank, J.S. & Quinn, J.T. (1979). Motor-output variability: A theory for the accuracy of rapid motor tasks. *Psychological Review, 86*, 415–451.

Southard, D. (1989). Changes in limb striking patterns: Effects of Speed and Accuracy. *Research Quarterly for Exercise and Sport, 4*, 348–356.

Stratton, R. (1996). Motivating your athletes and yourself. Coaching youth sports. http://www.tandl.vt.edu/rstratto/CYSarchive/CoachSept96.html

Stratton, R. (1997). Goal setting: the concept. Coaching youth sports. http://www.tandl.vt.edu/rstratto/CYSarchive/FeatureMay97.html

Suinn, R.M. (1980). Psychology and sport performance: Principles and applications. In R.M. Suinn (ed.), *Psychology in Sports: Methods and Applications*. Minneapolis, MN: Burgess, pp. 26–36.

Vealey, R.S. & Greenleaf, C.A. (2001). Seeing is believing: Understanding and using imagery in sport. In J. Williams (ed.), *Applied Sport Psychology*. Mountain View, CA: Mayfield, pp. 247–283.

Weinberg, R.S. & Gould, D.M. (1995) Foundations of sport and exercise psychology. Champaign, IL: Human Kinetics.

Wightman, D. C. & Lintern, G. (1985). Part-task training for tracking and manual control. *Human Factors, 27*(3), 267–283.

CHAPTER NINE

Practice Schedules

ollowing his total hip replacement surgery, Mr. Green was waiting for his first physical therapy appointment. He needed to relearn how to walk using his "new hip." He had already been warned that it would involve a lot of hard work and practice, but he was ready for the challenge. After all he had a goal: He wanted to walk his daughter down the aisle and be able to dance with her at her wedding.

The fact that practice is a critical component in the learning or relearning of a motor skill is not surprising. Nor is it surprising that the mastery of a skill takes time. To make the most of that practice time, the number of practice attempts should not only be maximized but also optimized. If Mr. Green's physical therapist has developed a thorough understanding of how practice context and distribution influence learning, his dream of walking his daughter down the aisle on her wedding day may become a reality.

Practice Context

If you were to observe a number of practice or training sessions, you would probably find that most practitioners employ the technique of practicing a skill repeatedly before moving on to either a different version of the task or a different task altogether. The logic underlying this approach is that by focusing on one thing at a time, the learner will be better able to concentrate, which will ultimately lead to performance enhancement. But let's take a look at what motor learning research says about this strategy. You may be surprised.

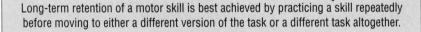

COMMON MYTH

Long-term retention of a motor skill is best achieved by practicing a skill repeatedly before moving to either a different version of the task or a different task altogether.

VARIABLE PRACTICE

A skilled performer can not only execute an action proficiently but can do so under a variety of conditions. A patient training to regain the use of hand function, for instance, may have a goal of being able to button his or her shirt independently. To accomplish this, the learner will have to manipulate a variety of buttons under numerous conditions, as buttons come in an assortment of shapes, textures and sizes and are used with an array of fabrics. Similarly, open skills, such as fielding a ground ball, require that the learner continually adapt his or her responses to conform to ever-changing environmental demands. But how is this capability to perform a skill in a variety of situations best developed?

Practice, according to Bernstein (1967), should "not consist in repeating the means of a solution of a motor problem time after time, but in the process of solving the problem again and again by techniques which are changed and perfected from repetition to repetition" (p. 134). Proponents of the Dynamic Systems Theory concur, suggesting that skill acquisition is best served through the modification of constraints, forcing learners to be engaged in a continuous search for task solutions (Newell & McDonald, 1992). In other words, movement and context variability is a necessary practice ingredient for skill development and generalizability. This notion is further supported by Schmidt's Schema Theory, which predicted that **variable practice** would enhance the development of one's schema. This, in turn, would enhance a performer's capability to accurately select the appropriate response specifications or parameter values to accomplish a movement goal.

variable practice: Practice schedule where multiple variations of a given task are practiced.

The theoretical prediction that variable practice benefits learning has received support from studies such as that conducted by Shea and Kohl (1991), who examined the effects of three different practice strategies on participants' capability to squeeze a hand dynamometer with 150 Newtons (N) of force. Two groups adopted a constant practice strategy where they practiced the task only at the criterion that was to be tested (150 N), while a third group followed a variable practice schedule in which the criterion condition was included. Results indicated that throughout the practice trials, the constant practice groups clearly outperformed the variable practice group. However, the results of the retention test revealed the opposite effect, indicating that greater learning gains were actually achieved by the variable practice group. Similar findings have been shown for the transfer of learning to a novel variation of a task (McCraken & Stelmach, 1977).

To fully understand the significance of these findings, we must revisit the distinction between learning and performance. Recall that learning is defined as a relatively permanent change in a person's capability to execute a motor skill, as a result of practice or experience. Performance, on the other hand, is a temporary expression of a skill. While constant practice has been found to have a greater influence on performance, variable practice has a greater influence on learning. Interestingly, constant practice is often the method employed by practitioners, but perhaps the rationale behind this is the success learners experience during practice. Given that the goal of practice is to foster learning, however, research does not support that constant practice is the best strategy.

CEREBRAL CHALLENGE #1

An argument sometimes made for the use of variable practice is that in an actual performance context, the same movement is never performed twice. Do you agree or disagree with this statement? Develop an argument to support your position.

Variable Practice Guidelines To maximize the potential benefits of variable practice, questions regarding how and when to implement variability into the practice session must be addressed. According to Gentile (2000), in order to determine how to implement practice variability one must first assess the nature of the skill being learned and the environment in which it will be performed. Then, depending on the outcome of that assessment, variations in the regulatory conditions (environmental conditions that specify the movement characteristics necessary to successfully perform a skill), nonregulatory conditions (those factors that are not inherently related to producing the appropriate motor response) or both should be systematically introduced in practice. For example, in open skills such as a learner fielding a ground ball, one's response must conform to the demands of an ever-changing environment. In this instance, presenting variations in both the regulatory (learner's position on the field, speed and trajectory of the ball, etc.) and nonregulatory conditions (performer's level of fatigue, crowd noise and other distractions) that might occur in the applied setting is recommended.

For open skills, variations in both regulatory and nonregulatory conditions should be systematically introduced in practice.

This same approach would apply to closed skills that involve inter-trial variability. A patient learning to button a shirt should therefore practice using buttons that differ in shape, size and texture while standing or sitting or with someone watching. But what about those skills such as springboard diving, where the objective of the performance is to consistently and accurately replicate a movement pattern? In such cases, practice should be designed so that the regulatory conditions remain constant, while a variety of potential nonregulatory conditions are presented.

CEREBRAL CHALLENGE # 2

1. Mr. Green, the gentleman in the opening story who is relearning how to walk following hip replacement surgery, is your patient. His goal, as you will recall, is to walk his daughter down the aisle and dance with her at her wedding. Explain how you will incorporate variable practice in this case. Be sure to include the variables that you will manipulate and a rationale for your plan.
2. Explain how you would implement variable practice with a skill of your choice.

Gentile's model provides the practitioner with guidelines regarding when to implement variable practice. According to Gentile, when introduced to a new motor skill, the learner has the goal of developing an understanding of the requirements of the task. Practice during this initial stage of learning should therefore facilitate the learner's development of a basic movement pattern. It should also be conducted in a manner so as not to overwhelm the novice learner, while providing opportunities for success to enhance confidence. These goals are best achieved through constant practice. Once the learner has acquired the basic movement pattern, however, variable practice strategies, as described above, should be introduced.

CEREBRAL CHALLENGE #3

Practitioners may continue to utilize constant practice rather than switch to variable practice once the learner develops an understanding of the basic movement pattern because with constant practice the learner will experience greater success during practice. We learned earlier that experiencing success in practice leads to greater motivation. What strategies might you employ to maintain motivation while incorporating a variable practice schedule?

CONTEXTUAL INTERFERENCE

Recognizing a clear advantage for the implementation of practice variability, the practitioner must next decide how to organize the practice session. More specifically, how should variability within a practice session be arranged?

The term 'interference' usually carries a negative connotation. But one form of interference, found to occur when practice is organized using *inter-task* variations (multiple skills) such as a set shot, a lay-up and a jump shot, as well as *intra-task* variations (within a single skill) such as buttoning an assortment of buttons, has been shown to facilitate learning (Battig, 1972, 1979). How much interference, or more specifically **contextual interference,** occurs is a function of how the tasks are integrated within a practice session. On one end of a range of possibilities, low contextual interference is found when practice trials are organized following a blocked schedule. In **blocked practice,** one variation of a skill is practiced repeatedly before practice attempts are given on another variation. For example, in a 30-minute practice, a hockey coach might have his players work on passing for 10 minutes, move on to wrist shots for the next 10 minutes and then dedicate the final 10 minutes to slap shots. Conversely, high contextual interference is found when multiple task variations are performed in a random order. Using this type of practice schedule, known as **random practice**, the hockey skills in the above example could be arranged as follows: passing, slap shot, wrist shot, slap shot, passing, wrist shot and so forth, provided that none of the variations is rehearsed twice in a row.

contextual interference: Interference that results from switching from one skill to another or changing the context in which a task is practiced from trial to trial.

blocked practice: Practice schedule where one variation of a skill is practiced repeatedly before practice attempts are given on another variation.

random practice: Practice schedule where multiple task variations are performed in a random order.

CEREBRAL CHALLENGE #4

1. How could random practice be utilized to practice the racquetball drive serve, lob serve and z serve?
2. How could random and variable practice be used to help Mr. Green relearn to walk?

The Contextual Interference Effect At the beginning of the last section we alluded to the fact that some degree of contextual interference facilitates learning. In fact, although practicing under conditions of high contextual interference (random practice) leads to poorer performance during acquisition (throughout practice), learning, which was established earlier to be the ultimate goal, is enhanced by practicing with high contextual interference as compared to practicing in a low contextual interference condition (blocked practice). This phenomenon is known as the contextual interference effect.

Two explanations have been offered to account for the contextual interference effect. The first, the elaboration hypothesis, contends that when random practice is used, multiple tasks are simultaneously housed in working memory, allowing for distinctions between the tasks to be more readily formulated (Shea & Morgan, 1979). This subsequently strengthens the memory representation of each skill, making it more readily available to the learner.

A second proposal, offered by Lee and Magill (1985) and known as the action plan reconstruction hypothesis, suggests that random practice facilitates learning by causing temporary between-trials forgetting of task solutions. Consequently, the learner is required to regenerate task solutions each time a particular skill variation is attempted. In blocked practice, this regeneration would only occur on the first trial of each block.

Limiting Factors Although the contextual interference effect has been shown to be quite generalizable, several limiting factors have been identified. First, the nature of the task appears to impact the contextual interference effect. This notion is based on Magill and Hall's (1990) hypothesis that the probability of eliciting a contextual interference effect is dependent on whether the task variations implemented were governed by the same generalized motor program. They suggested that practicing tasks controlled by different motor programs requires the learner to engage in more cognitive processing, which, in turn, leads to greater interference and enhanced learning. On the other hand, intra-task variations, which only require parameter modifications of the same program, are less likely to generate the critical level of interference to elicit the same effect. Magill and Hall further contend that practicing more dissimilar skills than similar ones would result in greater learning gains. Research has shown, however, that while this hypothesis appears to hold true in laboratory-based investigations (e.g., Hall & Magill, 1995, and Wood & Ging, 1991), results in applied settings are equivocal (see Brady, 1998). Several studies have shown that parameter-only modifications can elicit the contextual interference effect (Landin & Hebert, 1997; Sekiya, Magill, Sidaway & Anderson, 1994). Further research is needed to resolve this program/parameter debate.

Learner characteristics, such as age and skill level, are also thought to influence the contextual interference effect. Though limited in number, studies exploring contextual interference and age have found that blocked practice (low contextual interference) generally promotes greater learning for children (Brady, 1998; Hall & Boyle, 1993). Similarly, blocked practice advantages have been found for novice learners during the early stages of skill acquisition (Del Rey, Whitehurst & Wood, 1983; Hebert, Landin & Solomon, 1996; Landin & Hebert, 1997). Given that the initial stage of learning is characterized by a high degree of cognitive processing in order to develop an understanding of the movement, it is likely that the elevated level of interference created by random practice conditions simply overwhelms the learner (Magill & Hall, 1990). Conditions of high interference may therefore only be effective once a certain degree of proficiency is achieved (Del Rey, 1989; Del Rey et al., 1983; Hebert et al., 1996).

RESEARCH NOTE

To determine if the contextual interference effect would hold true for skilled performers, Hall, Domingues and Cavazos (1994) examined the influence of different batting practice schedules on the hitting performance of collegiate baseball players. Players received two additional batting practice sessions for six weeks, during which they received 15 fastballs, 15 curveballs and 15 changeups. The order of pitch presentation was dependent on group assignment. Players in the blocked group received 15 consecutive pitches of each type in repetitive blocks, while the random group received the same pitches but in random order. When tested under game-like conditions, the players in the random group outperformed those in the block group. These results demonstrated that the benefits of random practice are not limited to beginners but can also facilitate performance improvement of skilled performers.

While these results would imply that initial learning should be organized through blocked practice followed by random practice once the learner has acquired some degree of proficiency, Landin and Hebert (1997) suggested that in an applied setting, moderate levels of contextual interference might be superior. To create moderate contextual interference, a practitioner can use a repeated-blocked schedule of practice. For example, rather than taking 10 successive shots at each of four positions (blocked) or 1 shot from each position over 10 rotations (random), moderate contextual interference would be created by taking 5 successive shots at each of the four positions and repeating the rotation twice. Because the applied setting is typically characterized by the presence of a wide range of skill levels (Landin & Hebert, 1997) repeated-blocked practice, which combines the advantages of both blocked and random practice (Proteau, Blandin, Alain & Dorion, 1994), would theoretically accommodate more learners. Although moderate levels of contextual interference have been shown to facilitate learning (Landin & Hebert, 1997; Proteau et al., 1994), studies exploring this condition are limited and further research is needed to fully explore its potential.

FIGURE 9.1
Three practice variations (blocked, repeated-blocked and random) for practicing three different hockey skills (pass, slap shot and wrist shot) in a session.

Blocked practice	Pass x 20 Slap shot x 20 Wrist shot x 20
Repeated-blocked practice	Pass x 5 Slap shot x 5 } x 4 Wrist shot x 5
Random practice	Pass, Slap shot, Wrist shot, Slap shot, Pass, Wrist shot, Pass, Slap shot, Pass, Wrist shot, Slap shot, Wrist shot, Pass, Wrist shot, Slap shot, Pass, Slap shot, Pass, Wrist shot, Slap shot, Wrist shot, Slap shot, Pass, Wrist shot, Slap shot, Wrist shot, Pass, Slap shot, Pass, Wrist shot, Pass, Slap shot, Pass, Wrist shot, Slap shot, Wrist shot, Slap shot, Pass, Slap shot, Wrist shot, Pass, Wrist shot, Slap shot, Wrist shot, Slap shot, Pass, Wrist shot, Pass, Slap shot, Wrist shot, Slap shot, Pass, Wrist shot, Pass, Slap shot, Pass, Wrist shot, Pass, Wrist shot, Slap shot

CEREBRAL CHALLENGE #5

Reexamine your answers to Cerebral Challenge #4. How would you change them to implement a repeated-blocked practice schedule in each situation?

Practical Implications for Practice Organization A number of practical implications can be derived from the research on contextual interference. First, blocked practice should be used initially until learners get the idea of the movement. Once a basic proficiency level has been achieved, more moderate or high levels of contextual interference should be introduced in order to engage the learner in the higher cognitive processing activities that facilitate learning. Practice should therefore be organized using repeated-blocked and random schedules. For example, rather than serving to the same spot on each practice attempt, place colored cones in different positions around the court to vary serve placement. In tennis, practice the forehand and backhand in the same practice session in addition to varying the type of ball feed or the area of the court from which the learner hits the ball (Jackson, 2001). Design stations throughout the clinic where a patient can practice different manipulative skills. Vary the incline, direction and speed for patients relearning to walk. Remember, though, that this form of practice has the potential to adversely affect performance, which could lead to decreased motivation. Learners should therefore be educated regarding the future benefits of practicing under higher contextual interference conditions and encouraged to persevere.

Station work is an excellent method for implementing repeated-blocked or random practice.

CEREBRAL CHALLENGE #6

Station work is an excellent way to implement repeated-blocked or random practice. For example, in soccer, six stations could be set up around the field to practice the in-step kick, trapping, dribbling, volleying, throw-ins and heading the ball. A task card, like the example provided, would be located at each station describing the activity to be performed and the number of trials to be taken before rotating to the next station.

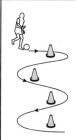

Starting on the inside of the first cone, dribble the ball through the cones using the inside of your foot going up and the outside of your foot coming back. Repeat 10 times then move to station #2.

1. Using a skill and or skills of your choice, design a station practice. Include in your design the rotation to be used, equipment needed, how you will label each station for easy visibility and what the task card at each station will say.
2. Speculate as to the potential weaknesses of this particular type of practice.

Practice Distribution

Thus far, our discussion regarding practice organization has focused on the scheduling of tasks and variations of tasks within a practice session. Practice organization also encompasses decisions regarding the duration and frequency of the practice sessions themselves, as well as the allocation of time within a single session. How should these decisions be made to best enhance learning?

MASSED VS. DISTRIBUTED PRACTICE

Practice distribution is defined in terms of the ratio of time that the learner is physically engaged in practice versus rest and can easily be manipulated by practitioners. Consequently, there is much interest in whether massed or distributed practice schedules are more beneficial for skill acquisition. **Massed practice** is defined as a schedule in which the amount of time allocated to rest between sessions or practice attempts is comparatively less than the time that the learner is engaged in practice. In **distributed practice**, the rest component between sessions or practice attempts is equal to or greater than the practice component.

The influence of massed versus distributed practice schedules on skill acquisition has been examined both across and within practice sessions. With respect to the duration and frequency of practice sessions themselves, research indicates a learning advantage for shorter, more frequent meetings (Baddely & Longman, 1978). In addition, Shea, Lai, Black and Park (2001) found that spacing practice sessions across days relative to spacing practice sessions within a day enhanced both performance and learning. Consequently, unless the decision as to how often to practice and for how long is out of the practitioners' control, as is often the case in physical education, for example, where the school dictates one's schedule, distributed practice is preferred.

The optimal practice distribution within a single session remains controversial. Following a review of the practice distribution literature, Lee and Genovese (1988) proposed that distributed practice is beneficial to both performance and learning but more so to performance. Furthermore, optimal practice distribution appears to be a function of the type of task being learned (Lee & Genovese, 1988, 1989). For continuous skills, it seems that distributed schedules offer a greater learning advantage than does massed practice (Lee & Genovese, 1988). Conversely, discrete skills appear to be best served through massed practice (Carron, 1969; Lee & Genovese, 1988, 1989).

Practical Implications for Practice Distribution Research on massed versus distributed practice offers the practitioner several guidelines for the scheduling of practice, training or rehabilitation sessions. First, learning is enhanced when shorter, more frequent practice sessions are scheduled. Consequently, it is better to practice three times a week for 30 minutes than once a week for 90 minutes.

massed practice: Practice schedule where the amount of time allocated to rest between sessions or practice attempts is comparatively less than the time that a learner is engaged in practice.

distributed practice: Practice schedule where the length of the rest component between sessions or practice attempts is equal to or greater than the time devoted to the practice component.

Distributed practice should also be used to avoid problems associated with high levels of fatigue. Prolonged fatigue can cause the learner to practice incorrect motor patterns, which will have an adverse effect on learning if the boundaries of the generalized motor program are exceeded. In addition, heightened levels of fatigue leave the learner more susceptible to injury. For new and complex skills, continuous tasks, tasks that inherently have high-energy requirements or tasks whose performance involves some degree of risk, shorter, more frequent work periods embedded with adequate rest intervals are therefore recommended. Examples of such tasks include figure skating, rock climbing and balancing on a wobble board. This same schedule should also be used for learners who lack the physical conditioning needed to sustain activity over extended periods of time. Additionally, practice should be scheduled such that conditioning is done towards the end of practice, while new skills or those that are highly technical are taught and practiced at the beginning of the session while the learner is still fresh (Jones, Wells, Peters & Johnson, 1993).

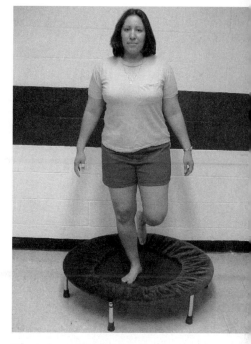

The inherent fatigue from balance exercises dictates the use of distributed practice.

For discrete skills such as archery, punting a football and a sit to stand transfer, practitioners should schedule short rest intervals between trials in an effort to maximize repetitions and enhance learning. Massed practice can also be effective when used with learners who have acquired basic skills, are motivated, are in good physical condition and have longer attention spans (Christina & Corcos, 1988; Jones et al., 1993). Finally, the fatigued conditions often present during competition can be simulated through massed practice. Provided that the levels of fatigue induced remain light to moderate, this strategy could enhance physical conditioning and performance in a game situation (Christina & Corcos, 1988). However, practicing when highly fatigued, as was discussed earlier, can have detrimental effects and should be avoided.

CEREBRAL CHALLENGE #7

Determine whether you would use massed or distributed practice for the following skills. Justify your answer.

a. Gymnastics vault
b. Free throw
c. The butterfly stroke
d. Dance routine

e. Performing a specific massage technique
f. Maintaining balance with an injured leg while standing on a trampoline (e.g., ankle rehabilitation)

Maximizing Time on Task

When a learner is resting, waiting in line or participating in a poorly designed drill, precious practice time is wasted. Given the amount of practice needed to become proficient at a skill, and the fact that there often exists a limitation in the amount of time available for such practice, this reduces the opportunity for learners to maximize their learning potential. Fortunately, strategies exist that can reduce down time and maximize time on task.

REST INTERVALS

Obviously, given the potentially harmful effects of high levels of fatigue (Arnett, DeLuccia & Gilmartin, 2000; Godwin & Schmidt, 1971), learners cannot be denied adequate rest. Ample rest can, however, be provided while filling the rest interval with another activity. This technique is commonly used in weight training, where an activity using a different muscle group is inserted into the rest interval. For example, if an athlete's workout regime calls for three sets of 10 repetitions of bicep curls and triceps extensions, the athlete can alternate between the two exercises. This strategy allows adequate recovery time for the biceps brachii muscle while the triceps are being conditioned. Similar results can be achieved through the implementation of contextual interference. In repeated-blocked or random practice, recovery is often "built in" to the program without having to completely stop activity. For example, in volleyball, a rotation could be designed where a player spikes, then moves to the setting position, then goes to the other side of the net to block, then provides cover behind the block and finally finishes the rotation by shagging a ball.

CEREBRAL CHALLENGE #8

Using a sport or rehabilitation activity of your choice, suggest possible activities that could fill the rest interval(s) and maximize practice effectiveness.

EQUIPMENT SUBSTITUTIONS

Research has shown that approximately 20 percent of a high school physical education student's time is spent waiting (Beauchamp, Darst & Thompson, 1990). One reason is the limitation placed on practice opportunities as a result of an insufficient amount of equipment. A youth soccer coach, for example, may have 20 team members but only eight soccer balls. Similarly, a physical educator teaching putting in a golf unit may only have seven holes on a putting green to which 35 learners must be assigned. The impact on wait time is obvious. However, by using alternative equipment, this problem can be remedied. In addition to the eight soccer balls, the coach could use playground balls of a comparable size to teaching dribbling and kicking skills. Likewise, the physical educator could give each student a tee to serve as his or her target. Surely if they can putt the ball to a tee, they will be able to get it into the hole. Similarly, softballs can serve as substitutes for shot puts, plastic grocery bags for juggling scarves, sand-filled tennis ball canisters for weights and bicycle tire inner tubes for surgical tubing. The possibilities are limited only by the practitioners' imagination. Be careful that the alternative equipment does not cause the learner to execute a pattern of movement that exceeds the boundaries of the generalized motor program being developed. If distinct movement pattern changes manifest as a result of the alternative equipment being used, the equipment should be modified or withdrawn.

CEREBRAL CHALLENGE #9

Using a sport or rehabilitation activity of your choice, generate a list of possible alternatives that could be used when an insufficient amount of equipment is available.

EXPLORATION ACTIVITY 9.1 Time on Task

EQUIPMENT NEEDED

10 people
3 soccer balls
Open area
Stopwatch

PROCEDURE

Form one large circle of 9 people with 1 person standing in its middle. The objective of the drill is to have the person in the middle try to get the ball while those forming the circle try to keep it away from him or her by passing it around.

1. Perform the drill for 60 seconds. How many times did each individual touch the ball? How motivated were the participants?
2. Have two additional people go into the middle from the circle. There should now be 3 people in the middle and 7 in the circle. Observe the activity over a 60-second period. How many times did each person touch the ball? How motivated were the participants? How did the intensity of the drill change?
3. Add two additional balls to the drill. Again, perform for a 60-second period. How many times did each person touch the ball? How motivated were the participants? How did the intensity of the drill change?
4. Can you suggest other strategies that could potentially be implemented to increase time on task?

DRILL DESIGN

To maximize time on task, drills should be designed to ensure the active participation of all learners. In addition, effective drills directly target the learning goal. Many traditional drills and activities fail to meet these criteria. For example, in volleyball, once a basic movement pattern for bumping and setting has been developed, two or three large groups (6–8 people) are formed, and learners are challenged to see how many times they can hit the ball before it touches the floor. Theoretically, it could be argued that this drill provides learners with the opportunity to practice the two newly learned skills, promotes random practice, enhances motivation and is therefore well designed. However, given the size of the groups, the number of potential contacts each learner will have with the ball is reduced. Moreover, the learners' goal orientation will be on not letting the ball hit the ground rather than on form. Consequently, the effectiveness of this activity should be questioned.

CEREBRAL CHALLENGE #10

1. Redesign the volleyball drill presented under "Drill Design" where two or three large groups (6–8 people) are formed and learners are challenged to see how many times they can hit the ball (bumping and setting) before it touches the floor. Explain why your drill is more effective.
2. What is the purpose of learning the weave in basketball? Do you think this is an effective drill? Justify your answer.

A Look Ahead

When planning practice and rehabilitative experiences, practitioners must decide how to best organize practice trials and distribute those trials across and within practice sessions to facilitate learning. Questions as to whether random or blocked practice should be implemented, when the use of massed or distributed schedules are beneficial and how to maximize time on task must therefore be answered. However, once the learner begins to practice a skill, the focus of the practitioner turns to error correction, and before an error can be corrected, its cause must be determined. Consequently, error detection will be discussed in the following chapter.

Summary

- For the introduction to a new motor skill, constant practice, where the learner practices only a single variation of a task, should be utilized. Once the learner has acquired the basic movement pattern, variable practice strategies, where the learner rehearses multiple variations of a given task, should be introduced.

- Variations in both regulatory and nonregulatory conditions that could be presented in an applied setting should be systematically introduced for open skills and those closed skills that involve inter-trial variability. For closed skills that do not involve inter-trial variability, learners should be exposed to a variety of potential nonregulatory conditions while the regulatory conditions of the skill remain constant.
- Increasing contextual interference, the interference that results from switching from one skill to another or changing the context in which a task is practiced from trial to trial, has been shown to facilitate learning.
- Low contextual interference occurs during blocked practice when one variation of a skill is practiced repeatedly before practice attempts are given on another variation, while high contextual interference is found when multiple task variations are performed in random order.
- Initial learning should be organized through blocked practice followed by random practice once learners have acquired some degree of proficiency.
- Repeated-blocked practice combines the advantages of both blocked and random practice.
- Learning is enhanced when shorter, more frequent practice sessions are scheduled.
- Distributed practice is recommended for novel and complex skills, continuous tasks, tasks that inherently have high-energy requirements or tasks whose performance involves some degree of risk. Massed practice can be effective when used with learners who have acquired basic skills, are highly motivated, are in good physical condition and have longer attention spans.
- Rest intervals, equipment substitutions and drill design should all be considered to maximize time on task.

Review Questions

1. Explain the concept of practice variability and its significance. Why is it important to make a distinction between learning and performance when answering this question?
2. What variables should be assessed to determine how and when to implement practice variability into the practice session?
3. Compare and contrast random and blocked practice.
4. What is the contextual interference effect?
5. Describe the two hypotheses that have been proposed to account for the contextual interference effect.
6. What limiting factors have been found to influence the contextual interference effect?
7. What practice strategy has been used to create moderate contextual interference?

8. Compare and contrast massed and distributed practice.
9. Why should prolonged high levels of fatigue be avoided?
10. List and explain three factors that can adversely affect time on task.

References

Arnett, M.G., DeLuccia, D. & Gilmartin, K. (2000). Male and female differences and the specificity of fatigue on skill acquisition and transfer performance. *Research Quarterly for Exercise and Sport, 71*(2), 201–205.

Baddeley, A.D. & Longman, D.J.A. (1978). The influence of length and frequency of training session on the rate of learning to type. *Ergonomics, 21*, 627–635.

Battig, W.F. (1972). Intra-task interference as a source of facilitation in transfer and retention. In R.F. Thompson and J.F. Voss (eds.), *Topics in Learning and Performance*. New York: Academic Press, pp. 131–159.

Battig, W.F. (1979). The flexibility of human memory. In. L.S. Cermak & F.I.M. Craik (eds.), *Level of Processing in Human Memory.* Hillsdale, NJ: Erlbaum, (pp. 23–44).

Beauchamp, L., Darst, P.W. & Thompson, L.P. (1990). Academic learning time as an indication of quality high school physical education. *Journal of Physical Education, Recreation and Dance, 61*(1), 92–95.

Bernstein, N. (1967). *The coordination and regulation of movements*. Oxford, England: Pergamon Press.

Brady, F. (1998). The theoretical and empirical review of the contextual interference effect and the learning of motor skills. *Quest, 50*, 266–293.

Carron, A.V. (1969). Performance and learning in a discrete motor task under massed vs. distributed practice. *Research Quarterly, 40*, 481–489.

Christina, R.W. & Corcos, D.M. (1988). *Coaches guide to teaching sport skills.* Champaign, IL: Human Kinetics Books.

Del Rey, P. (1989). Training and contextual interference effects on memory and transfer. *Research Quarterly for Exercise and Sport, 60*, 342–347.

Del Rey, P., Whitehurst, M. & Wood, J.M. (1983). Effects of experience and contextual interference on learning and transfer by boys and girls. *Perceptual Motor Skills, 56*, 581–582.

Gentile, A.M. (2000). Skill acquisition: Action, movement, and the neuromotor processes. In J.H. Carr, & R.B. Shepard (eds.), *Movement science: Foundations for physical therapy in rehabilitation* (2nd ed.). Rockville, MD: Aspen Publications, Inc, pp. 111–180.

Godwin, M.A. & Schmidt, R.A. (1971). Muscular fatigue and discrete motor learning. *Research Quarterly for Exercise and Sport, 42*, 374–383.

Hall, K.G. & Boyle, M. (1993). The effects of contextual interference on shuffleboard skill in children. *Research Quarterly for Exercise and Sport, Abstracts, 64*, A-74.

Hall, K.G., Dominguez, D.A. & Cavazos, R. (1994). Contextual interference effects with skilled baseball players. *Perceptual and Motor Skills, 78,* 835–841.

Hall, K.G. & Magill, R.A. (1995). Variability of practice and contextual interference in motor skill learning. *Journal of Motor Behavior, 27*(4), 299–309.

Hebert, E.P., Landin, D. & Solomon, M.A. (1996). Practice schedule effects on the performance and learning of low- and high-skilled studies: An applied study. *Research Quarterly for Exercise and Sport, 67,* 52–58.

Jackson, B. (2001, April). *Mixing and matching your repetitions: Contextual interference as a learning opportunity.* Paper presented at the meeting of the American Alliance for Health, Physical Education, Recreation and Dance, Cincinnati, OH.

Jones, B.J., Wells, L.J., Peters, R.E. & Johnson, D.J. (1993). *Guide to effective coaching: principles and practice.* Madison, WI: WCB Brown and Benchmark.

Landin, D. & Hebert, E.P. (1997). A comparison of three practice schedules along the contextual interference continuum. *Research Quarterly for Exercise and Sport, 68*(4) 357–361.

Lee, T.D. & Genovese, E.D. (1988). Distribution of practice in motor skill acquisition: Learning and performance effects reconsidered. *Research Quarterly for Exercise and Sport, 59,* 277–287.

Lee, T.D. & Genovese, E.D. (1989). Distribution of practice in motor skill acquisition: Different effects for discrete and continuous tasks. *Research Quarterly for Exercise and Sport, 60,* 59–65.

Lee, T.D. & Magill, R.A. (1985). Can forgetting facilitate skill acquisition? In D. Goodman, R.B. Wilberg & I.M. Franks (eds.), *Differing perspectives in motor learning, memory and control.* Amsterdam: North Holland, pp. 3–22.

McCraken, H.D. & Stelmach, G.E. (1977). A test of the schema theory of discrete motor learning. *Journal of Motor Behavior, 9,* 193–201.

Magill, R.A. & Hall, K.G. (1990). A review of the contextual interference effect in motor skill acquisition. *Human Movement Science, 9,* 241–289.

Newell, K.M. & McDonald, P.V. (1992). Practice: A search for task solutions. In R.W. Christina and H.M. Eckert (eds.), The Academy Papers, No. 25, Enhancing human performance in sport: New concepts and developments. *Proceedings of the American Academy of Physical Education* (pp. 51–59).

Proteau, L., Blandin, Y., Alain, C. & Dorion, A. (1994). The effects of the amount and variability of practice on the learning of a multisegmented motor task. *Acta Psychologica, 85,* 61–74.

Sekiya, H., Magill, R.A., Sidaway, B. & Anderson, D.I. (1994). The contextual interference effect for skill variations from the same and different generalized motor programs. *Research Quarterly for Exercise and Sport, 65*(4), 330–338.

Shea, C.H. & Kohl, R.M. (1991). Composition of practice: Influence on the retention of motor skills. *Research Quarterly for Exercise and Sport, 62*(2), 187–195.

Shea, C.H., Lai, Q., Black, C. & Park, J.H. (2001). Spacing practice sessions across days benefits the learning of motor skills. *Human Movement Science, 19*, 737–760.

Shea, C.H. & Morgan, R.L. (1979). Contextual interference effects on the acquisition, retention and transfer of a motor skill. *Journal of Experimental Psychology, Human Learning and Memory, 5*, 179–187.

Wood, C.A. & Ging, C.A. (1991). The role of interference and task similarity on the acquisition, retention and transfer of simple motor skills. *Research Quarterly for Exercise and Sport, 62*(1),18–26.

CHAPTER TEN

Diagnosing Errors

S ally was frustrated. She had spent hours with her coach working on her backhand. Her technique was flawless. But in competition, she was consistently contacting the ball too late. Her coach told her that her technique looked good; she just had to swing faster. But no matter how hard she tried she just couldn't fix the problem. She didn't know what else to do, and her coach offered no other suggestions.

Skill Analysis

Providing learners with information regarding the correctness of their performance as well as prescribing modifications for its improvement is an important aspect of the learning process. Before such information can be provided, however, practitioners must be able to accurately analyze performance and determine not only if an error exists but the cause of that error and how to fix it. The mechanism commonly used to determine the correctness of a response is observation of the performance. This form of assessment typically involves a comparison of the learner's technique to that which is representative of a highly skilled individual. Unfortunately, three potential limitations are inherent with this approach.

First, it should be noted that while there is a tendency to try to copy or adopt the technique of a champion athlete, that technique may not be best suited for that particular learner. There are many ways to perform a given technique, and athletes often develop their own idiosyncrasies. Practitioners must therefore develop a thorough understanding of biomechanics in order to determine the fundamental components of proper technique. In addition, learners may not share the same underlying abilities and attributes as the champion that they are trying to emulate, so certain techniques may be inappropriate due to individual differences.

A second limitation is that the flaw observed is not necessarily indicative of the underlying cause of the error. For example, an observer may see that a volleyball player is hitting the ball into the net on the serve. Upon seeing this, many practitioners may try to fix the player's arm swing or the amount of force generated, but if the athlete tosses the ball too far out in front of the hitting arm, this too would cause the player to hit the ball with too low of an angle to clear the net. In this situation, the toss, not the arm swing, should be corrected. Similarly, a right-handed hitter in baseball may be consistently fouling off to the right. One explanation for the error could be a slow swing speed due to the athlete taking the bat off of the shoulder and implementing a long, swooping swing. However, a second possibility is that the athlete is having difficulty identifying the pitch, causing him to delay the initiation of his swing.

The last example leads into the third limitation and the focus of this chapter. Errors are not always the result of poor technique. Many errors can be attributed to deficits in the area of motor learning. However, since we can only see the output of a learner's performance, there is a tendency to focus on the outcome of the movement and to provide feedback only about those technical aspects of the skill that can be seen (Rothstein, 1986). As a result, the underlying processes that led to the performance are often overlooked, as they are not directly observable. The purpose of this chapter is to identify potential errors that can manifest not because of poor technique but because of concepts related to motor learning and control.

Conducting an Observation

Accurate skill analysis begins with good observational skills. After all, you can't fix an error unless you first detect it and determine its cause. Observational and analytical skills do not come naturally to most human movement practitioners (Rink, 1998) but with practice and the understanding of how to conduct a systematic observation, these skills can be developed.

Unlike the still pictures presented in the Exploration Activity 10.1, human movement occurs both dynamically and quickly, leaving the observer with only fractions of a second to assess performance. Accordingly, good observations start with a plan (Hall, 1999). Prior to conducting an observation, the practitioner should identify both the purpose of the skill and its key elements. **Key elements** are specific body movements that are observable and affect the performance of the skill (Coaching Association of Canada, 1993). Their identification requires a thorough understanding of both the skill itself and biomechanics. Of further assistance are numerous textbooks, sport-specific

key elements: Specific body movements that are observable and that affect the performance of a skill.

books, web pages, journals and other movement practitioners. Once the key elements of the skill have been identified, those that will be the focus of the observation can be determined.

The second step in the observational plan is to determine the optimal viewing perspective from which to observe the skill and, more specifically, the key elements that have been chosen as the focus. In order to see all of the critical aspects of the skill, practitioners may need to watch the skill from several different positions. In addition, the distance at which you position

EXPLORATION ACTIVITY 10.1 Diagnosing Errors

EQUIPMENT

Stopwatch or digital watch
Diagram below
Partner

PROCEDURE

Examine the diagram below. Three differences exist between the two pictures. Find the three differences and time how long it took you to find them. Then, time someone doing a vertical jump. Be sure to note the time needed to complete each task.

QUESTIONS

1. What was the difference in time between how long it took you to find the three flaws and the performance of the vertical jump?
2. List differences in observing a static picture versus a dynamic movement for the detection of flaws.

Answers: 1. Arm position, 2. Front foot position 3. Collar is missing.

- Feet shoulder width apart
- Knees bent/body low
- Weight on balls of feet
- Glove open so pocket is up
- Opposite hand in area of glove

- Focus on the ball
- Get in position directly in front of ball
- Drop down, knee bent, body low to ground
- Reach out, glove open with palm side up and on ground in front of you
- Arms extended–reach ahead of feet to get ball

- Eyes down on ball
- Look ball into glove
- Close glove around ball
- Second hand covers ball
- Pull into the body

- In a continuous motion, rise up turning into the throwing position
- Step toward target and throw

FIGURE 10.1
Key elements of fielding a ground ball

yourself will vary depending on the focus of the observation. If you want to focus on the entire movement, for example, you will need to position yourself farther away from the learner, whereas a close-up view may be necessary to observe the performer's eye movements to determine where they are directing their visual focus. In addition, the position selected should ensure that the viewing area is void of distractions.

Another factor to consider is the number of trials that should be observed prior to making a judgment as to the quality of the performance. While no concrete number exists, analysis based on a single performance attempt should be avoided for several reasons. First, as we have learned, a characteristic of beginning learners is inconsistency in performance. Determining the consistent and/or critical error may therefore require repeated observations. In addition, the skill level of the observer as well as the complexity of the task itself should be taken into consideration.

Finally, the decision as to whether or not to capture the performance on videotape must be made. Videotape is useful, as it permits repetitive viewing by both the practitioner and the learner, it can be slowed, paused and advanced using the frame-by-frame function and it can capture movements that occur too rapidly (less than 1/4 of a second) for the human eye to see (Hall, 1999). Videotaping does have a few disadvantages. Learners who are not used to being videotaped can be intimidated and may subsequently alter their performance. Also, it is difficult to see intricate performance details when viewing the replay through the video camera versus a TV monitor.

CEREBRAL CHALLENGE #1

Using a skill of your choice, list the key elements and determine the optimal viewing perspective from which to observe each.

SKILL: _____

Key Elements	Observation Plan

Determining the Cause of an Error and Its Resolution

Once you have implemented your observation plan and detected the existence of one or more movement errors, you must determine their underlying cause. When observing skill performance, practitioners should start by asking themselves why they see a certain behavior. Why is the backhand late? Why is the patient losing his or her balance? Remember, as was indicated earlier, the answer may not be related to technique. Consequently, practitioners must be aware of the variety of potential sources of error that exist to ensure that corrections offered are both accurate and effective. Those sources can be grouped into five major categories: (1) errors due to constraints, (2) comprehension errors, (3) errors in selection, (4) execution errors and (5) sensory errors.

ERRORS DUE TO CONSTRAINTS

Constraints shape behavior. Accordingly, errors can emerge as a function of the task and/or environment relative to personal developmental level. A common error displayed by young learners executing a free throw, for example, is the projection of the ball in a shot put type manner. The adoption of this unorthodox pattern is not because the learner doesn't understand the correct technique, but because it is the only way that the learner can generate enough force to get the ball to a basket that is positioned too high. By lowering the basket to accommodate the developmental level of the learner, the practitioner can likely solve the problem.

Equipment can also create unwanted movement errors. A bat that is too heavy will alter a learner's swing pattern, crutches that are not properly

FIGURE 10.2
Cause of error schematic

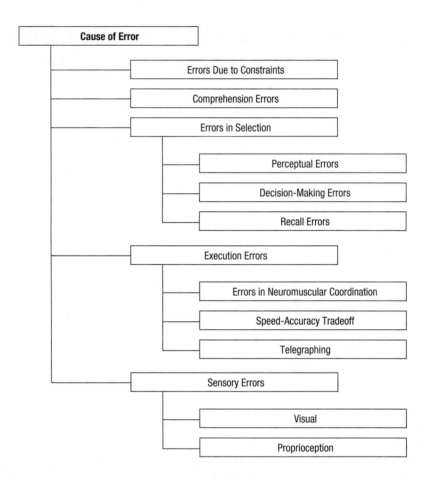

fitted will cause problems with a patient's locomotion and the speed of a treadmill can dictate the user's stride length and frequency.

 CEREBRAL CHALLENGE #2

Generate a list of potential errors that could occur in sport or rehab as a result of incorrect sizing of equipment, objects or implements.

COMMON MYTH

When teaching a youngster how to catch, you should toss the ball with a high arc in order to give them enough time to follow it and get underneath it for a successful catch.

Errors can also occur as a result of the structure of the task or drill. For example, by 5 or 6 years of age, the visual system develops to the point that objects moving in the horizontal plane can be efficiently tracked (Payne & Isaacs, 1999). However, it is not until a child is between the ages of 8 and 9 that she or he can track a ball traveling in an arc (Morris, 1980). The common practice of tossing a ball with a high arc to give a youngster more time to get under it actually makes the task much more difficult and reduces the learner's chances of catching success. Instead, until the age of 8 to 9, the ball should be thrown straight towards learners in a horizontal fashion in order to accommodate their visual development and increase their chances of success.

Other errors will arise when the environment moves from one that is closed, such as hitting off of a tee, to one that is more open, such as hitting a pitch. In these instances, practitioners should expect to see a decline in performance as learners adapt to the new demands imposed upon them. Prolonged regeneration of errors without signs of adaptation could, of course, indicate that the demands of the new task exceed the learner's current capacity. In such instances, the practitioner may have to revert to having the learner practice the skill in a more closed environment for a period of time.

Unless properly fitted, crutches can cause unwanted errors in locomotion.

Fear can also be a source of error. Beginning swimmers are often afraid of the water. Fear of the ball plays a factor in catching and striking. Fear of heights will have to be overcome before a learner can correctly rappel, ski jump or rock climb. Furthermore, performers may alter their technique because of a fear of reinjuring a recently rehabilitated limb. Finally, a different type of fear, the fear of failure, can have a negative impact on performance. To counter the fear of failure, practitioners should incorporate goal setting, provide opportunities for all learners to experience success in practice and create an environment where learners are not afraid to make mistakes.

COMPREHENSION ERRORS

A comprehension error occurs when the learner doesn't understand the requirements of the skill or what you want them to do. Whether due to not fully understanding the instructions given, a short attention span, limited attentional capacity, lack of motivation or countless other reasons, unless the learner understands the proper structure of the skill, errors will develop. In this instance, simply explain the skill again. Be sure to use terminology that is appropriate for the age and skill level of your learners, and avoid overloading them with too much information. Finally, check for understanding.

The fear of falling can interfere with a rock climber's performance.

Errors in comprehension can also occur when learners are trying to correct and refine their skills. While a practitioner may have made a learner aware of the existence of a problem, the learner may not fully understand what the error is or how it is being created. A useful tool in this situation is to videotape the individual's performance and provide the learner with the opportunity to see what he or she is doing wrong. In addition, learners must be taught to pay attention to the sensory consequences of their movements in order to develop their error detection and correct capabilities. Questioning strategies that engage learners in evaluating their performance prior to being given feedback are an effective strategy to accomplish this and will be discussed in detail in the next chapter. On the other hand, it may be the case that the learner understands the error but is uncertain about how to implement a change to correct the behavior. In addition to continued demonstrations and feedback, the use of guidance and/or a simulator may prove useful in this situation.

ERRORS IN SELECTION

The successful performance of many motor skills, such as a tennis backhand, is dependent not only on how the skill is executed but also on how quickly and accurately the performer assesses the situation and decides how to best respond. Any delays in the processes that lead to response selection not only influence the timing of the response but its quality as well. Practitioners must therefore be able to differentiate between moving slowly and initiating movement slowly. Slow movement execution is likely due to a problem with technique. On the other hand, if the movement is initiated slowly, the source of the error can likely be attributed to a perceptual or decision-making problem. This distinction, had it been considered, would have assisted Sally's coach in diagnosing her error. Since her technique was judged correct and speeding up the overall movement ineffective, the next step would be to examine Sally's response selection strategies.

Perceptual Errors Good decision making begins with good assessment. Unless the learner can quickly and accurately distinguish that which is task relevant from the abundant amount of stimuli present in the environment, delayed and/or incorrect response selection will occur. Movement errors can result when a learner doesn't know what cues to look for in the environment, can't distinguish between task relevant and irrelevant stimuli or focuses his or her attention on the wrong cues. In some instances, the learner may understand what cues are relevant but fail to look at the information-rich areas in the environment where those critical cues occur (Magill, 1998; Rothstein, 1986). This can equally hamper one's decision-making capabilities.

To determine the source of Sally's timing error, her coach must establish whether Sally can correctly read game situations. First, does Sally know what critical cues to look for? Second, is she able to detect that information during a game? If not, intervention strategies would focus on teaching what the critical cues are, prompting Sally to prepare her response sooner (e.g., begin your preparation as soon as the ball leaves the opponent's racket and get your racket into the backswing position by the time the ball bounces), directing her attention to where in the environment cues occur and providing extensive practice opportunities in a variety of situations that contain common task-relevant cues.

CEREBRAL CHALLENGE #3

You are teaching badminton to a 7th grade physical education class. You have been working with your students on the long serve and have noticed that many of them are having difficulty hitting the shuttlecock after they release it. Generate a list of possible reasons for the students missing the shuttlecock, and provide suggestions as to how you might try to correct the problem.

Level of arousal can also influence a learner's assessment proficiency. As we learned in Chapter 2, when arousal levels are too low, attentional focus becomes too broad and learners are unable to focus solely on task-relevant cues. On the other hand, when arousal levels are elevated to the point at which the learner becomes overaroused, attentional focus becomes so narrow that the learner may no longer be capable of effectively scanning the environment, leaving potentially significant stimuli undetected. Both situations may lead to inaccurate responses, as the performer lacks the necessary information for appropriate decision making.

Decision-Making Errors Many errors can occur as a result of problems in decision making. A learner who misjudges velocity, direction, height, weight, distance, trajectory of an object or position of opponents and/or teammates, for example, could select the wrong motor program or may select the appropriate motor program but apply erroneous parameters for a given situation. Paying attention to task-irrelevant stimuli, such as when a performer is tricked by a head fake, could also lead to momentary delays in responding. Furthermore, mispredicting the arrival of an object, person or musical cue could cause learners to mistime the initiation of their movement, causing them to respond either too early or too late. Again, these decision-making errors can be resolved by increasing the performer's ability to identify and locate critical cues and by developing a stronger cause-and-effect relationship between a specific cue and the appropriate response.

CEREBRAL CHALLENGE #4

Throughout the rehearsal, one dancer is consistently out of synch with the rest of the dancers. Suggest reasons as to why this may be occurring, and provide suggestions to correct the problem.

Response delays can also occur if the learner fails to reduce the number of response alternatives. According to Hick's Law, the higher the degree of uncertainty in a given situation, the longer it will take the learner to decide which response to make. By reducing the number of possible response alternatives, many decision-making problems can be resolved. Learners should be taught how to systematically look for key performance characteristics when assessing a situation, like a quarterback does during an option play. Increasing the learner's capability to identify potential predictors such as opponent or situational tendencies can also help reduce uncertainty. For example, each time Sally's opponent gets into trouble during the game, she hits a shot to Sally's backhand. Knowing this, Sally can better prepare her upcoming shot.

CEREBRAL CHALLENGE #5

An athlete is constantly being beaten when playing person-to-person defense. What will you look at to determine why he/she is unable to stay with his/her assignment? What recommendations might you offer to correct the problem?

Recall Errors Another common cause of movement errors is forgetting. Learners often have difficulty remembering movements and strategies because of the passage of time between practice sessions. Unless it is brought to their attention, some learners will even forget what you just told them to try to incorporate into their next attempt.

At times, learners will also be unable to recall what to do in a given situation. For example, in soccer, young learners are taught to play their positions, but in their excitement for the game, many forget about positioning and follow the ball. Many such instances occur where the learner is capable of performing the correct movement but simply forgets to do it at the appropriate time. Providing reminders and incorporating attention-focusing questioning strategies, such as "What are you going to focus on this time?" are usually sufficient to correct errors due to forgetting.

EXECUTION ERRORS

Sometimes the appropriate response to a situation is selected, but the learner cannot execute that response correctly. For example, a racquetball player might correctly choose a kill shot in a given situation but mishit the ball. This could happen for a number of reasons, including insufficient practice, and/or performing the movement too quickly.

Errors in Neuromuscular Coordination Practitioners must be able to distinguish between what learners can do and what they know (Christina & Corcos, 1988). Often movement errors occur not because of a lack of understanding but because the learner has not yet had enough practice time to establish the proper neuromuscular coordination (Wang & Griffin, 1998). In such cases the resolution of the error will likely result from providing additional opportunities to practice. However, in some cases, the learner does not possess the underlying abilities necessary to develop a high degree of skill proficiency or may lack the physical prerequisites to accomplish the task or a component of the task. Given that one's abilities are genetically determined, additional practice will not be a viable solution. If the problem stems from a physical deficit such as inadequate strength levels or poor range of motion, the deficit must first be addressed. In other words, the learner will have to improve his or her strength levels or range of motion before the correct performance of the skill will be possible.

Problems in neuromuscular coordination will also arise when a learner is trying to replace an established movement pattern with a new one. Throughout this process, negative transfer will occur in that the previously learned pattern will interfere with the acquisition of the new movement. Errors will result not from a lack of understanding or ability but because negative transfer must be overcome. This of course takes time and practice. Negative transfer can also occur between two skills that are similar in nature such as the golf swing and the baseball swing. Coordination errors will occur when an individual who has experience in one tries to resolve the similarities and differences with the other.

Finally, neuromuscular coordination can be compromised when a learner consciously attends to the specifics of a skill normally performed automatically when the learner attends to movement components that are otherwise performed automatically, the normal flow of the movement is interrupted. This can be seen when first-time users of a treadmill are told to walk the way they normally would. Until they become comfortable using the equipment and they are no longer thinking about how they normally walk, changes in gait pattern will be observed.

Speed-Accuracy Tradeoff Performance outcome can also be influenced by the speed-accuracy tradeoff. For example, if the windmill pitch is executed too fast, the pitcher will lose accuracy and have difficulty getting the ball in the strike zone. Similarly, movement patterns will not be performed accurately if patients perform their rehab exercises too quickly. By simply slowing down the speed of the pitch or the execution of the exercise, the error can be remedied.

In cases involving temporal accuracy, however, speeding up the movement can reduce errors. Sally's coach's suggestion to speed up her swing was therefore a good one. However, since increasing her speed did not fix the error, the coach should have continued to explore other potential causes.

Telegraphing In competition, success can be dependent on one's ability to gain an advantage over an opponent. This advantage is achieved by increasing the uncertainty in a situation for the opponent, causing a delay in their response. If an opponent is able to predict what event will occur and when it will occur, this advantage can be lost. The reason that a learner's serve, for example, is always easily returned could be that he or she is somehow revealing his or her intent, thereby allowing the opponent to prepare for it. The learner in this situation must be taught how to conceal his or her intentions when executing the skill.

CEREBRAL CHALLENGE #6

Generate a list of situations where a learner can gain an advantage by concealing their impending movement. Then generate a list of how a learner can inadvertently reveal their intent, allowing the opponent to anticipate the upcoming movement.

SENSORY ERRORS

Some errors are the result of limitations with sensory mechanisms of motor performance. Given the importance of vision and proprioception in both perception and the provision of feedback, interference with their contributions can be detrimental to learning and performance.

Visual Errors According to Knudson and Kluka (1997), movement errors can be made because the visual demands of the sport exceed what is physically possible. For example, learners could fail to see important cues because they were in midblink or because the event occurred too quickly. Shadows can also play havoc with the visual system and affect performance. Furthermore, the adoption of an improper vantage point can obstruct a learner's field of view. Obstructions can also be intentionally set, such as in hockey where one teammate attempts to block the vision of the goalie as another teammate shoots the puck.

Proprioception Errors Poor proprioceptive functioning can also impact performance and increase one's risk of injury. For example, vertigo, a disease that affects one's balance and equilibrium, can have a debilitating effect on a diver or gymnast. Poor proprioception can also cause a cross-country runner to react slowly in making the constant minor adjustments needed to maintain one's balance when running on an uneven surface. Patients with proprioceptive deficits could also lack control when performing everyday tasks. In this instance, alterations can be made to equipment, such as enlarging the handles of kitchen utensils to enhance their "feel" and make them easier to control. Finally, poor proprioception will affect kinesthetic awareness and could limit the learner's development of error detection and correction capabilities.

RESEARCH NOTE

Several researchers have proposed that a relationship exists between the type of footwear worn and gait and balance in the elderly (Sudarsky, 1990; Wasson, Gall, McDonald & Liang, 1990). According to Waked, Robbins and McClaran (1997), this relationship is a function of the shoes' effect on proprioception. Thirteen elderly male volunteers walked along a balance beam (height 3.9 cm; width 7.8 cm; length 9 m) barefoot and in six pairs of shoes that were identical except for their midsole thickness and hardness. Measures included balance failure frequency, foot position error and foot position awareness. Results showed that (1) stability and foot position awareness are related, (2) as midsole thickness increased, so did foot position error and (3) harder midsoles resulted in fewer foot position errors. Based on these results, the researchers concluded that foot position awareness is influenced by footwear midsole thickness and hardness, which subsequently affects stability. Interestingly, the elderly tend to prefer soft, thick running shoes. Stability problems could, the researcher concluded, be the fault of shoe preference.

Should the Error Be Corrected?

Once the nature of an error has been identified, Christina and Corcos (1988) suggest that three questions be considered prior to correcting it. First, is the learner capable of making the correction? The successful performance of the corrected technique will be dependent on whether the learner possesses the necessary underlying abilities. In addition, unless the learner has the physical prerequisites (strength level, range of motion, etc.) and/or intellectual capacity to perform the correction, changing the technique will be unsuccessful.

The second question to consider is how much time is needed for the learner to make the correction. This will obviously be dependent on the type of error being made. Errors that occur because of forgetting, for example, can easily be rectified through reminders. Similarly, parameter changes, such as increasing the speed at which the movement is performed, are relatively easy to implement. However, corrections involving fundamental changes in technique that will affect the motor program will take a great deal of time to learn. Throughout this process the learner will revert back to the cognitive stage of learning, and negative transfer will occur between the previously learned technique and the corrected technique, adversely affecting performance. The higher the negative transfer and the greater the amount of practice needed to not only learn the corrected technique but also integrate it with previously learned components, the longer it will take the learner to advance through the stages of learning (Christina & Corcos, 1988). Remember that timing is everything. If the decision is made to make such a correction two weeks prior to a major competition, the results could be disastrous.

The final question that must be addressed is whether the learner is motivated to make the correction. In some instances, learners will not be convinced that making the correction is the right decision. Also, if the correction involves the development of a new motor program, performance will deteriorate before it gets better and the learner will have to invest a considerable

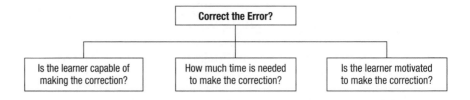

amount of time and practice to see the change through. Are they prepared
and willing to accept such a challenge?

CEREBRAL CHALLENGE #7

1. Generate a list of flaws that occur in your sport of choice, and determine whether
   those flaws would be time-consuming to correct.
2. You are coaching a high school varsity soccer team when you notice that one of
   your athletes has a fundamental flaw in his technique. He is a senior and does
   not have a chance at obtaining a college soccer scholarship. Will you try to fix
   the flaw? What considerations did you make to reach your decision?

A Look Ahead

Once an error has been detected and its cause identified and it is determined
that the error should be corrected, the next step is to provide the learner
with the necessary information to make the correction. Principles and guidelines exist on how to structure feedback in order to convey information that
will not only assist in improving skill proficiency but also reinforce and motivate the learner. These principles and guidelines will be explored in the
next chapter.

Summary

- When diagnosing errors, there is a tendency to focus on the outcome
  of the movement and to provide feedback only about those technical
  aspects of the skill that can be seen, but many errors can be attributed
  to deficits in motor learning.
- Considerations when conducting an observation include identifying
  the purpose and key elements of the skill, determining the optimal
  viewing perspective, deciding how many trials to observe prior to
  making a judgment regarding performance quality and choosing
  whether to videotape the learner(s) performing the skill.
- Errors can occur as a result of organismic, task or environmental
  constraints.

- Comprehension errors occur when a learner doesn't understand the requirements of the skill or what you want them to do.
- Errors in selection can be the result of problems in assessing the environment for task-relevant cues, decision-making or forgetting.
- Execution errors can occur when the learner has not had enough time to establish proper neuromuscular coordination, when movements are performed too quickly or when the learner reveals his or her intent, thereby allowing the opponent to anticipate the learner's movements.
- Errors in decision making and motor control can be the result of difficulties with vision and proprioception.
- Deciding whether an error should be corrected is dependent on the learner's capability to correct it, the learner's motivation and the amount of time available.

Review Questions

1. List and explain three possible limitations to using observations to assess performance.
2. What four considerations should be included when planning an observation?
3. When would you consider using a video camera to capture a learner's performance?
4. Once an error has been detected, a practitioner should always ask what question?
5. When working with children, why might it be useful to modify equipment size? Provide an example to support your answer.
6. What strategies might be useful in assisting a learner who is making a comprehension error? Fully explain your answer.
7. Three categories of errors can be made that are related to response selection. List and explain each.
8. What considerations should be made prior to deciding whether to correct a movement error?

References

Christina, R.W. & Corcos, D.M. (1988) *Coaches guide to teaching sport skills,* Champaign, IL: Human Kinetics Books.

Coaching Association of Canada (1993). *Coaching theory level I: National coaching certification program.* Gloucester, ON: Coaching Association of Canada.

Hall, S.J. (1999). *Basic biomechanics.* St. Louis, MO: WCB/McGraw-Hill.

Knudson, D. & Kluka, D. (1997) The impact of vision training on sport performance. *Journal of Physical Education, Recreation, and Dance, 68*(4), 17–24.

Magill, R.A. (1998). Knowledge is more than we can talk about: Implicit learning in motor skill acquisition, *Research Quarterly for Exercise and Sport, 69*(2), 104–110.

Morris, G.S. (1980). *Elementary physical education: Toward inclusion.* Salt Lake City, UT: Brighton.

Payne, V.G. & Isaacs, L.D. (1999). *Human motor development: A lifespan approach.* San Francisco, CA: Mayfield.

Rink, J.E. (1998). *Teaching physical education for learning.* St. Louis, MO: WCB/McGraw-Hill.

Robbins, S., Waked, E. & McClaran, J. (1995). Proprioception and stability: Foot position sense as a function of age and footwear. *Age and Aging, 24,* 67–72.

Rothstein, A.L. (1986). The perceptual process, vision and motor skills. In L.D. Zaichkowsky & C.Z. Fuchs, (eds.), *The Psychology of Motor Behavior: Development, Control, Learning and Performance.* Ithaca, NY: Mouvement Publications, pp. 191–214.

Sudarsky, L. (1990). Geriatrics: Gait disorders in the elderly. *New England Journal of Medicine, 322,* 1055–1059.

Waked, E., Robbins, S. & McClaran, J. (1997). The effect of footwear midsole hardness and thickness on proprioception and stability in older men. *Journal of Testing and Evaluation, 25*(1), 143–148.

Wang, J. & Griffin, M. (1998). Early correction of movement errors can help student performance. *JOPERD, 69*(4), 50–52.

Wasson, J.H., Gall, V., McDonald, R. & Liang, M.H. (1990). The prescription of assistive devices for the elderly: Practical considerations. *Journal of General Internal Medicine, 5*(1), 46–54.

CHAPTER ELEVEN

Correcting Errors

"How did that look?" asked the dancer. "I think I was able to keep my pelvis in line that time."

Such inquiries are commonplace as learners often turn to practitioners for feedback. That feedback, according to Chen (2001), is the most critical form of guidance that a practitioner can provide a learner. To ensure that feedback is effective in facilitating learning and performance, the type, content, frequency and timing must be carefully considered.

Types of Feedback

Feedback is a general term used to describe the information a learner receives about the performance of a movement or skill. That information can be available from both internal and external sources. **Intrinsic feedback** is response-produced information that is available to learners from their sensory system both during and as a consequence of performance. Examples include seeing the ball after you have released it and the feeling you get when you begin to lose your balance. **Augmented feedback,** on the other hand, is information received from an external source that supplements the learner's own sensory information. Examples of augmented feedback include a practitioner's comments, a videotape replay of the learner executing a skill and the distance, time or score resulting from one's performance that is posted by an official. Generally, this type of augmented information is presented to the learner following the completion of the movement and

intrinsic feedback: Response-produced information that is available to learners from their sensory system both during and as a consequence of performance.

augmented feedback: Information received from an external source that supplements the learner's own sensory information.

terminal feedback:
Augmented feedback that is presented following the completion of the movement.

concurrent feedback:
Feedback provided during the execution of a skill.

knowledge of results (KR):
Feedback that provides learners with information about the outcome of a response and is concerned with the success of the intended action with respect to the goal.

knowledge of performance (KP): Augmented feedback that provides information about the specific characteristics of the performance that led to the outcome.

is therefore labeled **terminal feedback.** There are occasions when augmented feedback can be provided during the execution of a skill. Termed **concurrent feedback,** examples include a coach yelling out split times for an athlete during a race or a therapist reminding a patient to keep a good pelvic tilt during an exercise.

Feedback can be further classified as knowledge of results or knowledge of performance. **Knowledge of results (KR)** is intrinsic or augmented feedback that provides learners with information about the outcome of a response and is concerned with the success of the intended action with respect to the goal. For example, a coach might tell a long jumper that his plant foot was 4 cm over the take-off board, a therapist could tell a patient the outcome of the functional reach test just performed and compare it with previous results or a personal fitness trainer might acknowledge the client's accomplishment of the correct execution of an exercise. In addition, a learner can see where the arrow hit the target or feel whether or not the ball was cleanly hit during the serve. Information regarding the specific characteristics of the performance that led to the outcome is known as **Knowledge of Performance (KP).** Informing a patient that she needs to shift her weight forward more before attempting to stand, telling a student that his elbow recovery in the freestyle should be higher or showing an athlete a video replay of a performance attempt are some examples.

CEREBRAL CHALLENGE #1

Read the following augmented feedback statements and determine whether they are an example of knowledge of results or knowledge of performance:

1. Your foot placement on the beam should be more angled.
2. You have to keep your head down and your eye on the ball.
3. That was great! You stayed on the wobble board for 28 seconds.
4. According to the radar gun, that pitch was 92 mph.
5. When you swing your leg through, try to pull your toes up.
6. You need to let the weight down more slowly.
7. Looking at the pattern of hits; you are shooting high and to the right.

FIGURE 11.1
Types of Feedback

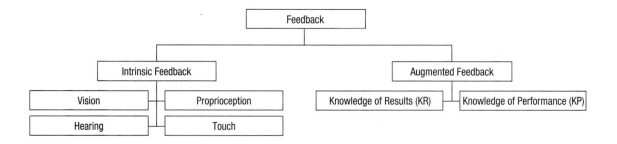

EXPLORATION ACTIVITY 11.1 Guidance properties of KR

EQUIPMENT

5 Paper clips
Partner
Blindfold
Pencil
Diagram below

PROCEDURE

One person, who is blindfolded, will attempt to pin the tail (paper clip) on the donkey. After each attempt, the partner will remove the paper clip and replace it with a pencil mark signifying where the tip of the paper clip had been placed. This process will continue for five trials. For the next five trials, the same blindfolded individual will be given KR that specifies which ring the paper clip had been placed into and whether it was on the left or right half of the vertical line drawn through the bull's-eye. As before, but using a different symbol, the partner will replace the paper clip with a pencil mark signifying where the tip of the paper clip had been placed. Following the completion of all 10 trials, the individual attempting to pin the tail on the donkey can remove the blindfold and look at the results.

QUESTIONS

1. What were the results of the two KR conditions (no KR vs. KR)?
2. Reflect on your thoughts during the two conditions. Were there any differences?
3. Under what conditions, in general, do you think it would be important to provide the learner with KR? Do any conditions exist where the provision of KR may not be necessary?

Functions of Augmented Feedback

Augmented feedback serves three major functions. First, it provides information about the correction of performance errors. This information could include a description of the correct and/or incorrect aspects of the performance, an explanation as to why an error occurred, the prescription of how to fix the error or informing the learner of the outcome of the performance (Christina & Corcos, 1988). This information helps guide the learner to modify subsequent movement attempts in an effort to enhance skill acquisition and performance.

Augmented feedback can also play a motivational role in the learning process. When learners receive information regarding their performance, they can compare it with preestablished goals to determine their progress. If that comparison indicates improvement, the learner will be encouraged to continue making an effort to achieve his or her goals. Statements such as "You can do it!" or "Hang in there, you are on the right track" can also help learners work through tough practices, difficult challenges and performance plateaus.

The third function that augmented feedback can serve is to reinforce the learner. When used in this manner, augmented feedback increases the probability of a response reoccurring on future attempts under similar circumstances. Statements and gestures that praise learners, such as "Great effort," "Way to get after the ball" or giving a learner a high five following a response can positively reinforce and therefore strengthen a behavior. Similarly, the satisfaction derived from an acknowledgment that the learner has successfully executed a response may instill the desire to replicate that

EXPLORATION ACTIVITY 11.2 Functions of Augmented Feedback

Observe a teacher, coach, therapist or yourself teaching a skill. Using the tally sheet below, identify whether each feedback statement given provided information for the correction of performance errors, was used to motivate the learner or was used to reinforce a behavior.

Information for Correction	Motivation	Reinforcement

1. What category received the most tally marks? The least?
2. Speculate as to why you obtained these results.
3. Speculate as to how effective the pattern revealed will be for skill acquisition.
4. What other observations are noteworthy?

action. Eliminating something negative can also reinforce behaviors. If you have learned how to drive a car with manual transmission, you may have experienced what's known as negative reinforcement. Until new drivers learn to coordinate their movements when shifting gears, the car will jump or stall. Because the new driver wants to avoid this embarrassing response, negative reinforcement serves to strengthen the desired coordinated movement.

Sources of Augmented Feedback

Perhaps the most common form of providing a learner with augmented feedback is through verbal descriptions and demonstrations. However, a number of additional sources exist through which feedback can be delivered.

AUDITORY FEEDBACK

In many instances, augmented feedback can take on an auditory form. For instance, consequent sounds that result from skill execution can assist learners in evaluating their performance. Information about rhythm can also be conveyed through clapping. In addition, auditory feedback exists in the form of buzzers and warning signals, such as the ground-proximity warning system found in aircraft.

VISUAL DISPLAYS

Performance feedback can also be visually displayed in a number of fashions. Game statistics can be charted on graphs, shot patterns revealed by inspecting targets and frame-by-frame photographs can display important information about the execution of numerous skill components. Computer graphics have also become a popular means of offering feedback. Children

FIGURE 11.2
Stick figure sequence and corresponding graph of ball velocity for the soccer throw-in.

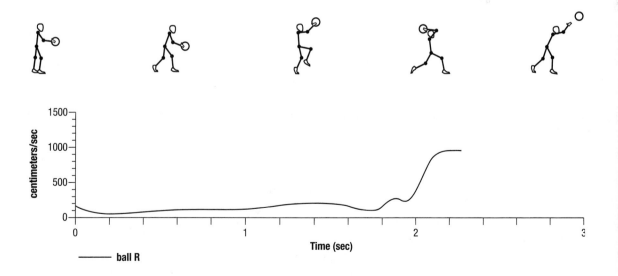

ball R

in some physical education classes are now tracking their progress using handheld pocket PCs to examine data obtained from heart rate monitors. Advances in technology have also made computer-based skill analysis tools accessible. These programs create stick figure representations of a movement and can calculate and graphically depict numerous kinematic variables, including time, displacement, velocity and angles. While studies exploring the effectiveness of kinematic feedback are limited, the results to date have found its impact to be positive (Swinnen, Walter, Lee & Serrien, 1993; Wood, Gallagher, Martino & Ross, 1992). Recent developments in real-time kinematic feedback systems (e.g., Hawkins, 2000) should provide further insights about the effectiveness of this form of information on skill enhancement.

Video Replay Another instructional resource that is receiving widespread use by movement practitioners is videotape. While videotape can capture performance attempts and store those images for repeated viewing, for it to be effective, learners have to understand what to look for and how to interpret what they are seeing. This capability is dependent on both the skill level of the learner and whether the replay is accompanied by cueing. In an extensive review of studies exploring the effectiveness of using videotape as a delivery mechanism of feedback, Rothstein and Arnold (1976) found that when learners were provided with cues to help direct their attention to the most important aspects of the performance replay, they were more able to utilize video as a source of information to facilitate skill acquisition, especially in the case of beginning learners. Without the benefit of attention-directing cues, the novice likely becomes overwhelmed by the magnitude of information presented (Newell & Walter, 1981). The benefits of including augmented cues with videotape feedback (VTFB) are not limited to novices. Recently a study of highly skilled gymnasts illustrated the value of augmented cues with VTFB extending previous findings into the realm of skilled performers (Menickelli, Landin, Grisham & Hebert, 2000).

Not only have the provision of cues that direct a learner's attention to specific technical aspects of the movement prior to the learner's viewing of the videotape replay been shown to be effective but so too have those that present information about the nature of the correction to be made. In a study by Kernodle and Carlton (1992), attention-focusing cues (e.g., "Focus on the left arm at the point of ball release") and cues that suggested what correction should be made (e.g., "Extend the left arm at ball release") were superior to the provision of KR (verbal information regarding outcome) and KP (videotape replay only) for the learning of the overhand throw. In addition, those participants receiving the information about the nature of the correction to be made displayed more advanced throwing technique as compared with the three other conditions.

Videotape Feedback Learning Stages Hebert, Landin and Menickelli (1998) identified four distinct stages through which athletes progressed when introduced to videotape. Darden (1999) later described these stages as shock, error detection, error correction and independence and suggested a number of practical tips based on the characteristics of each.

When learners are initially introduced to viewing themselves on videotape, they go through a period where they are preoccupied with their appearance. Before they can begin to use videotape feedback as an instructional tool, then, they must first get used to seeing themselves on tape. Until then, pointing out technical aspects of their performance will be futile.

In the error detection stage, learners begin to critically observe their practice attempts and identify specific performance errors. The provision of attention-focusing cues regarding the environment or aspects of the movement itself is now important to facilitate the development of error detection capabilities. As indicated earlier, learners are not always able to distinguish between task-relevant and task-irrelevant information. For example, if a projectile is involved in the performance, there is a natural tendency for learners to track it to see where it goes rather than looking at their technique. Learners should therefore be reminded to attend to the movement pattern in addition to the performance outcome (Darden, 1999).

With practice and guidance, learners will begin to make associations between specific technical elements and outcome and will progress to the third stage. It is here that learners can not only identify errors but also begin to understand why an error occurred. This, in turn, forms the basis for decision making with respect to the development of error correction strategies. Enhancing a learner's problem-solving skills should therefore be emphasized during this stage.

In the final stage, little, if any, dependency on teacher feedback remains. Learners can consistently identify and correct errors and should be encouraged to continue doing so. Self-guidance is therefore the focus of the final stage, independence.

EQUIPMENT AND DRILLS

Drills and equipment can also be a source of performance feedback. For example, the extended club drill is designed to provide learners with feedback as to whether their hands were too active during a chip shot in golf (Owens & Bunker, 1995). A second club is introduced to the learner's normal setup, creating an extension that projects above the waist. If, during the swing, the hands are too active, the shaft of the second club will touch the learner in the side.

Augmented feedback can also come from devices that monitor performance, such as a radar gun, or from equipment being used to perform the skill. For example, playing catch with a raw egg can be a fun but potentially messy strategy to teach the concept of absorption when catching. The egg, whether broken or intact following an attempt, provides augmented information to the learner regarding the performance. Many

The extended club drill is designed to provide learners with performance feedback.

teaching aids in golf, such as the hinged golf club, are also designed to provide feedback. If a flaw in swing mechanics occurs, the hinge will break, folding the club. Much of the aerobic fitness equipment found in health clubs is also designed to provide the learner with both concurrent and terminal feedback as to how many steps have been climbed, calories burned and distance rowed, ridden or run. Similarly, heart rate monitors and cycle computers have become a popular informational source. Finally, sophisticated flight simulators can capture measurements such as heartbeat, respiration rate, blood pressure, EEG, eye point of gaze, pupil size and blink rate. Following the completion of the flight, these physiological variables can be correlated with recordings such as stick input and aircraft response using specialized computer software to more fully inform the pilot of his or her performance.

CEREBRAL CHALLENGE #2

Generate a list of drills or equipment that is designed to provide learners with feedback in a sport or movement of your choice.

BIOFEEDBACK

biofeedback: Form of augmented feedback that measures physiological information that is concurrently available to a learner through some form of instrumentation.

When physiological measures are concurrently fed back to a learner through some form of instrumentation, the augmented sensory information provided is known as **biofeedback.** Shown to be effective in shaping behavior, biofeedback allows for the constant monitoring of physiological conditions during a response. For example, marathon runners might take their pulse during a workout or use a heart rate monitor to determine their level of intensity.

Using this information, learners are trained to alter and control their movements. For example, using a portable electrodermal response (EDR) feedback device, Peper & Schmid (1983-1984) were able to illustrate to the athletes of the United States Rhythmic Gymnastics Team how thoughts and feelings affected their physiological state. This information was then used to successfully help each athlete not only identify and stop negative thoughts and feelings but to enable them to restructure their self-talk, making it more positive.

Biofeedback is also particularly useful in teaching rehabilitation patients to regulate their movements. Using a computer-assisted feedback system that provided instantaneous feedback about muscle activity or joint angular excursions, Colborne, Olney, and Griffin (1993) examined the use of biofeedback for retraining gait in stroke patients. Muscle activity targets and joint motion along with cues regarding their specific timing during the gait cycle were provided throughout the training period. Based on their findings, the authors concluded that computer-assisted feedback is an effective tool for retraining gait in stroke patients.

Content of Augmented Feedback

To ensure that feedback is useful, regardless of the source used for its delivery, its content must be considered. Telling a learner that his or her shot missed when the outcome is clearly visible, for example, would be redundant. To best assist the learner then, what information should be depicted in a feedback statement? Should practitioners tell the learner what was done correctly, or should they focus on performance errors? Should performance errors be described, or would an explanation of how to modify the movement be more beneficial? How precise should the given information be?

ERROR VS. CORRECT FEEDBACK

One decision regarding the content of the augmented feedback involves whether to focus on the performance errors made or to highlight what was done correctly. To make this decision, the practitioner should consider the goal of giving the information (Magill, 2001). Recall that augmented feedback can serve three major functions. It can be used to motivate, reinforce or provide information regarding the correctness of a response in order to modify future attempts. When a learner is given information regarding the performance error made, he or she will use that feedback to modify future performances. Consequently, if the goal of the feedback is to facilitate skill acquisition, the practitioner should provide error-based information. If, however, the goal is to confirm the learner's progress and/or encourage continued persistence, practitioners should focus on the learner's achievements and highlight the correct features of the performance attempt. Magill suggests that a combination of both would be optimal. This recommendation is further supported by Fischman and Oxendine (2001), who advocate the use of a "sandwich" approach, where error correction information is sandwiched in between reinforcement and motivation. Using this strategy, the learner is first given information to reinforce correct performance. The next step would be to provide the learner with information to facilitate error correction. The sandwich is finalized by offering encouragement in order to motivate the learner to incorporate the error correction recommendations. An example of the sandwich approach using the dancer in the opening story might be, "Good! Your pelvis was in line that time. On this next trial, try to maintain your outward rotation while still concentrating on pelvic alignment. When you can combine both the pelvic alignment and outward rotation, your stability will improve and it will be easier to turn. You almost have it."

 CEREBRAL CHALLENGE #3

Rewrite the following statement incorporating the sandwich technique:
"No, no, no. You are doing it all wrong. When you hit the ball you have to be facing your target. How many times do I have to tell you?"

DESCRIPTIVE VS. PRESCRIPTIVE FEEDBACK

descriptive feedback:
Augmented feedback that describes the nature of the performance error made.

prescriptive feedback:
Augmented feedback that offers a suggestion as to how to correct an identified problem.

Knowledge of performance can be provided to a learner in two forms. The first, **descriptive feedback,** simply describes the nature of the performance error made. If a learner's outside-of-the-foot pass in soccer is inaccurate due to excessive spin, for example, the practitioner could state "You are putting too much spin on the ball." **Prescriptive feedback,** on the other hand, offers a suggestion as to how to correct the problem identified, for example, "You need to contact the ball just left or right of its midline to eliminate unwanted spin."

The use of either descriptive or prescriptive feedback is dependent on the skill level of the learner. Descriptive statements can only be effective if the learner understands their implications. Recall that novice learners are trying to develop an understanding of the movement's requirements. In addition, they may lack the capability to associate the cause of an error with the adjustments required to correct it. This implies that while descriptive feedback may be adequate for learners who have obtained a certain degree of skill proficiency, beginners would benefit more from prescriptive statements. Furthermore, a combination of both descriptive and prescriptive feedback, such as "You initiated your movement too soon. Wait until you see the pitcher's back heel lift off of the ground" could assist learners in formulating associations between errors and their corrections.

CEREBRAL CHALLENGE #4

Read the following augmented feedback statements, and determine whether they are an example of descriptive or prescriptive feedback:

1. Your plant foot is landing too far in front of you.
2. When you release the ball, continue to flex your wrist so that your fingers are pointing to the ground.
3. Pull your arms in faster.
4. The ball is behind your head when you contact it.
5. The heel-to-toe motion should be fluid.
6. Your knee is not reaching full extension.
7. Shift your weight forward before you take a step.
8. The racquet head angle is too low at contact.

PRECISION OF AUGMENTED FEEDBACK

Varying degrees of precision can be used to convey information to a learner. "Your angle of attack was only 30 degrees" and "The tip of the javelin was too low at release" are both legitimate feedback statements describing the same error. The question is whether the degree of precision used impacts a learner's capability to effectively utilize the information. Again, the skill level of the learner must be considered. During the early stages of learning, as the learner is trying to develop an understanding of the movement's requirements, the level of precision can be quite general and still be effective (Magill & Wood, 1986). Later in the learning process, when skills are being refined, more precise information becomes useful provided that the learner understands its meaning.

Augmented Feedback Frequency

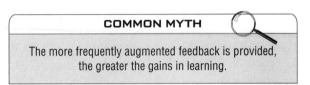

COMMON MYTH

The more frequently augmented feedback is provided, the greater the gains in learning.

Historically, it was thought that the more frequently augmented feedback was provided to a learner, the greater the gains in learning (Thorndike, 1931). According to this notion, then, an optimal learning environment would be one where the practitioner provided the learner with augmented feedback following each performance attempt. Contemporary research disputes this claim, however, and, as a result, has changed how practitioners should approach the question of how often augmented feedback should be given.

THE GUIDANCE HYPOTHESIS

According to the guidance hypothesis, although augmented feedback can guide a learner in the correction of performance errors, the provision of too much feedback can have a detrimental effect on skill acquisition (Salmoni, Schmidt & Walter, 1984; Schmidt, Young, Swinnen & Shapiro, 1989; Winstein, Pohl & Lewthwaite, 1994; Winstein & Schmidt, 1990). This detrimental effect is believed to be the result of the learner's development of an over-dependence on external feedback. When a learner receives augmented feedback at a high frequency, such as after every attempt, he or she begins to rely on its provision and abandons the processing of other important sources of information such as one's own internal feedback. Rather than being actively engaged in the learning process, then, it is thought that the learner instead tends to become a passive listener and fails to develop valuable problem-solving skills needed for future occasions when augmented feedback is no longer available. In contrast, the provision of augmented feedback at a lower relative frequency encourages learners to be reflective thinkers and enhances learning. The question yet to be resolved is exactly how much augmented feedback should be given to optimize learning. While research continues to investigate this question, several reduced-frequency feedback strategies exist that practitioners may consider.

Faded Feedback One reduced-frequency feedback strategy that has been shown to be effective is that of faded feedback (Winstein & Schmidt, 1990). In

faded feedback: Augmented feedback technique where learners are provided with a high frequency of feedback initially that is then gradually reduced.

faded feedback, learners are provided with a high frequency of feedback in the initial stages of learning to facilitate their understanding and acquisition of the basic movement pattern. Once a basic proficiency level has been achieved, however, augmented feedback should be gradually withdrawn. The actual schedule for reducing feedback frequency will be dependent on each individual learner's progress.

Bandwidth Feedback Another technique that fosters important information processing activities is bandwidth feedback (Sherwood, 1988; Smith, Taylor, & Withers, 1997). It too is based on the concept of providing more information during the early stages of learning and gradually reducing feedback as the learner improves. In **bandwidth feedback,** a range of "correctness" is predetermined, and augmented feedback is only provided on those trials where an error falls outside of this range. In the volleyball serve, for example, a range of correctness for the toss could be defined as between the shoulder and 1 foot in front of the shoulder. If the learner's toss falls within this range, no feedback would be provided, indicating that the toss was acceptable. If, however, the toss falls outside of the range, by being either too far backwards or forwards, the practitioner would then communicate information about its correction to the learner. The benefit of this approach is that feedback is systematically reduced according to the learner's level of proficiency. In addition, the learner receives positive reinforcement on those trials that do fall within the bandwidth, which will serve to strengthen the behavior that led to the outcome.

bandwidth feedback: Augmented feedback strategy where feedback is only provided on those trials where an error falls outside of a predetermined range of correctness.

Summary Feedback Summary feedback is an additional option that can be employed to avert the potentially harmful effects of augmented feedback on learning. In **summary feedback** the practitioner provides the learner with a summary of their performance following the completion of a certain number of trials. For example, in show jumping, a horse and rider have to negotiate numerous barriers. In this case, augmented feedback would be withheld until the series of jumps are completed. The learner would then be given specific feedback about each jump in the series. Watching a video replay of one's performance attempts following a given number of trials would be another example.

summary feedback: Augmented feedback that provides the learner with a summary of their performance following the completion of a certain number of trials.

Given the positive effect of summary feedback on learning (Schmidt, Young, Swinnen & Shapiro, 1989), a question of interest is the optimal number of performance trials that should be summarized. While research remains inconclusive, the answer may be a function of task complexity (Schmidt, Lange & Young, 1990; Swinnen, 1996).

Average Feedback Similar to summary feedback, and also found to be effective, is the technique of average feedback. In **average feedback,** a learner will receive augmented feedback following the completion of a certain number of attempts. This feedback will be in response to the average performance error that occurred in the series.

average feedback: Augmented feedback provided following the completion of a certain number of attempts regarding the average performance error.

For practitioners, average feedback offers several advantages over summary feedback. First, it may be easier to utilize. Second, it forces the practitioner to better focus the analysis. Finally, it reduces the possibility of overwhelming the learning with too much information.

CEREBRAL CHALLENGE #5

In Exploration Activity #1, when the performer was shown the pencil marks for each trial following the completion of all ten trials, he or she was given summary feedback. How would you redesign the experiment to provide bandwidth feedback? Average feedback?

Learner-Regulated Feedback An augmented feedback technique that has recently received attention is **learner-regulated feedback.** This strategy allows learners to control when augmented feedback is given. Rather than the practitioner determining when to offer feedback, learners are given augmented feedback only when they request it. In addition to both reducing and individualizing feedback frequency, this strategy actively involves the learner in the learning process (Chen & Singer, 1992; Janelle, Kim & Singer, 1995). By giving the learner the autonomy to control when and how much feedback they receive, retention of crucial information is enhanced (Chen, 2001, Hardy & Nelson, 1988; Holt, 1982; Zimmerman, 1989). This notion has been supported by the findings of numerous studies that learner-regulated feedback results in better retention than that achieved with traditional practitioner-controlled feedback (Chen, Kaufman & Chung, 2001; Chen & Singer, 1992; Janelle, Barba, Frehlich, Tennant & Cauraugh, 1997; Janelle et al., 1995).

Timing of Augmented Feedback

The presentation of augmented feedback can be broken down into three temporal intervals. The time from the end of one performance attempt to the beginning of the next performance attempt is known as the **inter-trial interval.** That interval is further broken down into the **feedback-delay interval,** the time from one performance attempt until augmented feedback is provided, and the **post-feedback interval,** the time from the provision of augmented feedback to the initiation of the next performance attempt. The latter two intervals will be examined in the following section, as both their length and the

learner-regulated feedback: Augmented feedback provided to a learner when he or she requests it.

inter-trial interval: Time from the end of one performance attempt to the beginning of the next performance attempt.

feedback-delay interval: Time interval from the completion of a performance attempt until the provision of augmented feedback.

post-feedback interval: Time interval from the provision of augmented feedback to the initiation of the next performance attempt.

Performance - - - - Feedback-Delay - - - - Provision of - - - - Post-Feedback - - - - Performance
Attempt #1   Interval   Augmented Feedback   Interval   Attempt #2

|- **Inter-response Interval** -|

FIGURE 11.3
Temporal model of augmented feedback presentation

nature of the activity that takes place within them influence performance-related feedback's effectiveness.

FEEDBACK-DELAY INTERVAL

COMMON MYTH

Augmented feedback should be delivered to learners immediately following their performance attempt.

One misconception regarding the timing of augmented feedback is that it should be provided to the learner immediately following a performance attempt. On the contrary, research has demonstrated that the instantaneous provision of augmented feedback has a negative impact on learning (Swinnen, Schmidt, Nicholson & Shapiro, 1990). By providing augmented feedback too soon, it is thought that learners are prevented from evaluating response-produced intrinsic feedback, impeding their development of error detection and correction mechanisms. How long should practitioners wait before giving feedback? It appears that learners simply need sufficient time, generally a few seconds, to process their own movement-produced feedback. Furthermore, delaying the provision of feedback for longer periods of time does not appear to adversely affect learning, although it is possible that an extended delay may cause the learner to forget the details of the practice attempt.

In addition to giving learners the opportunity to process intrinsic feedback, prompting learners to estimate their own performance errors before providing them with augmented feedback has also led to superior learning (Liu & Wrisberg, 1997; Swinnen et al., 1990). Chen (2001) recommends that practitioners assist learners in developing their self-evaluation skills by asking them questions during practice to provoke reflective thinking regarding practice attempts. A practitioner might, for example, ask a learner, "How was your follow-through that time?" or, "Why do you think the ball went off to the left?" Or the dancer in the opening of the chapter who indicated that she thought her pelvis was in line might be prompted further to explain how she came to that conclusion.

It should be noted that initially, learners might have difficulty responding to such questioning. Self-evaluation is a capability that must be developed. Practitioners can guide learners through the process by asking more specific follow-up questions that will lead learners to the answer. For example, a secondary question in the above follow-through example might be, "Do you think your arm came straight down, or did it cross your body?" Eventually, practitioner-learner interactions will become an exchange of ideas rather than the one-way passage of information, and the learner will develop the necessary problem-solving capabilities needed for further skill acquisition and performance enhancement.

RESEARCH NOTE

In a study by Liu and Wrisberg (1997) KR delay and subjective estimation of movement form were manipulated to examine their effects on throwing accuracy. Forty-eight participants were randomly assigned to one of four conditions: (1) immediate KR, (2) delayed KR, (3) immediate KR + subjective estimation of movement form and (4) delayed KR + subjective estimation of movement form. Their task was to throw a ball at a target placed on the floor as accurately as possible using their nondominant hand and in the absence of vision. Following the release of the ball, those participants in the immediate KR condition were permitted to track their ball and see it land on the target. Those in the KR-delay condition were only shown where their ball had landed on the target following a 13-second delay interval. In addition, participants in the subjective estimation groups were asked to rate their form in terms of force, release angle and trajectory either 2 seconds following the ball's landing (immediate KR + subjective estimation) or during the 13-second delay interval (delayed KR + subjective estimation). Results indicated that while the immediate KR groups displayed higher accuracy scores during practice, those in the delayed KR conditions were significantly more accurate during retention. Moreover, the performance accuracy of the subjective estimation groups was significantly higher during the no-KR retention tests. These findings support both the recommendation to delay the provision of feedback in order to give the learner time to process intrinsic feedback as well as the use of subjective error estimation to enhance learning and performance.

POST-FEEDBACK INTERVAL

During the post-feedback interval, the learner synthesizes the information received both intrinsically and extrinsically (via augmented feedback) and must formulate a new movement plan. Sufficient time must again be available to the learner to process and plan. Given that these operations are dependent on the complexity of the skill, the length of this interval will vary accordingly.

In some instances, learners may need to be reminded to engage in processing activities. By asking the learner what he or she is thinking about with respect to the upcoming attempt, not only can practitioners encourage active processing for movement modification but they can also check for understanding. Practitioners can further ensure understanding by observing the degree to which augmented information was able to assist the learner in modifying the subsequent response.

CEREBRAL CHALLENGE #6

Generate a list of guidelines for giving augmented feedback based on the information provided in this chapter.

A Look Ahead

Through augmented feedback, practitioners can guide, motivate and reinforce learners in an effort to enhance skill acquisition and performance. The effectiveness of the feedback provided is dependent on a number of variables, including type, source, content, frequency and timing.

This book has introduced you, the human movement practitioner, to the processes that govern movement acquisition and control. By understanding these concepts, principles and their applications, you can look ahead to the challenges you will face with the confidence that you will be able to make effective instructional decisions that will maximize your patients', students' or athletes' potential.

Summary

- Feedback is a general term used to describe the information a learner receives about the performance of a movement or skill.
- Feedback can be intrinsic, coming from one's own sensory system, or augmented in that it is supplied from an external source.
- Knowledge of results provides information regarding the outcome of a response and is concerned with the success of the intended action with respect to the goal.
- Knowledge of performance provides information regarding the specific characteristics of the performance that led to the outcome.
- Augmented feedback can function to provide information for error correction, motivation and reinforcement.
- Sources of augmented feedback include auditory feedback, visual displays, video replay, equipment and drills and biofeedback.
- In the sandwich approach, the learner is first given information to reinforce correct performance, then information regarding error correction, and then encouragement to motivate the learner to incorporate the recommendations provided.
- The provision of both descriptive and prescriptive information can assist learners in formulating associations between errors and their corrections.
- Learners need a high frequency of feedback in the initial stage of learning, but the frequency should be reduced as the learner becomes more proficient, or an overdependence on augmented information may occur.
- Methods used to reduce feedback frequency include faded, bandwidth, summary, average and learner-regulated feedback.
- Learners need time to process intrinsic feedback as well as formulate a new movement plan for the subsequent attempt.
- Prompting learners to estimate their own performance errors before providing them with augmented feedback results in superior learning.

1. Define the following terms: (a) feedback, (b) intrinsic feedback, (c) augmented feedback, (d) knowledge of results and (e) knowledge of performance.
2. Compare and contrast terminal and concurrent feedback.
3. Develop a flowchart to represent all of the categories and subcategories of feedback.
4. Compare and contrast positive and negative reinforcement.
5. What three functions can feedback serve?
6. Name the four stages of videotape feedback learning and the characteristics of each.
7. Compare and contrast (a) error-based and corrective feedback and (b) descriptive and prescriptive feedback.
8. What is the significance of the guidance hypothesis?
9. What strategies can be used to reduce the augmented feedback frequency?
10. The inter-response interval can be broken down into two additional intervals. Name and define each.

References

Chen, D.D. (2001). Trends in augmented feedback research and tips for the practitioner. *JOPERD*, 72(1), 32–36.

Chen, D.D, Kaufman, D. & Chung, M.W. (2001). Emergent patterns of feedback strategies in performing a closed motor skill. *Perceptual and Motor Skills, 93*, 197–204.

Chen, D.D. & Singer, R.N. (1992). Self-regulation and cognitive strategies in sport participation. *International Journal of Sport Psychology, 23*, 277–300.

Christina, R.W. & Corcos, D.M. (1988) *Coaches guide to teaching sport skills.* Champaign, IL: Human Kinetics Books.

Colborne G.R., Olney S.J. & Griffin, M.P. (1993). Feedback of ankle joint angle and soleus electromyography in the rehabilitation of hemiplegic gait. *Archives of Physical Medicine and Rehabilitation*, 74(10):1100–1106.

Darden, G.F. (1999). Videotape feedback for student learning and performance: A learning stages approach. *JOPERD*, 70(9), 40–45, 62.

Fischman, M.G. & Oxendine, J.B. (2001). Motor skill learning for effective coaching and performance. In J.M. Williams (ed.), *Applied Sport Psychology; Personal Growth to Peak Performance*. Mountain View, CA: Mayfield, pp. 13–28.

Hardy, L. & Nelson, D. (1988). Self-regulation training in sport and work. *Ergonomics, 31*, 1573–1583.

Hawkins, D. (2000). A new instrumentation system for training rowers. *Journal of Biomechanics*, 33(2), 241–246.

Hebert, E., Landin, D. & Menickelli, J. (1998). Videotape feedback: What learners see and how they use it. *Journal of Sport Pedagogy, 4*, 12–28.

Holt, J. (1982). *How children fail*. New York: Delacorte Press.

Janelle, C.M., Barba, D.A., Frehlich, S.G., Tennant, L.K. & Cauraugh, J.H. (1997). Maximizing performance feedback effectiveness through videotape replay and a self-controlled learning environment. *Research Quarterly for Exercise and Sport, 68*(4), 269–279.

Janelle, C. M., Kim, J. & Singer, R.N. (1995). Subject-controlled feedback and learning of a closed motor skill. *Perceptual and Motor Skills, 81*, 627–634.

Kernodle, M.W. & Carlton, L.G. (1992). Information feedback and the learning of multiple-degree-of-freedom activities, *Journal of Motor Behavior, 24*(2), 187–196.

Liu, J. & Wrisberg, C.A. (1997). The effect of knowledge of results delay and the subjective estimation of movement form on the acquisition and retention of a motor skill. *Research Quarterly for Exercise and Sport, 68*(2), 145–151.

Magill, R.A. (2001). *Motor learning: Concepts and applications*. St. Louis, MO: McGraw-Hill.

Magill, R.A. & Wood, C.A. (1986). Knowledge of results precision as a learning variable in motor skill acquisition. *Research Quarterly for Exercise and Sport, 57*(2), 170–173.

Menickelli, J., Landin, D., Grisham, W. & Hebert, E.P. (2000). The effects of videotape feedback with augmented cues on the performances and thought processes of skilled gymnasts. *Journal of Sport Pedagogy, 6*(1), 56–72.

Newell, K.M. & Walter, C.B. (1981). Kinematic and kinetic parameters as information feedback in motor skill acquisition. *Journal of Human Movement Studies, 7*, 235–254.

Owens, D. & Bunker, L. (1995). *Golf: Steps to success*. (2nd edition). Champaign, IL: Human Kinetics.

Peper, E. and Schmid, A.B. (1983/84). The use of electrodermal biofeedback for peak performance training. *Somatics IV* (3), 16–18.

Rothstein, A.L. & Arnold, R.K. (1976). Bridging the gap: Application of research on videotape feedback and bowling. *Motor Skills: Theory into Practice, 1*, 36–61.

Salmoni, A.W., Schmidt, R.A. & Walter, C.B. (1984). Knowledge of results and motor learning: A review and critical appraisal. *Psychological Bulletin, 95*, 355–386.

Schmidt, R.A., Lange, C.A. & Young, D.E. (1990). Optimizing summary knowledge of results for skill learning. *Human Movement Science, 9*, 325–348.

Schmidt, R.A., Young, D.E., Swinnen, S. & Shapiro, D.E. (1989). Summary knowledge of results for skill acquisition: Support for the guidance hypothesis. *Journal of Experimental Psychology: Learning, Memory and Cognition, 15,* 352–359.

Sherwood, D. E. (1988). Effect of bandwidth knowledge of results on movement consistency. *Perceptual and Motor Skills, 66,* 535–542.

Smith, P. Taylor, S., & Withers, K. (1997). Applying bandwidth feedback scheduling to a golf shot. *Research Quarterly for Exercise and Sport, 68(3),* 215–221.

Swinnen, P S. (1996). Information feedback for motor skill learning: A review. In H.N. Zelaznik (ed.), *Advances in Motor Learning and Control.* Champaign, IL: Human Kinetics, pp.37–66.

Swinnen, P.S., Schmidt, R.A., Nicholson, D.E. & Shapiro, D.C. (1990). Information feedback for skill acquisition: Instantaneous knowledge of results degrades learning. *Journal of Experimental Psychology: Learning, Memory and Cognition, 16,* 706–716.

Swinnen, P.S., Walter, C.B., Lee, T.D. & Serrien, D.J. (1993). Acquiring bimanual skills: Contrasting forms of information feedback for interlimb decoupling. *Journal of Experimental Psychology: Learning, Memory and Cognition, 19,* 1321–1344.

Thorndike, E.L. (1931). *Human learning.* New York: Century.

Winstein, C.J., Pohl, P.S. & Lewthwaite, R. (1994). Effects of physical guidance and knowledge of results on motor learning: Support for the guidance hypothesis. *Research Quarterly for Exercise and Sport, 65,* 316–323.

Winstein, C.J. & Schmidt, R.A. (1990). Reduced frequency of knowledge of results enhances motor skill learning. *Journal of Experimental Psychology: Learning, Memory and Cognition, 16,* 677–691.

Wood, C.A., Gallagher, J.D., Martino, P.V. & Ross, M. (1992). Alternate forms of knowledge of results: Interaction of augmented feedback on modality in learning. *Journal of Human Movement Studies, 22,* 213–230.

Zimmerman, B.J. (1989). Models of self-regulated learning and academic achievement. In B.J. Zimmerman & D.H. Schunk (eds.), *Self-Regulated Learning and Academic Achievement Theory, Research and Practice: Progress in Cognitive Development Research.* New York: Springer-Verlag, pp. 1–26.

Your effectiveness as a practitioner will be dependent on your ability to integrate multiple motor learning and control concepts and principles. Two scenarios and corresponding questions follow that have been designed to provide you with the opportunity to apply what you have learned in this book to the school physical education setting and to the clinical setting. Remember to consider the learner, the task and the environment in which the task is performed in all cases.

Physical Education Teaching Scenario

As part of your teacher preparation, you must complete several observations of a physical education class at the local junior high school. You decide to observe an 8th grade coeducational class that has just started a unit on soccer. There are 30 students in the class, including Chris and Morgan. Chris's movement experiences have been limited and predominantly acquired through physical education. Morgan, on the other hand, is very active and has played baseball, softball and basketball and runs track.

1. During your first observation, the teacher introduces dribbling. Following the *initial* description and demonstration, the students are paired up for a drill. In this drill, one student is to dribble the ball to the other side of the gym while his or her partner tries to take the ball away. The goal of the drill, the teacher emphasizes, is to dribble without looking at the ball. As the drill progresses the teacher notices that everyone is either losing the ball or totally focusing their vision on it. (a) Explain why this is not an effective drill. (b) Suggest an alternative drill that would be more effective for this group of learners, and provide a comprehensive rationale for your suggestion.
2. When you arrive for your observation the following day you notice that there are not enough soccer balls for everyone. Apparently the soccer coach borrowed some of the balls and had not yet returned them. In order for everyone to have a ball for the lesson on passing, the teacher has decided to replace the missing soccer balls with playground balls that are similar in size. (a) Assess the potential advantages and disadvantages of this strategy. (b) Based on your assessment, would you agree or disagree with using the playground balls in this situation? Justify your answer.
3. The next skill to be introduced to the class is trapping. (a) Which method, part or whole, would you use if you were going to teach this skill? (b) What factors did you take into consideration when making your decision? Fully explain your answer.

4. When teaching trapping, the teacher makes a reference to cushioning or absorbing the ball like you would when fielding a softball or baseball. (a) What strategy is the teacher using to try to facilitate learners' understanding of the concept? (b) Will this cue be equally effective for both Chris and Morgan? Why or why not?

5. (a) Which method, segmentation or simplification, would you suggest using to teach learners the skill of heading a soccer ball? Defend your selection. (b) Outline how you would design the learning experience using the method that you selected.

6. (a) Design a drill that incorporates both random practice and variable practice to assist your learners in refining their dribbling, trapping and passing skills. (b) Would incorporating random and variable practice be equally effective for both Chris and Morgan? Explain.

7. Chris is having a tough time passing the ball, and the teacher goes over to help. Having analyzed Chris's attempts, the teacher provides the following extrinsic feedback: "No, that's not it. You are too tense. Why are you so uptight? Your head isn't straight, and you aren't kicking through the center of the ball—no wonder it doesn't go straight! Can't you do better than that?" (a) Rewrite this statement so it provides Chris with more effective feedback. (b) Explain why your rewrite is more effective.

8. Chris has come a long way in practice and has become quite proficient in shooting. However, every time the ball is passed near the goal, the defender steals it before Chris can get the shot off. The teacher decides that Chris's shooting technique is all right but that Chris is taking too long to react to the ball. (a) Generate a list of potential reasons for Chris's inability to respond quickly in this situation. (b) Provide suggestions for each reason given in order to correct the problem.

Rehabilitation Scenario

You have just started working at a rehabilitation clinic. One of your first cases is a patient who had a below-the-knee amputation (BKA) of the left leg. The patient has been fitted with a prosthetic and is ready to start balance training, transfers training (e.g., to the car) and gait training.

1. The psychological effects that accompany the amputation of a limb are a significant factor to consider during the patient's rehabilitation. A patient's level of motivation, for example, will directly influence the learning process. Frustration can lead to a loss of motivation when patients are not progressing as fast as they had anticipated. What strategies will you employ to motivate the patient during the rehabilitation process?

2. A major concern for the patient, as is common for those learning to use a lower limb prosthesis, is the fear of falling. (a) What arousal level might you expect to be associated with the fear of falling? (b) How might that influence the patient's training? The performance of activities of daily living? (c) What strategies will you incorporate into the patient's rehabilitation program to reduce the fear of falling?

3. Describe how you could incorporate goal setting into the rehabilitative process for this patient. Include an example of a goal that might be appropriate in this situation.

4. Given the loss of proprioception, patients will have difficulty learning to equalize stride length. What alternative feedback mechanisms could be used to compensate for the patient's lost proprioception?

5. In order to effectively design variable practice experiences, the nature of the skill and the contexts in which it will be performed must be assessed. Generate a list of variations that should be incorporated into prosthetic training for (a) learning to fall safely, (b) transfers (e.g., to the car) and (c) gait (both indoors and outdoors).

ANSWERS TO PHYSICAL EDUCATION SCENARIO

Question 1 This is not an effective drill for several reasons. First, the learning goal expressed by the teacher, to dribble the ball without looking at it, is too advanced. Given that only an initial explanation and demonstration of the skill has been given, most of the learners in the class would be in the cognitive stage of learning. Consequently, they should be given the opportunity to practice the skill in order to develop a basic understanding of the idea of the movement. Once learners have developed some proficiency in dribbling, the next step in the progression would be to learn to do so without looking at the ball.

Second, the drill does not target the learning goal. According to the teacher's instructions, the goal of the drill is to dribble to the opposite side of the gym without looking at the ball. By placing a defender in front of the dribbler, the goal of the drill for the learner becomes one of protecting the ball.

Third, by placing a defender in front of the learner whose task is to try to take away the ball, the context in which the skill is being performed becomes open and in turn more complex. Given that learners are in the cognitive stage, the attentional demands needed for movement production will be high. The additional demand imposed by the defender exceeds the learner's attentional capacity, causing interference to occur. The result is either a decline in the level of performance or a disregard for one of the tasks. This was evident in that the learners were either losing control of the ball or totally focusing their vision on it.

Question 2 Two factors should be considered here. The advantage to utilizing the playground balls is that the amount of time on task will increase. The question the practitioner must ask prior to implementing this strategy is whether the use of the playground balls will cause the learner to execute a pattern of movement that exceeds the boundaries of the generalized motor program being developed. Provided that distinct movement pattern changes would not manifest as a result of using the alternative equipment, this is a good strategy to implement.

Question 3 Given that the skill is high in task organization and low in task complexity, whole practice would be recommended.

Question 4 The teacher's use of a reference to cushioning the ball like you would when fielding a softball or baseball is an example of attempting to capitalize on positive transfer. Any time you attempt to capitalize on the use of transfer, it is important to be sure that the skill or concept you refer to has been well learned. Given Morgan's past experiences with baseball and softball, the reference will likely be effective. For Chris, who has limited movement experiences, the reference will not likely be meaningful, and the idea the teacher is trying to convey will not be communicated effectively.

Question 5 Again, task organization and task complexity must be assessed to determine which method, segmentation or simplification, should be used. First, the skill would be considered relatively high in task organization. Second, given that heading requires a learner to coincidently time his or her actions to an oncoming ball, the movement is somewhat complex in nature. That complexity can be easily reduced, however. Practice could start by having learners place a small piece of masking tape on the middle of their forehead. Then, using lighter balls, such as beach balls, learners could throw their ball up into the air and try to hit it with the masking tape spot on their forehead. As they become proficient at this, they could progress to a slightly harder ball such as a volleyball or playground ball and finally to a soccer ball. In addition, learners could progress from self-toss to partner toss. Tosses should initially be predictable and from close range, progressing to further away and unpredictable.

Question 6 One partner would dribble the ball down the field and then pass it to the other partner, who would trap it, then dribble it down the field before passing it back to his or her partner. Variations in distance, speed, foot used, type of pass, type of trap and the like would be incorporated.

High levels of contextual interference can be overwhelming if the learner is still trying to generate an understanding of the movement. Given the past experiences of Morgan and Chris, it is possible that Morgan may progress through the learning process at a faster rate and be ready to handle a drill of this nature while Chris may not. The answer is dependent on the learner's degree of proficiency when the drill is introduced.

Question 7 The sandwich approach would be more effective in this situation. Using this strategy, the learner is first given information to reinforce correct performance. The next step would then be to provide the learner with information to facilitate error correction. The sandwich is finalized by offering encouragement in order to motivate the learner to incorporate the error correction recommendations. The following is an example:

"Good! Your contact with the ball is much stronger. On this next trial, focus on kicking through the center of the ball. That will make the ball go straight. Let's try again. You almost have it."

This rewrite is more effective because it confirms the learner's progress, encourages continued persistence and offers prescriptive feedback, which is more beneficial for novice learners.

Question 8 The error in this situation is a delay in responding. There may be multiple reasons causing this delay. First, the practitioner must establish whether Chris can correctly read game situations. Does Chris know what critical cues to look for? Can Chris detect that information during a game? If not, intervention strategies would focus on teaching what the critical cues are, prompting Chris to prepare a response sooner, directing Chris's attention to where in the environment they occur, and providing extensive practice opportunities in a variety of situations that contain common task-relevant cues. Second, Chris's attentional focus may be either too broad or too narrow, depending on the level of arousal. Third, the delay in responding may be a function of problems with decision making. Reducing the number of possible response alternatives and increasing the learner's capability to identify potential predictors such as opponent or situational tendencies could resolve such problems.

ANSWERS TO REHABILITATION SCENARIO

Question 1 Throughout the learning process the patient must be provided with opportunities to experience some degree of success. This will lead to feelings of achievement that will further motivate the learner to practice. The patient must also be taught that challenges are an integral part of the learning process. Positive feedback and the provision of encouragement and reinforcement are also critical. The monotony of repeated training can be reduced if the therapist makes practice fun, introducing variety into the training protocol when possible. Another powerful motivational technique is goal setting. It will be discussed in detail in Question 3.

Question 2 One would expect that the fear of falling would result in a high level of anxiety, leading to high levels of arousal. Fear of falling will obviously influence the patient's motivation to perform various activities. Furthermore, an overdependence on the uninvolved limb is likely to occur. As patients progress, high arousal will influence their attentional focus, and performance of activities in more open environments will likely be compromised (e.g., walking through a crowd). In order to reduce a patient's fear and subsequent anxiety, practitioners must not only teach them to fall safely (in a way to minimize the risk of injury) but also what to do in the event of a fall. In addition, balance and coordination exercises in standing that reinforce good posture should be incorporated in the initial stages of the rehabilitation protocol.

Question 3 Several steps should be taken to incorporate goal setting into the rehabilitative process. First, a combination of short-term, long-term, performance and process goals should be set. Those goals should be challenging yet realistic, specific, measurable and specify a target date for their completion. Second, the patient should be included in the goal-setting process and encouraged to frequently evaluate his or her progress. Third, the practitioner must be supportive and provide positive reinforcement throughout the rehabilitative process.

An example of a goal that might be appropriate in this situation would be: "Patient can perform an independent and safe transfer to a bed, while being spotted by the therapist, 8 out of 10 times by the end of week two."

Question 4 To assist patients in developing a frame of reference for various activities, they should be given the opportunity to experience a variety of positions and movements across a broad assortment of environments. Focus patient attention on the feelings associated with a movement to help them recognize and interpret the proprioceptive cues received from other sources. In addition, assist learners in developing their self-evaluation skills by asking them questions during practice to provoke reflective thinking regarding practice attempts. Information regarding movement and body position is also available through visual feedback. Other alternative feedback mechanisms could include the use of biofeedback (e.g., a load monitoring device), mirrors and video replay.

Question 5

(a) Manipulate height and position. (*Note:* Safety is a priority.)

(b) Manipulate where the transfer occurs. Examples include the bed, wheel chair, toilet, tub, shower, floor, car and a variety of furniture.

(c) Manipulate the surface (smooth, rough, carpeted, uneven), train on stairs, ramps, curbs, elevators and escalators, ambulate and maneuver in narrow places, crowds, managing doors, stepping over obstacles, etc.

GLOSSARY

Ability A genetic trait that is prerequisite to the development of skill proficiency

Afferent Carrying to; meaning sensory input in the nervous system

Affordances Action possibilities of the environment and task in relation to the perceiver's own capabilities

Ambient visual system Visual system that functions at a subconscious level and is thought to be responsible for spatial localization and orientation

Amplitude Size of a movement

Anxiety An emotion resulting from an individual's perception of a situation as threatening

Arousal A general physiological and psychological activation of the organism that varies on a continuum from deep sleep to intense excitement

Associative stage The intermediate stage of learning in Fitts and Posner's model

Attention cueing A practice technique where the learner directs his or her attention to a specific aspect of the skill during its performance as a whole

Attentional focus The process used to selectively attend to specific environmental information

Attractor state Preferred states of stability or patterns towards which a system spontaneously shifts

Augmented feedback Information received from an external source that supplements the learner's own sensory information

Automaticity A capacity to perform a skill with little or no conscious control

Autonomous stage The advanced or final stage of learning in Fitts and Posner's model

Average feedback Augmented feedback provided following the completion of a certain number of attempts regarding the average performance error

Backward chaining Part practice technique whereby the parts of a skill are presented and practiced in a sequence that progresses from the final skill component to the initial one

Bandwidth feedback Augmented feedback strategy where feedback is only provided on those trials where an error falls outside of a predetermined range of correctness

Bilateral transfer When practice with one limb enhances the rate of skill acquisition with the opposite limb on the same task

Biofeedback Form of augmented feedback that measures physiological information that is concurrently available to a learner through some form of instrumentation

Blocked practice Practice schedule where one variation of a skill is practiced repeatedly before practice attempts are given on another variation

Cerebral cortex The outermost layer of the cerebrum

Choice RT The reaction time resulting from a situation involving a choice as to how to respond

Closed skill A skill for which the object or context to be acted on or within is very stable and predictable allowing the performer to control the performance situation

Closed-loop control A mode of control whereby feedback is used in error detection and correction

Cognitive stage The initial or beginning stage of learning in Fitts and Posner's model

Concurrent feedback Augmented feedback provided during the execution of a skill

Constraints The boundaries that limit the movement capabilities of an individual

Contextual interference Interference that results from switching from one skill to another or changing the context in which a task is practiced from trial to trial

Continuous skill A skill whose beginning and ending points are either arbitrary or determined by some environmental factor rather than by the task itself

Control The manipulation of variables within a movement to meet the demands of a given situation

Control parameters Variables that move the system into new attractor states

Coordination The process of constraining a system's available degrees of freedom to organize an efficient movement pattern that will effectively achieve the goal of the task

Cue Utilization Hypothesis A paradigm where changes in attentional focus occur according to arousal levels

Declarative knowledge Information used to decide what to do in a given situation

Degrees of freedom problem How we control the available degrees of freedom to produce a particular movement

Descriptive feedback Augmented feedback that describes the nature of the performance error made

Discovery learning Teaching strategy where a learning environment is created that engages the learner in attempts to solve a movement problem through exploration of a variety of possible task solutions

Discrete skill A skill whose beginning and end points are clearly defined

Distributed practice Practice schedule where the length of the rest component between sessions or practice attempts is equal to or greater than the time devoted to the practice component

Efferent Carrying away from; meaning motor output in the nervous system

Episodic memory The memory of personal experiences and events that are associated with a specific time and context

Event anticipation Prediction of what event will happen

External focus of attention Focusing one's attention on the effects of his or her actions on the environment

Exteroceptors Receptors located at or near the body's surface that detect stimuli outside the body and provide information about the environment

Faded feedback Feedback technique where learners are provided with a high frequency of feedback initially that is then gradually reduced

Feedback-delay interval Time interval from the completion of a performance attempt until the provision of augmented feedback

Fine motor skill A motor skill involving very precise movements normally accomplished using smaller musculature

Fixation The focusing of one's visual attention on a specific object

Fixation/diversification Second and final stage of learning in Gentile's model; involves matching the new movement pattern to the particular environment in which it is to be performed.

Fixation emphasizes consistency of movement and is the objective for closed skills. If the environment is variable, the diversification of the movement pattern is emphasized to promote flexible behavior

Focal visual system Visual system that functions to identify objects primarily located in the central region of the visual field

Foreperiod The time interval between the presentation of a warning signal and a stimulus

Forward chaining Part practice technique whereby the parts of a skill are presented and practiced in a sequence that progresses from the initial skill component to the final one

Fractionization Part practice technique where skill components that are normally performed simultaneously are partitioned and practiced independently

Freezing the degrees of freedom Strategy whereby the learner freezes or fixes the movement possibilities of a joint, causing the limb(s) to function as a single unit or segment in order to accomplish the goal of the task

Generalized motor program Abstract representation of a class of actions or pattern of movement that can be modified to yield various response outcomes

Getting the idea of the movement The first stage of learning in Gentile's model, characterized by the learner trying to develop an understanding of a movement's requirements

Golgi tendon organs Proprioceptors located at the junction of a tendon with a muscle that indicate the level of tension development in a tendon

Gross motor skill A motor skill that places less emphasis on precision and is typically the result of multi-limb movements

Guided discovery Discovery learning technique where the practitioner designs a sequence of questions, each of which elicits a single correct response discovered by the learner

Hick's Law Relationship between the number of movement choices and the time needed to prepare a response where the higher the degree of uncertainty in a given situation, the longer the time needed to decide which response to make

Imagery Technique involving the visualization or cognitive rehearsal of a movement in the absence of any physical execution

Individual differences Relatively stable and enduring characteristics that make each of us unique

Internal focus of attention Focusing one's attention on a specific body movement

Interneuron Nerve cell that lies between a sensory and a motor neuron in a reflex arc

Interoceptors Receptors that detect stimuli from the internal viscera and provide information about the internal environment

Inter-trial interval Time from the end of one performance attempt to the beginning of the next performance attempt

Intrinsic feedback Response-produced information that is available to learners

from their sensory system both during and as a consequence of performance

Invariant features Relatively fixed underlying features that define a motor program

Inverted-U principle The relationship between arousal and performance where there exists an optimal level of arousal for peak performance

Key elements Specific body movements that are observable and that affect the performance of a skill

Knowledge of performance Feedback that provides information about the specific characteristics of the performance that led to the outcome

Knowledge of results Feedback that provides learners with information about the outcome of a response and is concerned with the success of the intended action with respect to the goal

Learner-regulated feedback Augmented feedback provided to a learner when he or she requests it

Learning A relatively permanent change in a person's capability to execute a motor skill as a result of practice or experience

Learning style Individual preference for receiving and processing new information

Massed practice Practice schedule where the amount of time allocated to rest between sessions or practice attempts is comparatively less than the time that a learner is engaged in practice

Memory The ability to store and recall information

Modal strength The preferred perceptual mode through which a learner takes in and processes information

Motivation An internal condition that incites and directs action or behavior

Motor control The neural, physical and behavioral aspects that underlie human movement

Motor learning The study of the processes involved in acquiring and refining motor skills and of variables that promote or inhibit that acquisition

Motor program An abstract representation of a movement plan, stored in memory, that contains all of the motor commands required for carrying out the intended action

Motor skill A goal-oriented act or task that requires voluntary body and/or limb movement and must be learned

Movement time The time interval between the initiation of a movement and its completion

Muscle spindles Proprioceptors located between the skeletal muscle fibers in the muscle belly that indicate how much and how fast the muscle's length is changing

Negative transfer When the learning of a new skill or its performance under novel conditions is negatively influenced by past experience with another skill or skills

Open skill A motor skill that is performed in an unpredictable, ever-changing environment

Open-loop control A mode of control whereby action plans are generated that contain all of the information necessary to complete a response

Outcome goals Goals that are concerned with the final result of a competition relative to one's opponent

Parameters Flexible features that define how to execute a generalized motor program

Part practice method Teaching strategy that involves breaking the skill down into natural parts or segments, practicing those parts separately until they are learned and then integrating them to perform the skill in its entirety

Perception The process by which meaning is attached to information

Perceptual narrowing The narrowing of attentional focus with increasing levels of arousal

Performance The act of executing a skill

Performance goals Goals that are concerned with self-improvement

Performance plateau A period of time during the learning process in which no overt changes in performance occur

Phase shift Change in the state of stability of a system causing a spontaneous reorganization into a new form

Photoreceptors Light-sensitive cells located in the eyes

Positive transfer When the learning of a new skill or its performance under novel conditions is positively influenced by past experience with another skill or skills

Post test Skill performance test administered directly following a practice period that is used to find out what a learner can do after practicing a skill

Post-feedback interval Time interval from the provision of augmented feedback to the initiation of the next performance attempt

Power law of practice Law that states that when learning a new skill, there tends to be a large initial improvement in performance, which slows later in practice

Precue Clues in the environment that if detected can assist a learner in anticipating

Prescriptive feedback Feedback that offers a suggestion as to how to correct an identified problem

Proactive inhibition Interference that results when old memories interfere with the retention of new ones

Procedural knowledge Information regarding skills, operations and actions

Procedural memory The memory of information regarding how to do something

Process goals Goals that direct the performer's focus to achieving some technical element during skill execution

Proprioceptors Receptors that provide information regarding body position and movement by detecting changes in muscle tension, joint position and equilibrium

Psychological refractory period (PRP) Delay in responding to a second stimulus in a situation where two stimuli, each of which requires a different response, are presented in succession within a short period of time

Random practice Practice schedule where multiple task variations are performed in a random order

Rate limiters Constraints that function to hinder the ability of a system to change

Reaction time The interval of time between the moment that a stimulus is presented to when a response is initiated

Reflex An automatic, involuntary response to stimuli

Reflex arc The simplest pathway by which a reflex occurs

Regulatory conditions Environmental factors that specify the movement characteristics necessary to successfully perform a skill

Response time The time interval from the moment that a stimulus is presented to when a response is completed; combination of RT and MT

Retention test Skill performance test given following a period of no practice that measures the persistence of improved skill performance

Retroactive inhibition Interference that results when new learning impedes the retention of older memories

Schema A rule or relationship that directs decision making when a learner is faced with a movement problem

Segmentation Part practice technique that separates the skill into parts according to spatial or temporal elements

Selective attention The ability to attend to or focus on one specific item in the midst of countless stimuli

Self-organization Spontaneous emergence of a movement pattern as a result of the ever-changing constraints placed on the learner

Self-talk Development and use of cues by learners to help guide themselves through an action or a movement sequence

Semantic memory The memory of general knowledge that is developed by our experiences but is not associated with time

Serial skill A motor skill composed of a number of discrete skills whose integrated performance is crucial for goal achievement

Simplification Part practice technique that reduces the level of difficulty of the task or some aspect of the task for the learner

Speed-accuracy tradeoff A trade-off that exists between speed and accuracy such that an emphasis on speed negatively impacts accuracy and vice versa

Stimuli A change in the environment that evokes a response

Stimulus-response compatibility The extent to which a stimulus and its required response are naturally related

Summary feedback Augmented feedback that provides the learner with a summary of their performance following the completion of a certain number of trials

Task analysis The breaking down of a skill into its component parts and corresponding underlying abilities

Tau Optic variable that provides time of contact information by taking the size of the retina image at any position of an object's approach and dividing it by the rate of change of the image

Taxonomy A model into which skills are classified

Temporal anticipation Prediction of when an event will happen

Terminal feedback Augmented feedback that is presented following the completion of a movement

Transfer When the learning of a new skill or its performance under novel conditions is influenced by past experience with another skill or skills

Transfer test Measurement of the adaptability of a response determined by testing a learner's ability to use a skill in a novel context or manner

Variable practice Practice schedule where multiple variations of a given task are practiced

Verbal cue A word or concise phrase that focuses the learner's attention or prompts a movement or movement sequence

Visual search The manner by which the performer directs his or her visual attention while trying to locate critical regulatory cues

Zero transfer When past experience with another skill or skills has no influence on the learning of a new skill or its performance under novel conditions

NAME INDEX

SUBJECT INDEX